Hell Upon Water:
Prisoners of War in Britain
1793–1815

HELL UPON WATER

PRISONERS OF WAR IN BRITAIN
1793–1815

by

PAUL CHAMBERLAIN

The History Press

For Melissa,
For her patience and tolerance of a history enthusiast

British Library Cataloguing in Publication Data:
A catalogue record for this book is available
from the British Library

Copyright © Paul Chamberlain 2008
ISBN 978 1 86227 466 2

First published in the UK in 2008 by
The History Press
The Mill, Brimscombe Port,
Stroud, Gloucestershire GL5 2QG

Printed in Great Britain

Contents

Acknowledgements

A visit to Portchester castle in the 1980s drew my attention to some French names carved into the stonework. I had heard tales of French prisoners being held there during the Napoleonic Wars, but had not realised the significance of this site in the story of that conflict. After twenty-three years of immersing myself in the subject, with conference papers, talks to local groups, magazine and journal articles, and involvement in the Norman Cross Eagle Appeal along the way, here is the result of that research.

One of the pleasures of such a study is that many individuals and organisations would contact me for information, but invariably tell of a story they knew relating to just some of the many thousands of prisoners of war who left their mark on Britain two hundred years ago. These snippets of information made me realise that the prisoners of many nationalities who were brought to Britain have left an indelible mark on many local communities.

Many individuals have provided me with a piece of the story and I thank them for their time and consideration. These include Paul Bennett, David and Janet Bromley, Sue Brunt, Stella Child, Michael Crumplin, Ian Fletcher, Peter Fry, John Grehan, Kenneth Hillier, Dave Hollins, the late Martin Howe, Peter Lee, Olive Main, J. David Markham, Sheila Millard, Keith Oliver, Ben Robinson, Karen Selby and Helen S. Smith.

Of the many institutions and organisations which have answered my queries and made information readily available I mention first and foremost the staff at the National Archives, Kew, where much of the research for this book was performed. However, I am grateful for the help provided by the staff at the British Library, Bank of England Museum, Bishops Waltham

Society, Dartmoor Prison, Dartmouth Museum, Gosport Borough Council, Museum of Transport Glasgow, Guildhall Museum Rochester, Hampshire Museums Service Winchester, Liverpool Museum and Art Gallery, National Army Museum London, National Maritime Museum Greenwich, Oxfordshire County Museum, Perth Museum and Art Gallery, City Museum Peterborough, Petersfield Historical Society, Portchester Castle, Central Library Portsmouth, Portsmouth Museums Service, Plymouth Museum and Art Gallery, Royal Marines Museum Southsea, Royal Naval Museum Portsmouth, Science Museum Kensington, Tiverton Museum, The National Library of Wales and Wardown Park Museum Luton.

Thanks should also go to Jamie Wilson at The History Press, who patiently waited for this book from an initial idea some years ago through to the miracle of actually getting into print, and to Clare Jackson for guiding me through the book submission process.

Last but not least, thanks should also go to my patient and very tolerant wife Melissa who has put up with my endless disappearances to Kew or to churchyards (often with her in tow) to photograph yet another old gravestone.

Paul Chamberlain

Abbreviations used in chapter notes:

BL	British Library, London.
BoE	Bank of England Archive Section
NAM	National Army Museum, London.
NMM	National Maritime Museum, Greenwich.
TNA:PRO	The National Archives (Public Record Office), Kew.

CHAPTER 1

Marching Into Captivity

The eighteenth century was period of frequent conflict as the European powers jostled for continental supremacy, at the same time expanding their overseas empires, while attempting to limit the imperial ambitions of their rivals. The century saw France, Spain and Holland arrayed as frequent enemies of Great Britain. The War of the Spanish Succession (1701–1714), the War of the Austrian Succession (1740–1748), the Seven Years War (1756–1763) and the American Revolutionary War on the side of the American colonists were all clashes in which these nations fought against Britain. Each war was characterized by conflict on land and sea across the globe, and resulted in many prisoners of war arriving in Britain. As the century progressed, armies and navies became larger, and consequently the numbers of prisoners taken became greater.

The extent of the conflict during the American Revolution prompted an attempt at regulating the business of repatriating prisoners of war. Exchange of prisoners had always been erratic, but in 1780 a treaty was agreed between Britain and France stating that vigorous attempts would be made to exchange all prisoners of war as speedily as possible after capture, man for man, rank for rank. If there were no prisoners of equal rank to exchange, then the numbers would be made up of a proportion of lesser ranks, or a cash equivalent could be substituted.[1]

This treaty was regarded as the gentlemanly way to conduct prisoner of war affairs, but it only worked when there were gentlemen on both sides who could reach an agreement. However, 1789 saw events in France that changed the situation. The French Revolution removed French gentlemen from the scene, either by guillotining them or forcing them to flee for their lives. While these momentous events were changing the social and political climate in that country, they were also to change the conduct of war.

Prior to 1789, European conflict was conducted in a 'civilized' manner between monarchs who, while pitting their relatively small but professional armies against each other, respected their mutual positions as heads of state. The French Revolution, under the banner *liberté, égalité, fraternité*, overturned the idea of royal and aristocratic privilege. This had two immediate effects. First, the French were infused with a national fervour to export their revolutionary principles to the rest of Europe. Second, this forced the nations of Europe to co-operate against a common foe. War was about to be waged on a scale never seen before.[2]

The Revolutionary War began in 1792 with the French demonstrating the effectiveness of a *levée en masse* by fighting off an Austro-Prussian alliance, at the same time as the abolition of the monarchy by the National Convention in Paris. 1793 began dramatically with the execution of Louis XVI in January; the following month resulting in France declaring war upon Britain, Spain and the United Provinces (Holland). While countries such as Spain and Holland later found themselves allied to France, Great Britain remained an implacable foe until the short-lived peace resulting from the Treaty of Amiens in 1801.

War between Britain and a France now under the First Consul Napoleon Bonaparte (he became Emperor in 1804) erupted in 1803. Again Britain found herself at war, actively or otherwise, against most European nations as alliances were made and broken. This war lasted until the defeat of the Emperor in 1814. After a short-lived exile to Elba he returned to claim the French throne, only to be finally defeated in the Waterloo campaign of 1815.

To understand how the war prison system developed in Britain, it is important to look at the events and activities that generated the reason for its existence: prisoners of war. During the period 1792–1815, over 200,000 prisoners of war arrived in Britain. Of this total, 122,440 were taken during the Napoleonic Wars 1803–15. The highest prisoner population in any one year was 72,000 in 1814.[3]

During the Revolutionary War the British Army fought an abortive campaign in the Low Countries during 1793–94. This generated prisoners, some of whom were sent to Britain while others remained in Holland (on board some prison hulks in the Scheldt) and in Germany awaiting exchange. Aside from this conflict and an Anglo-Russian invasion of Holland in 1799, the British Army was not to campaign again on the continent of Europe until the Peninsula War in 1808.

Nineteenth century historians viewed the British Army as a projectile fired by the Royal Navy, and in the 1790s many such firings took place as colonies belonging to France and her allies were attacked. Islands in the West Indies, Malta, French settlements in India and the Dutch colony at the Cape of Good Hope all fell to combined operations mounted by the British.[4] While the politicians gained valuable bargaining counters at future peace negotiations and British merchants gained new markets to be exploited, the Admiralty acquired thousands of prisoners of war, men, women and children, soldiers, sailors and civilians. Although many of these were held locally until exchanged, the majority were transported to Britain to fill the land prisons and hulks.

The West Indies was a rich source of captives. One prison ship was stationed at Martinique but found to be insufficient for the numbers being taken, but as the authorities there regarded their prisoners as being 'troublesome brigands and Negros taken in arms', they were only too glad to transfer responsibility to the naval authorities in Britain. Sir Ralph Abercrombie sent 4,000 such prisoners to Britain from this theatre in 1796.[5]

When the Dutch enclave at the Cape fell in 1796 many soldiers and civilians were taken prisoner. The Governor, Abraham Sluysken, was sent to England to reside on parole at Hambledon, Hampshire, together with his staff and servants.[6] Occasionally a campaign produced captives who did not spend time in Britain, such as when a British army ended Napoleon's dreams of oriental conquest in Egypt in 1801. The French troops involved were fortunate in that they were allowed to return to France and no doubt the Admiralty shared their relief, as by this time the war prison establishment had expanded dramatically.

11

While the army captured enemy nationals in large batches as French, Dutch and Spanish territory fell, the Royal Navy was generating a constant flow of inmates for the prison depots as soon as hostilities began. Upon war being declared between Holland and Britain in 1796, the Admiralty immediately detained enemy ships sitting in British ports. This resulted in a large haul, for there were seven Dutch warships berthed in these ports at the time, one in Ireland, one at Leith, and five at Plymouth. This was a typical occurrence. Throughout the Revolutionary and Napoleonic Wars many merchant vessels and some warships were 'detained by the Admiralty' when they were in Britain's harbours on the assumption of hostilities.[7]

The Royal Navy attacked enemy warships and merchant vessels whenever and wherever they could be found. During the blockade of the French and Dutch coastline many small vessels were captured such as whalers and local civilian craft. There was a restriction on attacking coastal fishing vessels as these were part of the local community. War was waged against nations, not local inhabitants who often supplied the Royal Navy with intelligence and fresh produce, although this limitation was ignored if the fishing vessel was found to have an armed soldier on board. This prohibition did not apply to the fishing and whaling fleets that operated in the North Sea and around Greenland; these were national fleets supplying the nation at war and so were legitimate targets. Coastal vessels supporting the commerce of France were often escorted into Portsmouth and Plymouth with the naval officers concerned receiving prize money and the captured French men and boys a berth in the hulks (many youths were taken to sea to learn the profession).[8]

The Admiralty had an ambivalent attitude towards individuals of neutral countries onboard enemy ships, and enemy nationals' onboard neutral vessels. In May 1796 their Lordships were inundated with requests from the Danish, Prussian and Swedish Consuls to release their nationals who were taken prisoner on board Dutch vessels. Earlier that year Mr Dobree, the Agent for prisoners of war on Guernsey, informed the authorities in London that he had detained some American vessels that had arrived partly navigated by Frenchmen. He wished to know if they should be regarded as captives or set free. The reply was:

> Orders have been given for detaining as prisoners of war all Frenchmen who may be found onboard neutral vessels arriving in the Ports within His Majesty's dominions.[9]

Taking captives from neutral vessels was hardly an approach that would win friends abroad.

There was a further reason for closely examining the crews of all vessels, both enemy and neutral. Nobody loves a traitor to their country, least of all the British during the war with Revolutionary France. Revenue cutters often captured French privateers in the Channel such as the *Rose* Revenue Cutter that boarded one such vessel and found that the Master and most of the crew were actually British. The ship was taken to Plymouth where it was ordered that a strict examination be made of the crew, and any found to 'be subjects of His Majesty' should be properly secured and not regarded as simple prisoners of war. The French Corvette *La Revanche* was captured while under the command of a sailor named Cooper, and a detailed investigation performed to ascertain whether he was American or British.[10] This sort of legal quibble was to have serious consequences during the latter part of the Napoleonic War.

The war with Revolutionary France came to an end with the signing of the Treaty of Amiens in 1801. The Admiralty lost no time in returning to the continent the many thousands of prisoners of war in England and instigating the dismantling of the prison establishment. However, it was fortunate that only a few of the older hulks had been broken up by 1803, as by then relations between Britain and France had deteriorated, resulting in the resumption of hostilities. Immediately the Royal Navy began snapping up prizes upon the oceans, with large numbers of prisoners coming from enemy vessels in the Channel, as the Navy enforced a blockade of French ports.

Napoleon's proposed invasion of England generated an increase in sea traffic as vessels for this enterprise were constructed and moved along the coast. French efforts involved the construction of invasion craft not only in and around the Channel ports such as Boulogne, Ambleteuse and Calais, but as far east as the Rhine, in Dutch ports and Toulouse. These vessels were assembled on the Channel coastline, and the Royal Navy attempted to disrupt this shipping whenever it could, bringing some of the erstwhile invaders to England, but not in the victorious manner they had envisaged. The Emperor's invasion hopes were postponed indefinitely by the campaign of Trafalgar in which 7,500 prisoners of war, both French and Spanish, were taken.[11] The year 1805 also saw the Admiralty planning a new prison in the windswept Dartmoor countryside, to accommodate the increasing naval harvest of prisoners. The structure was intended to be more economical to run compared to the equivalent number of hulks.

The principal nationalities taken at this time were French, Spanish and Dutch. While the majority was taken at sea, occasional large hauls resulted from the capture of enemy colonies throughout the world, especially in the West Indies which was a major theatre of the war. However, the year 1808 saw the Spanish rise up against their erstwhile allies the French, giving Britain an opportunity to attack the French on the continent. Thus began the campaign in the Iberian Peninsula, which was to generate on occasion an overwhelming number of captives. The conflict involved successful sieges such as Ciudad Rodrigo and Badajoz, generating 1,100 and 3,700 prisoners respectively. Many enemy soldiers were taken during or immediately after the battles in Spain and Portugal, one example being the Battle of Salamanca at which over 7,000 prisoners were captured.[12] The constant maneuvering of the British, Portuguese and Spanish forces resulted in a continuous flow of prisoners to Lisbon and from there to England. The battles and sieges may have generated large numbers of prisoners, but the constant patrols and skirmishes produced a steady trickle of captives.

It was not only British operations that generated captives. The Spanish Juntas did not have the facilities (both practical and administrative) to confine large numbers of prisoners of war, and so Spanish forces handed the majority of enemy soldiers taken by them over to Britain. Although the Spanish held many

French prisoners on hulks in Cadiz and on the island of Cabrera, the treatment afforded them was so minimal that from 1810 many of them were sent to England. Spanish guerrilla activity produced captives, both from the military and from the large civilian population following the French armies such as Bernard Tolede, a French hotel manager 'taken by the inhabitants in Spain, 11th November 1812'.[13]

The numbers of prisoners being shipped from Lisbon to English ports necessitated an increase in the prison ship establishment. Dartmoor Prison, planned to house the many prisoners arriving during the invasion scare, was finally ready for receiving prisoners in early 1809. This and the re-opening of Portchester Castle in 1810 were fortuitous, as by this time it was obvious that the Iberian Peninsula was to be a major theatre of war. Even this did not immediately alleviate the over-crowding problem in the prisons. That year Wellington was requested not to send any more prisoners from the Peninsula to England for the time being, as there was no room for them. He replied by sending 20,000 French captives to England in 1810–11, as he simply did not have the resources to house, feed and guard them in Spain or Portugal. His problem was compounded by the large numbers of soldiers deserting from French service. Wellington wrote:

> Two battalions of the Regiment of Nassau, and one of Frankfurt having quitted the enemy's army and passed over to that under my command ... I now send these troops to England.[14]

Many of the soldiers in the French Armies were drawn from throughout the French Empire and satellite nations, and included Germans, Italians, Poles and Swiss troops. As the war dragged on, many thousands of such men were captured in battle or as a result of desertion from French service.

While the war at sea included naval engagements both large and small that generated inmates for the war prisons of Britain, there was a continuous sea-going conflict fought by both sides against enemy trade. Naval vessels did capture enemy merchantmen, but the latter were also at considerable risk from privateers.

Privateers were privately owned and armed vessels issued with a licence, or letter of marque, to attack enemy merchant shipping. Such vessels operated from both British and French ports, and were provided with large crews to man the prizes they took. As soon as war was declared in 1793 both sides fitted out privateers to raid the enemy shipping lanes to destroy their commercial capacity and capture seamen, thus weakening the enemy's naval power.

As French and Dutch colonies fell into British hands, the market for goods manufactured in France and Holland diminished so merchants in these countries turned to financing privateers to maintain their trading interests. As Britain acquired new colonies, so British commerce benefited from these markets. More merchant vessels plying the seas meant more French privateers were fitted out to attack them, and this in turn resulted in increased activity by the Royal Navy to combat the menace. With the decline in overseas trade for France, more goods were sold in Europe, which meant an increase in French coastal shipping. This produced more prizes for the Royal Navy and for the many privateers operating from the ports in southern England and the Channel Islands.

From 1793 to 1797 an increased naval blockade of France further reduced the markets available to French merchants, many of whom invested in privateering. This threat to British trade did not reach serious proportions until 1797, thereafter gradually declining until 1802. French privateer activity never reached the same level during the period 1803 to 1815 as it did the previous decade, the peak being in 1807–08.[15]

The year 1797 caused many problems for the Admiralty in relation to prisoners of war. This year saw the mutinies at Spithead and the Nore, and news of these events encouraged French merchants to invest in privateering ventures, their reasoning being that these mutinies would seriously affect Britain's capacity to enforce the naval blockade and to wage war at sea. 1797 saw a peak in the number of French privateers fitted out and launched into the Channel. 1797 also saw a peak in the number of French privateers captured by the British. The previous year had generated 2,448 privateer crewmen for the war prisons; in 1797 a total of 7,094 were taken, while the following year the number had dropped to 5,894, declining still further until 1801.[16]

What the French failed to understand was that while the main British fleets were temporarily incapacitated, those ships maintaining the blockade of the French coast – the frigates, cutters and sloops – were largely unaffected by the mutinies and continued their patrol of the Channel. The fact that more privateers were venturing forth from French ports only served to hand prizes to the Royal Navy on a plate. Revenue Cutters in the Channel also captured such enemy vessels.

Ships of the Royal Navy employed a number of ruses to ensnare enemy privateers, as generally the latter were faster and more maneuverable. Cinema-goers will be familiar with one method used by the Royal Navy to capture privateers, which was to pretend to be a merchant ship by displaying a total lack of discipline and a casual attitude in handling the ship. The guns were hidden and most of the crew below deck. When the unsuspecting privateer was within range, the covers were thrown off and the crew rushed on deck to open fire. By this time it would be too late for escape and the privateer would become a prize to line the pockets of the jubilant British seamen. The film *Master and Commander* (based upon the books by Patrick O'Brian) sees Captain Jack Aubrey employing this technique to lure the French privateer *Acheron* within range of his hidden guns. This was an effective and common technique utilized in the English Channel and the West Indies. Another ruse was to fly the flag of a friendly or neutral state until the privateer came within range. This flag was then run down and the naval ensign hoisted.[17]

When a privateer was taken the first act was to put a prize crew on board and secure the enemy crew in the hold. The vessel was sailed to the captor's home port, and this included not only mainland Britain and the Channel Islands, but bases in the West Indies and Canada. Many French privateer crewmen were disembarked at British ports in the West Indies prior to being transferred to England.[18]

On arrival in Britain the seamen were sent to the nearest land prison or prison ship with space for them, while the officers were conveyed to London under guard to be examined by the

Admiralty. They were asked questions to elicit who they were, the origin of their ship plus details of their voyage and cargo, which were confirmed by the ships papers if they had not been thrown overboard. It was important to establish the nationality of the crew, who could be from throughout the French coastal ports, northern Europe, the Mediterranean and North America. Most, however, were usually categorized as 'French' or 'Dutch' in the *General Entry Books for Prisoners of War* depending on the nationality of their ship. Occasionally British sailors joined the crew of French privateers and capture by the Royal Navy could find them on trial for treason.[19] Soldiers taken on land or at sea were categorized according to the army in which they were serving, so German soldiers captured in Spain were categorised as 'French'.

Napoleon's Berlin Decree of November 1806 inaugurated the Continental System, ordering that Britain was to be blockaded; all trade with her should cease; British nationals and goods were to be seized; and no ship was to be allowed to enter a French port after leaving a British one. This was the French response to the failure of peace negotiations and the British order of the previous May that declared that the European coast from Brest to the River Elbe was formally blockaded. The Royal Navy virtually closed all ports (i.e. those from which British commerce was excluded) to neutral shipping which had failed to first call at a British port and pay duty on their cargoes. A British Order in Council of 7 January 1807 was an effort to prevent neutrals from carrying goods between French ports. This activity against each nation's trade encouraged French merchants to fit out privateers, many of which then fell victim to the blockade by the Royal Navy.

Napoleon's Milan Decree of 1807 outlawed all neutral shipping that submitted to British rules. The principle neutral nations at that time were Denmark and the United States of America, both countries that prospered through their neutrality. The Danes had suffered many of their merchant vessels being detained by the Royal Navy during 1805 and 1806 when they were suspected of carrying enemy property or contraband. If these vessels were proved to have been engaged in trade that could benefit the enemy, the cargo, and in some cases the ship itself, were condemned as a lawful prize and the captors being awarded prize money. This was an arrangement that suited the Royal Navy to the detriment of the Danish merchant community and Anglo-Danish relations.[20] In the summer of 1807 the British Government took the decision to strike against the Danes, launching an attack on Copenhagen. This was to prevent the Danish fleet from falling into the hands of Napoleon and swelling his naval forces. While this aim was dramatically achieved after a bombardment of the city and dockyard, it led to seven years of war with what remained of the Danish Navy in the Baltic region. Many thousands of Danes, both soldiers and seamen, became captives of the British, although these two countries had better diplomatic relations when it came to the exchange of prisoners compared with the situation between Britain and France.

American maritime trade also suffered considerably from the French Decrees and British Orders in Council, as American vessels were barred from any direct traffic between the West Indies; any colony of a belligerent; and any but its own or a British port. There were many in the USA who were prepared to go to war to maintain the right to free trade.[21] To enforce the regulation of trade, the Royal Navy was empowered to stop and search any ship on the high seas. If that was not bad enough in American eyes, there was also the serious quarrel over impressment.

Britain experienced a continual shortage of seamen to man her ships. Vessels of the Royal Navy had a reputation for harsh conditions and indefinite service on board, and whenever possible many British seamen deserted to the American merchant service where the conditions and treatment were better. Indeed, many American ship owners positively welcomed deserting British seamen, finding such experienced sailors an asset to their vessels. The British response was the search of neutral ships and the seizure of any crewmen considered Britons. It was often difficult to identify British nationals and many American seamen were impressed in 'error'. Frequent complaints were lodged by the United States over the impressment of its nationals.

Public opinion in the USA finally forced President James Madison to sign a declaration of war against Great Britain on

18 June 1812. The Americans had as their war aims the restoration of maritime rights; an end to impressment; the final destruction of the Indian threat to the frontier lands (this threat often being materially supported by Britain) and the annexation of Canada.

This act had three effects that influenced the prisoner of war population held by Britain. First, the resulting land campaign in Canada generated many prisoners. Second, American privateers attacked British merchant vessels in the West Indies, the Atlantic and even around the coast of Britain. Third, those American seamen who had been pressed into service on board His Majesty's ships immediately gave themselves up as prisoners of war. The records contain many entries regarding such seamen. Charles Parditt 'gave himself up on board HMS *Ocean*, being an American subject' in November 1812. HMS *Aboukir* lost four of her crew in this way in the same month, and the situation was the same on board many other ships of the Royal Navy.[22]

In July 1812 six American merchant vessels arrived in Portsmouth harbour unaware that their country was now at war with Britain. These ships were 'detained by the Admiralty' and their crews passed into captivity. The *Leonidas* was one such example. Her captain, Benajah Liffingwell, was allowed to reside on parole at Odiham, Hampshire, while his crew was sent to the hulks at Chatham. The ship's cook, Thomas Wood, was discharged a few months later as he had been born in Newcastle, Northumberland. Although he was technically still a British subject (at that time Britain did not recognise the right of an individual to change their nationality), his age (55 years) and the fact that he had never served in the Royal Navy did not class him as a traitor.[23]

The American invasion of Canada and the naval activity on the Great Lakes produced a regular harvest of prisoners of war, many of whom were confined in the Americas, but many found themselves transported to Britain, a fact that caused controversy in the United States. Regular exchange of prisoners of war took place in the Americas between British and US forces, but the distance across the Atlantic precluded any regular exchange cartels. American prisoners were shipped to Britain as the facilities for their confinement were more extensive and efficient there.

Public opinion in the Unites States considered this to be a harsh policy, as once an American arrived in Britain as a prisoner his chance of exchange was minimal. The lack of regular exchange cartels returning these prisoners from Britain gave rise to the infamous Dartmoor massacre which will be related in a later chapter. American prisoners in Britain were also taken in the Atlantic or around the European coastline as they attempted to trade with the continent.

While merchant vessels and privateers were considered fair game for attack and capture, fishing vessels of all the belligerents were officially left alone as the attitude was that governments waged war on each other, not on local communities. The privateer owners of Guernsey however, had other ideas. In 1796 these ships were seizing French fishing vessels 'with an avidity too common to their interested dispositions'. The Admiralty ordered the release of these vessels and their crews as fishermen were not to be regarded as prisoners of war. The proprietors of the privateers insisted that they were only carrying out their instructions, although they backed down when the Admiralty threatened to withdraw their *letters of marque*. It has to be noted however, that fishing vessels with a soldier on board were considered military craft and their crews sent into captivity.[24]

Their Lordships could also be merciful to fellow seamen who became prisoners of war through no fault of their own. In 1796 the merchant vessel *D'Hiver* from Cherbourg was driven ashore and wrecked near Shoreham. Instructions were given for the crew to be immediately returned to France.[25]

The principle events related thus far were responsible for generating the bulk of the prisoner of war population in Britain. However, captives came from many other sources. Britain's allies handed over prisoners for safekeeping, as Britain's war prison system was regarded as the most efficient of the time, and as British gold financed her allies' participation in the conflict, accepting responsibility for captives was another means of supporting their war effort. During the Peninsular conflict both Spain and Portugal sent French prisoners to the British, and even detained American vessels and their crews, although these countries were not involved in the Anglo-American War.

During the Waterloo campaign the Prussian Army sent nearly 7,000 French captives to reside in Dartmoor Prison and the surrounding parole depots.[26]

It would be wrong to assume that all the prisoners of war residing in Britain were French or American. Napoleon's Empire stretched over many countries, while other European nations were allies of France at one time or another. The war prisons of Britain contained captives from Austria, the Balkans, Denmark, France, the myriad German States, Holland, Italy, Naples, Poland, Prussia, Russia, Spain, Sweden, Switzerland and the United States of America. Prisoners were of Caucasian, mulatto and negro stock. Many women and children were taken prisoner in enemy colonies, on board merchant vessels, and in the wake of the armies fighting on the Continent, but were not regarded as combatants. Aside from their families, the staff and servants of senior military and civilian officials passed into captivity.

Prisoners even came from the ranks of the British army and navy. Private Fremeaun was serving in His Majesty's 90th Regiment of Foot in 1811; being French he was discharged and imprisoned at Chatham. His story had a happy ending, as he applied to the Admiralty for liberty since he was not in the French service and had committed no crime. He also produced certificates from two British officers giving him a good character.[27]

When a soldier or sailor became captive his initial treatment was at the hands of the military and naval force who acquired him. Generally there was no personal animosity between British soldiers and sailors and their opposing counterparts. Any rough handling that an enemy prisoner of war received at the hands of his British captors was usually due to the common soldier or seaman's desire for plunder, rather than aggression towards a vanquished foe. Once a prisoner had been taken, the attitude towards him was usually indifference or occasionally sympathy for the plight of a fellow serviceman. Private William Wheeler wrote an account of his military adventures during the Peninsular campaign. When wounded he was conveyed to hospital via a Spanish boat in the company of other injured soldiers, including a number of Frenchmen. He soon struck up a friendship with a French corporal with whom he shared a blanket, and they passed the time with songs, anecdotes and pipes of tobacco.[28]

The successful storming of the citadel of Badajoz resulted in some of the worst excesses committed by British soldiers whilst on campaign. The men ran riot in the town, venting their anger and bloodlust upon the inhabitants and any French soldier rash enough not to have surrendered. The enemy soldiers who laid down their arms were quickly (and probably gratefully) marched from the citadel. Edward Costello wrote:

> We saw a number of Frenchmen guarded by our soldiers, coming over the bridge. They were the prisoners taken in the Fort San Christobal which but a hour or two previously had surrendered. These were soon surrounded by our men, who began examining their knapsacks, from whence a number of watches, dollars etc. were quickly extracted ...[29]

British officers were courteous and sympathetic towards their captured counterparts whenever circumstances permitted, as Surgeon James McGrigor recalled at Badajoz.

> In one street, I met General Phillipon, the governor, with his two daughters, holding each by the hand; all three disheveled, and with them were two British officers, each holding one of the ladies by the arm, and with their drawn swords making thrusts occasionally at soldiers who attempted to drag the ladies away. I am glad to say that these two British officers succeeded in conveying the governor and his two daughters safely ... to the camp.[30]

On campaign the British usually treated their prisoners of war correctly. Costello wrote of the Peninsula campaign that the military would not hesitate to use force 'to preserve our French prisoners from being butchered by the Spanish and Portuguese irregulars'.[31]

Senior officers taken prisoner were treated with the greatest respect. Admiral Villeneuve was allowed to wear his sword, retain his staff officers and given some choice as to his town of residence after surrendering at Trafalgar. General Ruffin was mortally wounded at the Battle of Barrosa in March 1811 and taken prisoner. When he died on board HMS *Gorgon* off Plymouth on 15 May of that year he was conveyed to Portsmouth where he was buried with full military honours at what is now the garrison church, although the gravestones are too weathered to locate his exact burial site.[32]

Prisoners of war were initially held in the nearest convenient castle, monastery or town, until arrangements could be made to transfer them to Lisbon for transport to England. The rank and file marched under escort, while the officers often faired somewhat better. Baron Lejeune tells how after he was stripped naked by Spanish irregulars he was clothed, provided with money and entertained by British officers before being sent in a carriage to Lisbon.[33]

There were usually sufficient troops available for the escort of small numbers of prisoners, and they could be transported on board supply ships unloading in port. Whilst in transit the prisoners were guarded by either marines or soldiers depending on what troops were available. Captives crossing the Atlantic from the West Indies were often guarded by soldiers being sent home due to ill-health, as was the case in 1796 when fifteen transports arrived at Plymouth with nearly 2,000 negroes captured in the French service. The guard had been provided from the 15th, 21st, 34th, 46th, 3rd Battalion 60th, and 61st Regiments, and comprised officers, NCOs, drummers and invalids. Their ill-health at the start of the two-month voyage had been exacerbated by a shortage of medical supplies, and the troops were noted as having 'been sickly on the passage ... upwards of one hundred of them have died'. On disembarkation it was noted that many of the prisoners had smallpox.[34]

If the prisoners of war were conveyed by naval transport they were landed at a Port near a prison depot, which meant Portsmouth, Plymouth or Chatham. Later in the war prisoners were sent directly from Lisbon to Perth Prison via Leith, Scotland. Privateers landing captives did so at their home port, handing their charges over to the naval or military authorities there. On board these ships the prisoners were confined in the hold and guarded by the privateer crew themselves.

Once in Britain a prisoner would be guarded by the military who escorted their charges to the assigned place of confinement. Officer prisoners were allowed a passport plus expenses and traveled by coach to their parole depot. Prisoner rank and file were usually marched to the depots, but on occasion the canal system was used to transport them to depots inland such as Norman Cross. The journey from the coast to Land Prisons far inland could take some days, with the prisoners being lodged in barns and other large buildings on route. On the wall of the White Lion public house in Stevenage is a plaque noting that French prisoners were lodged overnight in the barn at the rear of the building, as they were being marched north along the Great North Road (now the A1) to Norman Cross. Subsistence of such prisoners was in the hands of the local inhabitants who were always diligent in submitting their expenses for supplying food, straw for bedding and candles.[35]

A large body of foreign prisoners always excited interest amongst the inhabitants of a country town or village through which they passed, and the soldiers had to be especially vigilant in keeping the two populations apart. The *Reading Mercury* of 13 October 1800 reported that bands of 300 and 600 French prisoners of war passed through the town. The same newspaper recorded that 500 Frenchmen halted at Reading on their way to Norman Cross in June 1806, while seven years later a local diarist wrote that a large party was marched down London Street and lodged in the stable at the Saracen's Head Inn, 'presenting a very miserable appearance'.[36]

Once at a Prison Depot, the prisoners were in the care of the Transport Office of the Admiralty.

Notes

[1] State Paper: *For the Exchange of Prisoners of War Between Great Britain and France*. Published in the *Morning Chronicle*, 27 September 1798. This is a version of the agreement that was first established in 1780.

[2] Haythornthwaite, Philip J. *The Napoleonic Source Book* (New York, 1990).

[3] Abell, Francis. *Prisoners of War in Britain 1756–1815* (London,1914), p.10.

[4] Fregosi, Paul. *Dreams of Empire: Napoleon and the First World War, 1792–1815* (London, 1989), p.29–43.

[5] TNA:PRO WO40/8. War Office Unnumbered Papers 1796.

[6] NMM ADM/MT/415. Admiralty Letters 19 February 1796.

[7] ibid. 16 February 1796.

[8] NMM ADM/MT/416. Admiralty Letter 4 October 1796.

[9] NMM ADM/MT/415. 16 February 1796.

[10] NMM ADM/MT/416. July 1796.

[11] Clayton, Tim & Craig, Phil. *Trafalgar: The men, the battle, the storm* (London, 2004), p.363–367.

[12] Gates, D. *The Spanish Ulcer: A History of the Peninsular War* (London, 1986), p.331 and 358.

[13] TNA:PRO ADM103/612. List of Parole Prisoners L-Z.

[14] Gurwood, Lt.Col. J. *Selections from the Dispatches and General Orders of Field Marshal the Duke of Wellington* (London, 1851). Dispatch 856, 14 December 1813.

[15] Crowhurst, Patrick. *The French War on Trade: Privateering 1793–1815* (Gower Publishing, 1989), p.1–24.

[16] ibid. p.207–209.

[17] ibid. p.38–39.

[18] NMM ADM/MT/416, 4 October 1796.

[19] ibid. July 1796.

[20] Munch-Petersen, Thomas. *Defying Napoleon: How Britain bombarded Copenhagen and seized the Danish Fleet in 1807* (Sutton Publishing, 2007), p.38–59.

[21] Reilly, Robin. *The British at the Gates* (London, 1976), p.25–35.

[22] TNA:PRO ADM103/342, *General Entry Book of American Prisoners of War 1812–15.*

[23] ibid.

[24] NMM ADM/MT/416, 4 October 1796.

[25] NMM ADM/MT/415, 10 February 1796.

[26] TNA:PRO ADM103/144, *General Entry Book of American Prisoners of War at Gibraltar, 1812–1815*; ADM103/145, *General Entry Book of French Prisoners of War at Gibraltar, 1803–1813*; ADM103/98, 99, 100, *General Entry Book of French Prisoners of War at Dartmoor Prison,* 1815.

[27] TNA:PRO ADM105/52, Prisoners' Applications, 1811.

28 Liddell Hart, Captain B.H. (Ed.), *The Letters of Private Wheeler 1809–1828* (The Windrush Press, Stroud, 1993), p.145–147.

29 Costello, Edward. *The Adventures of a Soldier or Memoirs of Edward Costello* (London, 1841), p.175–176.

30 McGrigor, James. *The Autobiography and Services of Sir James McGrigor; Late Director General of the Army Medical Department* (London, 1861) p.276.

31 Costello, ibid. p200.

32 Pescott Frost Collection, p121.

33 Lejeune, Baron Louis François. *Memoirs of Baron Lejeune* (London, 1897) p103.

34 WO40/8. War Office Unnumbered Papers 1796.

35 NMM ADM/MT/415. The Mayor of Penzance submitted a bill of £3 12s 8½*d* to the Admiralty for providing supper for 12 French officers and 62 Common Men, carriage of their baggage, candles to illuminate their meal, 40 bundles of straw as bedding, and expenses for men carrying the straw and serving supper. These prisoners were from the captured Privateer *Courer*, brought into Penzance by HMS *Porcupine*.

36 Childs, W.M. *The Town of Reading during the Early Part of the Nineteenth Century* (London, 1910) p.60.

CHAPTER 2

For The Public Service

While on official business to Portsmouth and Plymouth, Commissioner Ambrose Searle decided to visit Stapleton Prison 'without warning ... for the Public Service' to investigate the 'more than common degree of sickness there' during the early months of 1801. He reported:

> I was sorry to observe that neither the Agent, or principal Clerk, or any other proper person belonging to the Department and paid by us, were on the spot, and giving attendance on so special a duty as the receipt and examination of the prisoners.

Discrepancies were found in the amount of food ordered and actually supplied to the prisoners, while much of the meat and bread was of poor quality.[1]

Prisoners of war were the responsibility of the Admiralty, and of all the Admiralty Departments during the late eighteenth to early nineteenth centuries the Transport Office had a reputation for efficiency. Gentlemen such as Ambrose Searle perpetuated this reputation by their attention to every detail of the confinement of prisoners of war.[2]

Until 1795 all business relating to these prisoners was in the hands of 'The Commissioners for taking care of sick and wounded seamen, and for exchanging prisoners of war', popularly known as the 'Sick and Hurt Board'. This department of the Admiralty had been formed in 1702 with an office first at Crutched Friars in the City of London, then Tower Hill, finally arriving at its permanent site at Somerset House in the 1780s. The main function of this Board was administering the health of seamen, and they appointed Agents, usually surgeons, at the ports of Deal, Dover, Fareham, Gosport, Portsmouth, Plymouth, Rochester, Yarmouth, Guernsey, Jersey and Kinsale. Until the outbreak of war with Spain in 1739 the Board was instigated only in wartime, but after this date it had a permanent establishment, albeit reduced during times of peace. In 1746 there were also agents at Bristol, Berwick, Exeter, Falmouth, Glasgow, Hull, North Shields, Saltash and Weymouth, with overseas depots at Gibraltar and Port Mahon. Some of these ports were used to handle and house prisoners of war during the conflicts of the eighteenth century, so that during the early years of the French Revolutionary War small prison depots could be found at a number of these sites. The Sick and Hurt Board administered prisoners of war until this function was transferred to the Transport Board in 1795.[3]

The Transport Board came into existence on 4 July 1794, with responsibility for all naval transport of troops and baggage; naval stores both at home and abroad; plus a long list of minor duties including even the procurement of annual presents for the Indians in Upper and Lower Canada!

The first Commissioners of the Board were Captain Hugh Cloberry Christian RN, who was appointed Chairman; Captain Philip Patton RN; and Mr Ambrose Searle (a civilian appointee). Patton and Searle were to assist the Chairman. Searle had much experience of administrative matters, having been private secretary to Lord Howe in America. A civilian secretary and other naval officers were also appointed to help in the smooth running of the transport service, many of these men having gained administrative experience whilst employed in the various sections of the old Navy Board Department. Alexander Whitehead was the Transport Board's secretary throughout the Revolutionary War, while Captain Rupert George RN became Chairman of the Board when Christian vacated the post in June 1795 after becoming Rear-Admiral of the Blue. Captain John Schank RN replaced Philip Patton when the latter left the Board in 1805 to take his flag.

On 25 September 1795 the Board gained two further members, a sea officer and a civilian commissioner, when all business relating to prisoners of war was transferred from the Sick and Hurt Office. The Transport Office had gained a reputation for efficiency from its inception, and it was considered in the best interests of the Service for the war prisons to be transferred to this department. In 1806 the Transport Office was divided into three sections; a branch relating to the transport service; another for sick and wounded seamen (the Sick and Hurt Board was abolished and its medical functions transferred); and the third for prisoners of war. This organisation continued until the Board was dissolved in 1816.

All members of the Board acted together at one table and business was dealt with by consultation and agreement. When a decision was made the initials of the members present were affixed to it and the necessary orders given for its implementation. The Secretary ensured that the minutes were properly kept and supervised the general conduct of the office. The Board met from Monday to Saturday throughout the war and relayed all information regarding its activities to the Admiralty. These activities were indeed considerable, with the administration of the prisoner of war business generating a vast amount of work.[4]

Transport for prisoners had to be organised, from their place of capture and within Britain once they arrived here. Accommodation had to be found; they needed feeding and clothing; their health required constant attention; contracts had to be arranged with civilians near the prisons; staff had to be employed at each depot. Aside from this day-to-day administration, there were exchange cartels to be organised, and every penny of expenditure had to be accounted for to a Parliament where members took great interest in the cost of the war against France, and often used the subject of prisoners of war and their exchange to attack the government.

If this was not enough work to keep the Transport Office busy, there was also a vast amount of correspondence to deal with from anyone with even the remotest interest in prisoners of war, including King George III, Government Ministers, Members of Parliament, Prison Staff, Charitable organisations, foreign embassies, prisoner's families, and the prisoners themselves. Every letter was answered and every request or complaint investigated, often after the Board had requested further information from all interested parties.

The Board appointed an Agent at each depot who was responsible for the staff, prison and prisoners. These Agents had to report regularly on the state of affairs at their depots, and were kept on their toes by regular visits from the Board's Commissioners, who reported their observations. The Commissioners were the main power within the prisoner of war system and had a reputation of being firm but fair, within the regulations governing the system. They ensured that the Agent and staff at each depot performed their duties, and made recommendations to, and occasionally admonished, those employees who were lax in their work or who abused the system. Before ordering any changes at a depot, they obtained as much information on the matter as they could from the prison staff, prisoners and any civilians who were involved. They were always accessible to the prisoners, and would investigate any complaint from the captives, no matter what their nationality. All information obtained was reported at the Board's meetings.

The Commissioners made a point of transmitting any good ideas they found to other depots, so that the whole system would benefit. For example, in 1807 Commissioner Towry found that the surgeon at Stapleton Prison had a very effective remedy for his pneumonia patients. This information was conveyed to the Board and he ensured that other depots knew of it.[5] The Commissioners maintained a benevolent attitude towards the prisoners. However, they would only tolerate requests and complaints going through the proper channels; if the prisoners attempted to change things without recourse to the authorities, then the authorities would come down very hard upon them. In 1807 the prisoners at Mill Prison, Plymouth, were obviously finding their quarters rather stifling, so they took it upon themselves to make some ventilation holes in the roof. A Commissioner visiting the depot ordered that these holes were to be closed up and the expense of the repairs charged to the prisoners. He wrote:

> To prevent anything of its kind in future, I would recommend all the prisoners hammocks to be numbered, and the first person or persons found sleeping near the new air holes, removed, put on short allowance, and otherwise punished, if found necessary.[6]

The Agents at the Land Prison and Ship Depots were naval officers of the rank of Captain, chosen for their administrative abilities. The Agents at the parole depots were gentlemen of some standing in the community such as lawyers, but not tradesmen who might have a commercial interest in the prisoners in their charge, and who might very well exercise authority at their own discretion without reference to any higher authority. This was found to be the case with the Agent at Fareham, whom the Military Governor of Portsmouth complained was only a tradesman after all, and thus totally unsuitable for the position he held![7]

Each prison ship depot had an Agent in overall command, with each hulk having its own commanding officer. The latter were lieutenants and the Board received many applications from naval officers unable to obtain a sea-going appointment. The Board attempted to employ only officers of good character. Lieutenant Joseph Williams RN, residing at Portsmouth, found that he was not the only officer asking for employment with the Transport Office. The Secretary to the Board sent him a reply in January 1810 stating:

> I am ... to acquaint you that your name will be put on the list of candidates for the command of prison ships under this Department, but I am at the same time to apprise you that there are very many before you on the list; and it is necessary you should transmit testimonials from the captains you have served with.[8]

While the Board tried to employ only good officers, some bad characters slipped through the net, or perhaps the mundane and sometimes brutal conditions on board the hulks had an adverse effect upon these men. As with all sea-going vessels, the hulks kept a log recording each day's activities. Many of the entries are concerned with the weather, the receipt of stores and punishments inflicted upon the naval crew of the ship.[9] Many prisoners asserted that these officers were drawn from the dregs of the Royal Navy, and in some cases the Board's Commissioners were inclined to agree with them. Commissioner Otway, writing from Plymouth in 1799, remarked:

> On enquiry into the character and conduct of the various persons employed at the prison and on board the prison ships, they seem to be as fit for their respective situations as under all the circumstances can be expected.

Commissioner Boyle, visiting the Portsmouth hulks in 1813, gave specific examples of dubious Commanders:

> Lieutenant Harley of the *Suffolk* I found extremely drunk at 10 o'clock, and I understand that is generally the case with him. Lieutenant Peding, 2nd of the same ship, is also a most drunken character. Lt. Voller, 2nd of the *Guildford*, who is absent on leave, I should recommend to the Board to be immediately discharged for reasons unnecessary to point out in a public letter, but which I will communicate on my return.[10]

However, there were good officers in the prison ship establishment. Captain Miller, in command of the prison ship depot at Portsmouth, employed a French officer to collect complaints from the prisoners that he then attempted to remedy.

Generally the officers given employment performed their duties well, though within the constraints of the Board's regulations. The visits by the Commissioners ensured that they did their job and did not exceed their allotted budget. Agents were paid a salary of £200 per annum (in 1797), and allowed expenses for travel on official business, stationery, furniture for an office, and minor items such as candles for lighting and coal for heating their rooms. Anything beyond this had to be sanctioned by the Board, and indeed, the Transport Board was very strict over what was and what was not allowable as expenses. The Transport Office was accountable to an elected Parliament for all expenditure.

Prison Staff

Each Agent had a staff consisting of civilian employees to assist in the running of the depot. In the prison ship depots the organisation consisted of the Agent, a First Clerk and an Interpreter (often the same person), a Second Clerk, and one or two boatmen. This Agent had overall command of the depot. Each hulk had a Lieutenant RN commanding and a crew of a Master's Mate, two Midshipmen, fifteen seamen and four boys (*Arvé Princess*, Portsmouth, 1810). In addition each ship had a civilian staff of a Clerk/Steward and a Surgeon.[11,12]

At each of the hulk depots there was at least one Hospital Ship which employed a Surgeon, one to six Assistant Surgeons (the number varied according to the number of sick on board, and usually comprised both British and French employees), a Clerk, a Matron, and a Sempstress.[13]

A large prison such as Portchester Castle required an efficient staff. When the depot was reopened as a war prison in 1810, Captain C.W. Paterson RN was appointed Agent. His staff consisted of four Clerks (the First Clerk, a Mr Colepeper, not only received a salary of £78 per annum for clerical duties, but was paid an extra £30 as an Interpreter), a Steward, five Turnkeys, a Messenger, and three Labourers. If maintenance work was required within the prison and the existing labour force was insufficient, then up to eight French labourers could be employed on a temporary basis and paid at the standard prison rate of 3*d* per day.

Next to the Agent in a prison the most important administrator was the Surgeon, who had responsibility for all aspects of the prisoner's health. Those inmates suffering from illness or injury were treated under his supervision in the prison hospital. He had responsibility for ensuring adequate stocks of clothing, bedding and medicines in the hospital, and that they were of good quality. He regularly inspected the sanitation facilities of the prison, examined the food brought by the contractors, and its storage, and generally advised the Agent on all health matters.

He was assisted by a locally-recruited staff, often supplemented with French Surgeons in captivity who would volunteer to serve in the prison hospitals, and as they were officers entitled to parole they were allowed to roam outside the prison walls, though within the usual parole regulations. In 1810 four French Assistant-Surgeons on parole at Odiham volunteered to administer to the sick in Portchester Castle. They had accommodation in the village of Portchester, and their willingness to serve whilst in captivity was looked upon favourably for the purpose of exchange. They were paid one shilling per day and given hospital rations, in addition to their parole allowances.[14]

Extra staff were employed if circumstances warranted it, such as when a large number of negroes in the service of France was taken in the West Indies and sent to Portchester Castle. Commissioner Searle wrote in December 1796 that these West Indians had suffered greatly from the English climate since their arrival, with 'frostbite, catarrhal and pulmonic complaints and dysenteries' causing a high mortality amongst them. With the arrival of smallpox Searle ordered that two more Assistant Surgeons and another Dispenser be added to the hospital establishment. He also ordered that a close watch be kept on the other prisoners as he felt that the health of the negroes had been affected by the European captives who robbed and plundered the negroes, 'considering themselves as a superior race of beings to the unfortunate blacks'.[15]

Nurses in the hospitals were recruited from amongst the prisoners, and in 1797 some disgruntled inmates of Portchester Castle complained to the French Agent in London about their employment at the prison. The Transport Board investigated and found that the reason for their complaint was the discharge of some nurses who were discovered to be stealing the rations given to sick prisoners. The report about the prison hospital painted a very favourable picture of the sort of treatment experienced by prisoners of war who fell ill whilst in captivity. The surgeon, Mr Blatherwick, was very highly thought of by the prisoners, and he was found to keep a very clean and efficient hospital. All patients were regularly visited between the hours of 11.00am and 12.00 noon, and the nurses were selected from amongst the 'most orderly and well-behaved' of the prisoners. The sick were given an extra ration of rice and mutton, some of which was being purloined by members of the nursing staff. The Board wholeheartedly agreed that any nurse who was complained of was to be immediately discharged back into the prison if the complaint was found to be justified. It was two of the nurses thus discovered who had complained to the French Agent, and this gentleman readily concurred with the Board when it stated that the complaints were totally unwarranted.[16]

While prisoners who abused the trust given to them could cause trouble, civilian employees of the Board gave their masters just as many problems. Mr Colepeper was transferred from the prison establishment at Plymouth to take up his appointment at Portchester. He no doubt thought that he could evade payment of £10 12s 11d Property Tax owing at his former place of work, but the Transport Office thought otherwise. This Department kept very accurate records of its employees and ensured that every penny of tax was paid. Captain Paterson was instructed to deduct the debt from Colepeper's salary. Throughout the records there are instances such as this, where careful attention is given to the amounts paid to staff, and the amount of tax owed by them. Tax evasion was obviously repugnant to the Transport Board.[17]

One of the perks of being a turnkey at a prison, be it for civilian or military prisoners, was permission to sell Small Beer to the prisoners and keep the profit. The Board allowed this within the war prisons, provided the retail price of the locally obtained beer did not exceed 8d per gallon. Some turnkeys abused this privilege. Commissioner Boyle discovered that in 1810 John Stacey had a very nice position both as turnkey at Portchester Castle and as proprietor of a nearby Public House (the Crown Tavern, now Crown House in the village of Portchester). He indulged in a very lucrative trade of selling strong beer to the prisoners. This practice was forbidden and Stacey given the choice of giving up his Public House or his position as turnkey. It seems that drunken prisoners were not to be encouraged at any depot.[18]

Indeed, inebriated staff were not encouraged either, partly because they were rendered incapable of performing their job, and partly as it set a bad example to the prisoners. Mr Bell, the Chief Clerk at Portchester Castle, was discharged in June 1810 (after only a few months in the post) 'in consequence of his being unfit for the situation by habitual drunkenness'.[19]

Prison Regulations

All prison depots were subject to a set of regulations, by which all staff and prisoners were expected to abide. In addition to these rules, each barrack block within the land prisons and each deck on board the hulks had a committee to police the prisoners and maintain some sort of good behaviour. The official regulations were posted in a prominent place at the depots so that all inmates could read and understand them. These rules were stated thus:

By the Commissioners for Conducting His Majesty's Transport Service, and for the Care and Custody of Prisoners of War.
Rules to be observed by the Prisoners of War in Great Britain, Ireland etc.

1. The Agent's orders are to be strictly obeyed by all the prisoners; and it is expressly forbidden, that any prisoners should insult, threaten, ill treat, and much less strike the turnkeys, or any other person who may be appointed by the Agent to superintend the police of the prison, under pain of losing turn of exchange, of being closely confined, and deprived of half their ration of provisions, for such time as the Commissioner may direct.
2. All the prisoners are to answer to their names when mustered, and to point out to the Agent any errors they may discover in the lists, with which he may be furnished, in order to prevent the confusion which might result from erroneous names: and such prisoners as shall refuse to comply with this regulation, shall be put on half allowance.
3. Should any damage be done to the buildings by the prisoners, either through their endeavouring to escape, or otherwise, the expense of repairing the same shall be made good by a reduction of the rations of provisions of such as may have been discovered, all the prisoners confined in the particular building so damaged,

shall contribute by a similar reduction of their rations towards the expense of the said repairs.

4. Such prisoners as shall escape from prison, and be re-taken, shall be put into the Black Hole, and kept on half allowance, until the expenses occasioned by their escape are made good; and they shall moreover lose their turn of exchange, and all Officers of the Navy or Army so offending shall, from that time, be considered and treated in all respects as common men.

5. Fighting, quarrelling, or exciting the least disorder is strictly forbidden, under pain of a punishment proportionate to the offence.

6. The prisons are to be kept clean by the prisoners in turns, and every person who shall refuse to do that duty in his turn, after having received notice of the same, shall be deprived of his rations, until he shall have complied.

7. The prisoners are from time to time to inform the Agent of the clothing or other article which they may stand in need of, and have money to purchase; and the Agent shall not only permit them to purchase such articles, but also take care that they are not imposed on in the price.

8. The prisoners in each prison are to appoint three or five, from among their own number, as a committee for examining the quality of the provisions supplied by the Contractor; for seeing that their full rations, as to weight and measure, are conformable to the Scheme of Victualling; and if there should be any cause of complaint they are to inform the Agent thereof; and should he find the complaint well-founded, he is immediately to remedy the same. If the Agent should neglect this part of his duty, the prisoners are to give information thereof to the Commissioners, who will not fail to do them justice in every respect.

9. All Dealers (excepting such as trade in articles not proper to be admitted into the prison) are to be allowed to remain at the principal gate of the prison from six o'clock in the morning until three in the afternoon, to dispose of the merchandise to the prisoners; but any of the prisoners who shall be detected in attempting to introduce into the prison spiritous liquors, or other improper articles, or in receiving or delivering any letter, shall be punished for the abuse of this indulgence, in such manner as the Commissioners may direct.[20]

Prisoners had some control over their environment, and could approach the Agent at any time with problems or requests. If he failed to give satisfaction in his response, then they could contact the Commissioners direct, or complain to the French Agent in London. The prisoner committee officially sanctioned by the Transport Board was also used to maintain discipline and exercise some control over their colleagues. Each such group of prisoners asserted control over their fellows by first being elected by majority decision, usually from amongst the more educated and socially superior men, and secondly by establishing their own set of regulations in addition to the official rules. According to Benjamin Waterhouse the committees were re-elected every four weeks, and consisted of a President and twelve Counsellors.[21] Benjamin Palmer was an American prisoner at Dartmoor, keeping a diary of his stay in Britain, in which he related the regulations imposed by the committee of which he was Secretary, due to his ability to read and write.

Regulations in Dartmoor Prison No.7, 11 October 1814
(Secretary: Benjamin Palmer)
Regulations established by the Committee appointed by the majority of the prisoners.

Article 1
Any person or persons who shall be found guilty of gambling for money or any other thing shall pay two shillings each. Any shopkeeper who shall be found guilty of allowing gambling in his shop for anything whatever shall pay the sum of eight shillings, and for the second offence shall not be allowed to keep shop.

Article 2
Any person or persons who shall be found guilty of taking down the lights hung up for the benefit of the prisoners shall forfeit the sum of one shilling and two shillings for the second offence.

Article 3
Any person or persons who shall be found guilty of treachery or theft or uncleanliness shall receive corporal punishment, according to the degree and nature of the offence, and as the Jury shall determine.

Article 4
Any person or persons who shall be found guilty of making any nuisance (except in the Necessary) shall be made to clean the same and pay one shilling.

Article 5
Any person or persons who shall be found guilty of washing in the well shall pay one shilling for every such offence.

Article 6
Any person or persons who shall be found guilty of disturbing the prisoners after 10 o'clock at night shall pay one shilling.

Article 7
No persons shall be molested or brought to trial for any misdemeanour before he became a prisoner in Dartmoor Prison.

Article 8
Any person or persons who shall make a smoke in the prison after the doors are shut, or before they are opened in the morning shall for every such offence forfeit one shilling, unless the doors are shut in the day, and then the consent of the Committee must be obtained to make a fire.

Article 9
Any person who shall have cause of complaint shall make the same known to the Committee whose decision shall be definitive unless they shall see fit to call a jury.

Article 10
Any person or persons who shall be summoned to attend as a Juryman shall refuse or neglect to attend at the place appointed without any reasonable excuse shall for every such offence pay one shilling.

Article 11
All moneys collected by fines shall be appropriated to defray the expenses of pens, ink and paper etc., and to pay the Constable

Criers for their trouble, and it shall be the duty of the Committee to appoint a person to receive the money and to keep a regular account of all receipts and disbursements.

Article 12
It shall be the duty of the Committee to appoint three men out of the said Committee, one to attend in the Cook House and two to attend outside and inspect the provisions.

Article 13
Any person who shall defraud his fellow prisoners by contracting debts he is not able to pay shall be brought to trial, and must abide by the sentence of the Jury.

Article 14
Any one of the Committee who shall be guilty of a breach of any of the foregoing Articles, shall pay double.[22]

Punishments

The official regulations stated that any failed escapees would be incarcerated in the Black Hole, or *cachot*, on short allowance of rations until the cost of their recapture should be made good. The Black Hole was also used to confine troublesome prisoners.

On board the hulks this room was usually situated in the hold, and was about six feet by six feet, with only a small window high up for ventilation. There was a bench on which to sit and a simple tub for a latrine. In the Land Prisons this place of confinement was a small structure usually erected for the purpose. At Dartmoor this was at first a small building in the Infirmary yard, but it was of such poor construction that inmates frequently broke out and mingled with the other prisoners.[23] In 1811 a much stronger cell was constructed utilizing French labour. The floor was of granite blocks each weighing over a ton, which was intended to prevent prisoners from tunnelling out. Such stone was also used to construct the walls and roof and the new cachot was approximately 45 by 25 feet. There were no windows and only two ventilation openings under the vaulted roof. The door was of solid wood plated with iron panels, with a small opening through which food could be passed to the prisoners.[24]

At Portchester Castle there were four Black Holes; three were situated in the medieval part of the castle, and the fourth in the room over the Land Gate where today can be seen a number of inscriptions carved into the stonework by prisoners incarcerated there. Some of these carvings record the offence of *De Zarte* – desertion from prison – an obvious euphemism for an attempt to escape, and the length of the prisoner's detention. Many of these inscriptions date from the earlier wars of the eighteenth Century.

Prisoners who continually attempted escape or caused trouble in the Land Prisons were sent back to the hulks, where conditions were somewhat less wholesome than on land, and where the security was more appropriate for such men. Even such high security confinement did not deter the hardened characters, and many hulk commanders were at their wits' end with some prisoners. Jacques Friteau was confined in the Black Hole of the *Crown*, but still caused problems for the authorities when he attempted to set fire to this room! Mathieu Lesur was a nineteen-year-old seaman sent from the *Crown* to the *Vengeance* who:

> ... has been concerned in several attempts to cut out ... is extremely impertinent to every officer in the ship ... during the last week has been detected twice in the act of attempting to get away ... threatened the clerk's life ... ordered to be confined to the Black Hole in irons on short allowance until further orders.

This punishment was applied to many other violent, quarrelsome, outright ugly characters.[25]

The crimes for which prisoners of war could be punished were many and varied. The records for Dartmoor Prison give an insight into the trouble the captives could cause. These are taken from the entries for the prison cachot.

1812

24 February	Louis Constant and Olivier de Camp, for striking a sentinel on duty.
20 May	Jean Delchambre, for throwing a stone at a sentinel and severely cutting his head.
19 August	F. Lebot, for throwing a stone at the postman, as he was returning from Tavistock.
4 September	Jean Swan, for drawing a knife on the hospital turnkey.
24 September	S. Schamond, for throwing down a sentinel and attempting to take away his bayonet.
20 October	W. Johnson, for throwing stones at a sentinel.

1813

13 March	P. Boissard, for striking a turnkey and threatening to murder him on the first opportunity.
28 March	J. Beauclere, for threatening to stab Mr Moore, because he could not procure employment for him on the Buildings.
6 April	F. Le Jeune, for being one of the principal provision buyers in the prison (i.e. illegally purchasing the rations of other prisoners, for resale at a profit), and for repeatedly writing blood-thirsty and threatening letters.
10 April	M. Girandi and A. Moine, for being guilty of infamous vices.[26]

Other punishments available to the authorities included reducing the ration of the offender, and sometimes of his messmates as well. It was therefore in the interests of a whole mess to maintain discipline. A man could be deprived of his chance of exchange by placing his name at the bottom of the list. While the actual chance of an exchange was not a foregone conclusion, and became more remote for the French prisoners as the war progressed, depriving a man of his one slim prospect of returning home was a frightful punishment.[27]

The prisoners tried to maintain discipline themselves by administering punishments other than simple fines. In

Dartmoor any American who tried to enlist in British service but was discovered by his colleagues had the letter 'T' for traitor pricked into his forehead with India ink.[28] Benjamin Palmer wrote that an informer, if tried and found guilty by his colleagues, would be condemned to sweep the decks of the prison ship whilst wearing a piece of canvas on his hat with 'I am an Informer' written upon it.[29] Bad language earned the perpetrator the same punishment of sweeping the decks. Whipping was used to punish serious crimes, although the Board actively discouraged this. In December 1815 a French prisoner was admitted to the hospital at Dartmoor with 'a lacerated back from severe punishment in the prison'. An investigation was ordered and the prisoners told not to administer their own punishments, and warned of the consequences if a prisoner died because of such treatment.[30]

For more serious crimes, such as forgery of coins and banknotes or murder, the prisoner would find himself at the mercy of the law of the land, rather than the prison regulations. Nicholas Deschamps and Jean Roubillard were tried at Huntingdon Assizes for forging £1 banknotes. At the time this was a capital offence and they received a sentence of death, but this was commuted to imprisonment in Huntingdon Gaol until peace came in 1814, when they were released.[31] Prisoners of war occasionally killed each other, either by plain and simple murder or in a duel fought over some dispute, no matter how trivial. Incarceration together for years at a stretch was bound to test a man's temper and tolerance of others.

George Johnson was hanged for the murder of Jonathan Paul, a fellow American at Dartmoor, after being found guilty at Exeter Assizes in March 1815. In the case of such trials, the jury was usually composed of half British and half French or Americans (as appropriate), to ensure that there could be no accusations of injustice. A jury composed of half English and half French jurors found two Frenchmen guilty of forgery. They were sentenced to hang, despite a request to be shot. Louis Herquiada was hanged at Winchester in March 1808 for killing a fellow prisoner on board the *San Damaso*. Occasionally an example would be set by executing the prisoner at his depot in front of all the other prisoners, as was the case with a Spaniard hanged at Mill Prison for murder in 1806. Prisoners were sometimes acquitted after trial. In 1809 two Frenchmen quarreled onboard a Portsmouth hulk and one was stabbed to death. The Court at Winchester inflicted no punishment as it was clearly proved that the victim had brought death upon himself by his passionate temper![32]

The Garrisons

While the Admiralty was responsible for the administration of the prisoners of war, their security was in the hands of the military. The hulks were garrisoned by detachments of Royal Marines supplemented with forces drawn from the militia, and as the three prison ship depots corresponded to the three Marine Divisions, troops for the task were conveniently situated nearby.

The Royal Marines was one branch of the British military that regularly recruited from amongst the prisoner of war population. This source of men resulted in a wide cross-section of European nationalities being represented within the Corps. In the 1790s Dutch prisoners were a source of recruits with many being permitted to enlist. In May 1796 the Admiralty approved of a party of 80 Dutch prisoners enlisting as Marines from Portchester Castle. In April 1799 permission was granted to recruit from Austrian and German prisoners.

The Napoleonic period produced an ever-increasing demand for manpower within the Corps, and prisoners of war were again enlisted in large numbers. The Portsmouth Division reported that from 1 May to 30 June 1804 167 recruits were raised, of which 62 were foreigners from the prisons. A return for Plymouth dated 1 January 1811 showed that of 928 ranks serving on shore (many as guards on board the hulks) a total of 406 were foreigners, consisting of 158 Prussians, 126 Germans, 98 Dutch, 7 Swedes, 5 Portuguese, 4 Maltese, 4 Spaniards, 3 Danes and 1 Russian.[33]

One can imagine the initial language difficulties incurred in training and commanding such a heterogeneous collection of troops, and this was a reason for leaving such men in the depots rather than sending them to sea. As one of the duties of the Marines was to guard the hulks, the employment of foreign-speaking troops on board was an advantage in controlling the prisoners. Useful this may have been to the authorities, but guarding erstwhile colleagues cannot have been a popular task, and some prisoners asserted that ex-prisoners of war made for very brutal guards.

Even the English members of the Corps often posed a problem. A spell of duty on board a prison ship was not a popular posting, and many Marines had their health impaired by such a task. In 1808 10 sergeants and 42 privates were certified as unfit for any further service after duty on the hulks.[34] As was usual with ships in harbour, the men were allowed to bring women on board. In 1798 Private James Whitton, part of the garrison on the *Sultan*, brought a woman onto the ship. This woman was, apparently, very drunk and Whitton began to beat her. The Sergeants attempted to restrain him, whereupon he called one 'a lousy drunken rascal' and struck him in the face. The other Sergeant also received a torrent of abuse, both NCOs being informed by Whitton that 'if he had a knife about him he would run it through their bloody hearts'. He was fortunate to receive 300 lashes, similar offences often resulting in the perpetrator being hanged.[35] Events such as this cannot have induced confidence and respect amongst the prisoners of war for their guards. The ships logs for the hulks record many instances of punishments being awarded to marines on board. On board the *Bahama* George Brown was given 48 lashes for contempt, neglect, disobedience and drawing his bayonet on his superior officer on 19 July 1809. The following month William Hartly was recorded as having been given two dozen lashes for contempt and neglect of duty. On 12 September of the same year Richard Courtney received 36 lashes for desertion and neglect of duty, while a week later James Williams received 48 lashes for contempt, disobedience and selling wine to the prisoners. Many of the seamen on board these vessels received similar punishments for identical crimes.[36]

There was often a shortage of marines to garrison each of the ships, so detachments of the militia were often sent on board. John Kincaid recalled that while he was an ensign in the

North York Militia he found himself encamped on the lines at Chatham, where his regiment did duty on board the hulks in the Medway. He wrote that his post was 'for the greater period with a guard on board the old *Irresistible*, which was laden with about eight hundred heavy Danes'.[37] The log of the *Vengeance* at Portsmouth recorded that on 20 October 1809 soldiers from the Northampton Militia were disembarked and replaced by forty-one men of the Inverness Militia. These men remained on board until 21 December when they were replaced by forty marines, who stayed for only three days prior to being transferred to the *Assistance*, to be replaced by forty Rosshire Militia who had been doing duty on board that prison ship.[38]

The Army supplied troops for guarding prisoners on land. Each Land Prison had a garrison consisting of about 500 soldiers, this being the case with the larger depots such as Dartmoor and Norman Cross. parole depots did not have troops specifically assigned to guard the parole prisoners, but the local troop of Yeomanry could be, and occasionally was, called upon to assist in quelling any disturbance amongst these men.

Throughout the period the Army complained about having to provide garrisons for the Land Prisons, in addition to the many other duties expected of the British soldier. The Army had to find troops for overseas service, both for field armies and for garrisons in the ever-expanding British Empire. At home the Army was deployed to repel any French invasion, at the same time often being called upon to quell civil disturbance. While a full-scale invasion by France never materialised, there was always the fear that the enemy would launch raids on parts of the country, releasing and arming such prisoners of war that were nearby, and wreaking havoc in the countryside. In 1779 a Franco-Spanish fleet had sailed up the Channel to attack Plymouth or Portsmouth. While this attempt failed due to lack of organisation and an outbreak of disease on board the ships, this potential disaster for Britain was still fresh in the minds of many military commanders during the early years of the Revolutionary War. The French invasion of Fishguard in 1797, and the landing of French troops in Ireland the following year in support of an Irish rebellion, confirmed their fears.

Other events in the country required the presence of soldiers to maintain order. Periodically there were civilian riots over high prices and low wages. In 1795 there was a serious bread crisis because of the poor corn crop, and 178 food riots were reported around Britain. Further riots occurred in 1800–1801 and 1811–12, mainly over the high price of bread and many of these disturbances involved revolutionary agitators.[39] Naval mutinies at Spithead and the Nore in 1797; further trouble in Ireland in 1803; and the French invasion threats of 1798 and 1803–05 all greatly worried many of the military commanders around Britain.

General Sir William Pitt was Military Governor of Portsmouth in 1794 and the incarceration of prisoners of war in the area was of great concern to him. He wrote to Lord Amherst about Forton Prison, complaining that it was only 200 yards from the Gosport Lines and that he considered it unsafe and unwise to have so many prisoners near to such important defence works, especially if the French conducted operations along the south coast. Guarding the prisoners also depleted the Gosport garrison. Lord Amherst replied that he understood the problem and Pitt's concern, as Forton 'has long been complained of ... the position and state of the prison is in every respect the most dangerous and I may say absurd that can be.'[40]

The situation was alleviated later in the year by opening Portchester Castle as a major depot. General Pitt explained the situation in the Portsmouth area in a letter dated 1 September 1794. In this report he noted that sending many to Hilsea Barracks and then on to Portchester had reduced the number of prisoners at Forton. There were now 4,282 prisoners at the latter depot, with 1,049 left at Forton, while 106 were sick at Hilsea. The strength of the garrison in the Portsmouth area was as follows:

Regiment	Strength	Location
Royal Invalids	266	Portsmouth
South Gloucester Regiment	563	Portsmouth and Docks

West Middlesex Militia	532	Gosport – guarding Forton Prison, the convicts working on the defences, the magazine at Priddy Hard, and Haslar Hospital.
Anglesea Militia	79	Fort Monckton and Haslar Hospital.
Denbigh Militia	294	Portchester Castle.
Oxford Militia	587	Portchester Castle.
Flintshire Militia	119	Hilsea Barracks, guarding the prisoners of war; and Fort Cumberland, guarding convicts.
Total number of troops	2,440	

There was concern that this garrison was too small to guard so many prisoners of war and defend Portsmouth in the event of enemy attack. Aside from the 5,437 prisoners confined in the depots, there were additional captives on parole at Alresford (160 prisoners), Bishops Waltham (88 prisoners) and Petersfield (222 prisoners). These officers had to be watched even though they were not actually guarded by troops, and Pitt considered that such men were in a position to cause trouble in the countryside.[41]

The British Army of the time consisted of Regulars, Militia, Fencibles and Volunteers. In the first category were the Line Regiments who provided troops for service wherever they were required, both at home and abroad. The Militia were regular soldiers but raised for home defence only, each county forming one or more battalions according to its population, and these units usually served outside of the county in which they were raised. This was to avoid any conflict of loyalty if they were used to suppress civil unrest, and as they were the main troops used for guarding prisoners of war this meant that they would not have local knowledge that could assist prisoners in escaping. In 1803 an Act of Parliament raised the Army of Reserve, which was a failure in producing more troops for home service, but which did result in the formation of Garrison Battalions the following year. These too were used for guarding the prison depots. Fencible regiments, both infantry and cavalry, were formed during the 1790s for service in Great Britain and Ireland only. While they were not used as garrisons for the prisons, they were used extensively to escort captives through the country to the depots; to assist in any quelling any disturbances in the prisons; and to recapture escaped prisoners. The Volunteers were units of locally formed troops who drilled for a few hours each week and were available in the event of invasion. They were also a useful local police force if any parole prisoners caused a disturbance.[42]

Britain was divided into military districts, each of which was allocated both regular and volunteer forces, to be dispersed as their duties required. While recruits had to be found for overseas service, troops also had to guard military installations; defend the country in the case of invasion; support the civil authorities; and guard prisoners of war. As the Napoleonic conflict progressed, many militia soldiers were induced to enlist in the regular regiments. Militia battalions that were 600 strong in the early years of the war became depleted and could not make up their numbers. This meant that while one such unit was sufficient to guard a prison depot in the early period, by 1810 it was necessary to use two or three militia battalions – often with a detachment from a regular regiment's depot – to make up a garrison of 500 men. This was a serious problem for military commanders who had prison depots situated in their districts, and parole depots containing large numbers of officers in the surrounding countryside.

In 1810 it was decided to alleviate the situation by moving many of the parole officers to Scotland and the north of England, and to create new prison depots in that area. This eased the problem for the military commanders in the southern half of England. However, Lord Cathcart, commanding the forces in Northern Britain, expressed surprise and concern that all future prisoners of war were to be sent to the northern part of the country. He had heard that many officers were to be sent on parole to that area, with consignments already on their way, before he had even had a chance to express his opinion of the scheme! He asked for a delay of six to eight weeks so that he could organise the security of these captives, plus he pointed out that there would be problems in accommodating troops in the proposed areas of confinement. When he was informed that 15,000 prisoners of war would eventually be held in the north of the country he expressed his concern to all who would listen. His garrison strength was 6,129 Regulars and 7,053 Militia, and after all other duties had been taken into consideration, he would have only 2,500 troops available to guard the prisoners and not enough artillery available locally in case of need. Circumstances did not bring as many as 15,000 captives to his sphere of responsibility, but this did not prevent continual complaints about too many prisoners and not enough troops.[43]

Militia regiments, when part of the complement of a military district, were assigned to prison depots for only a few months at a time. For example, the Cheshire Militia was stationed at Mill Prison, Plymouth, in January 1813. The following month they were marched to Dartmoor, returning to Plymouth in May. This was typical of the duties of such battalions, being moved around the depots every few months and spending no more than six months at one location. From 1810 it was often necessary to have two or more battalions on duty at a depot together. At Norman Cross in 1812 from January until the end of April the garrison comprised the West Essex and the 2nd Yorkshire West Riding Militia. In May the Bedfordshire and the Yorkshire North Riding battalions replaced them. Until 1814 such was the case at this depot, with at least two such units there at any one time.[44]

Often it was necessary to move the militia to a depot very quickly, especially if a large consignment of prisoners was about to arrive. In April 1812 the Bedfordshire Militia was on garrison duty in Littlehampton when they received orders to march to Norman Cross, as a large batch of prisoners was about to arrive from Spain. They commenced their march on 28 April with the men being conveyed in waggons and the officers in post-chaises to speed the journey. They arrived at the depot on 4 May.[45]

The following chapters will relate how soldiers of the garrisons were involved in the various activities of the prisoners they were guarding, be it as agents in selling bone models or as accomplices in escape attempts. Guarding prisoners of war was a tedious duty and the soldiers involved often had an ambivalent attitude to their charges. If they could make money out of the business then so much the better, but many took their duties very seriously indeed. As Charles Dupin later wrote:

> the prisons are habitually guarded by a militia, whose sentinels have shown themselves, on many occasions, too eager to fire upon the prisoners ... Several prisoners of war have, in this manner, been killed on the spot ...[46]

As will be related, this eagerness to use their muskets was in evidence on a number of occasions, and culminated in the infamous Dartmoor Massacre of 1815. If a musket ball would not stop a troublesome prisoner, then many soldiers were quite willing to use the bayonet. These then were the men who guarded prisoners of war.

Notes

[1] TNA:PRO ADM105/44. Commissioners Report 15 May 1801.

[2] Ambrose Searle was also a very religious man, and obviously had the affairs of his fellow men at heart, for he wrote a number of religious and moral pamphlets during his life copies of which exist in the British Library.

[3] Crimmin, P.K. *The Sick and Hurt Board and the health of seamen c1700–1806*. Journal for Maritime Research December 1999, http://www.jmr.nmm.ac.uk

[4] Condon, M.E. *The Establishment of the Transport Board - A Subdivision of the Admiralty, 4 July 1794*. The *Mariners Mirror 58*: 69–84, 1972.

[5] TNA:PRO ADM105/44. 30 April 1807.

[6] ibid. 28 October 1807.

[7] WO40/8. War Office Unnumbered Papers from Sir William Pitt relative to Prisoners of War in the Neighbourhood of Portsmouth, 20 October 1796.

[8] TNA:PRO ADM98/261. Letters relating to prisoners of war at Portsmouth, 19 January 1810.

9   TNA:PRO ADM51/2183. Log of the *Bahama* Prison Ship 1 July 1809
    – 30 June 1811.
10 Branch-Johnson, W. *The English Prison Hulks* (London, 1957) p.55.
11 TNA:PRO ADM104/8.
12 TNA:PRO ADM98/261. 17 January 1810.
13 TNA:PRO ADM105/44. 7 May 1801.
14 TNA:PRO ADM98/252. Admiralty Letters to Agent, Portchester
    Castle. 24 May and 6 June 1810.
15 TNA:PRO ADM105/44. 19 December 1796.
16 TNA:PRO ADM102/844. August 1797.
17 TNA:PRO ADM98/252. 13 April 1810.
18 ibid. 20 September 1810.
19 ibid. 25 June 1810.
20 TNA:PRO ADM105/44. Commissioners Reports.
21 Waterhouse, Benjamin M.D. *Journal of a Young Man of Massachusetts*,
    1816. p.64. This work was written by Dr. Waterhouse from an account
    related to him by an ex-prisoner of war. He was never a prisoner
    himself. Nevertheless, it is an accurate account of life in the British
    war prisons, as corroborated by other authors.
22 Palmer, Benjamin Franklin. *The Diary of Benjamin F. Palmer,
    Privateersman. While a prisoner on board English warships at sea, in the
    prison at Melville Island and at Dartmoor.* (The Acorn Club, Connecticut
    1914) p244–46.
23 Abell, p235.
24 Joy, Ron. *Dartmoor Prison Volume One: The War Prison 1809–1816.*
    (Halsgrove Publishing, Tiverton, Devon 2002) p40.
25 TNA:PRO ADM103/85. General Entry Book of French Prisoners of
    War on board HMPS Crown.
26 Thompson, Basil. *The Story of Dartmoor Prison.* (London, 1907) p93–95.
27 Walker, p64.
28 Waterhouse, p113.
29 Palmer, p26.
30 TNA:PRO ADM98/229. Correspondence to Agent at Dartmoor
    Prison, August 1815.
31 Walker, p66–67.
32 Pescott-Frost Collection p60.
33 Donald, A.J. and Ladd, J.D. Royal Marines Records 1793–1836. (City
    of Portsmouth, 1982) p310.

[34] TNA:PRO 185/73, 26 April 1808. Letter from Major-General George Elliot to the Admiralty.

[35] Lowe, J.A. (Editor) *Records of the Portsmouth Division of Marines 1764–1800*. (City of Portsmouth 1990) pxxxv.

[36] TNA:PRO ADM51/2183 ibid.

[37] Kincaid, John. *Random Shots from a Rifleman* (Spellmount, Staplehurst, Kent, 1998) p.14–15.

[38] TNA:PRO ADM51/1981. Log of the *Vengeance*, 20 October 1809.

[39] Seaman, L.C.B. *A New History of England 410–1975*. Harvester Press, Brighton, 1981. p363-372.

[40] NAM WO40/6. Papers from Sir W. Pitt relative to prisoners of war in the neighbourhood of Portsmouth, 15 April 1794 and 19 April 1794.

[41] ibid. 1 September 1794.

[42] For a detailed account of the often complex organisation of the British Army during the Napoleonic Wars see Haythornthwaite, Philip J. *The Armies of Wellington* (London 1994).

[43] NAM 7412–28,–6,–7,–11. Letters from Lord Cathcart to Horse Guards, 1810.

[44] NAM 8211–24. Statement of the different changes of Quarters of the Militia Forces in Great Britain since 1 January 1812.

[45] Burgoyne, Lt. Col. Sir John M. *Regimental Records of the Bedfordshire Militia from 1759 to 1884*. (London 1884) p.63.

[46] Dupin, Charles. *Voyages dans La Grande Bretagne, Entrepis relativement aux Services Publics de la Guerre, de la Marine. et des Ponts et Chaussées, en 1816–17–18–19, et 1820. Deuxieme Partie, Force Navale*. (l'Institut de France, Paris 1821) p.27.

CHAPTER 3

These Floating Tombs

The Medway is covered with men of war, dismantled and lying in ordinary. Their fresh and brilliant painting contrasts with the hideous aspects of the old and smoky hulks, which seem the remains of vessels blackened by a recent fire. It is in these floating tombs that are buried alive prisoners of war – Danes, Swedes, Frenchmen, Americans, no matter. They are lodged on the lower deck, on the upper deck, and even on the orlop deck ... Four hundred malefactors are the maximum of a ship appropriated to convicts. From eight hundred to twelve hundred is the ordinary number of prisoners of war heaped together in a prison ship of the same rate.[1]

Captain Charles Dupin penned this narrative in 1816 as part of a report to the French Government on the conditions experiences by prisoners of war at the hands of the British. The psychological effect of the hulks was later referred to in an account written by Baron de Bonnefoux in 1835.

It is difficult to imagine a more severe punishment; it is cruel to maintain it for an indefinite period, and to submit to it prisoners of war who deserve much consideration, and who incontestably are the innocent victims of the fortune of war. The British prison ships have left profound impressions on the minds of the Frenchmen who have experienced them; and an ardent longing for revenge has for long moved their hearts, and even today when a long duration of peace has created enemies, I fear that, should this harmony between them be disturbed, the remembrance of these horrible places would be reawakened.[2]

These gentlemen conveniently ignored the similar conditions experienced by British soldiers and seamen at the hands of the French, and the often brutal treatment of foreign prisoners of war in France. It has also to be remembered that these men were writing for a French audience after Frenchmen had experienced these hulks, and so it was most unlikely that they would praise the British prison system.

While conditions on the hulks could be worse than in the land prisons, it was not only the prison authorities that were responsible for the environment. Many prisoners contributed to their environment, whether in a positive or negative manner, so much so that life onboard varied according to the outlook of the prisoners themselves. The picture portrayed by men such as Dupin and Bonnefoux has been presented as true ever since, with many historians confusing the war prison ships with the convict hulks, which were administered separately and whose conditions were indeed horrendous.

At the start of the Revolutionary War the few prisoners who arrived in Britain were housed in land prisons such as Forton or Liverpool. By 1794 it was obvious that new prisons were urgently required for the ever-increasing prisoner of war population, and this prompted the Sick and Hurt Board to use old warships as prison hulks. Such vessels had been used during the Seven Years War, and in North America forty-two vessels were used during the American Revolution. This experience of their use was put to good effect during the wars with France, when prison ship depots were instigated at Chatham, Plymouth and Portsmouth.

The use of hulks was controversial. With the revolt of the American colonies, felons could no longer be transported across the Atlantic. This posed a serious problem for the authorities in Britain who had a large number of convicted criminals awaiting transport but nowhere to send them. To overcome this problem (temporarily, or so it was thought at the time, and a few years before transportation to Botany Bay became an option), convict hulks were installed at Chatham, Portsmouth and Woolwich. The convicts laboured on public works and the combination of hard labour, poor diet and unsanitary living conditions resulted in a high mortality during the first two years of their establishment.

The 1780s had seen increasing efforts by such reformers as John Howard to improve the hulks, if not abolish them completely. Their use was defended on the grounds of cost and convenience.[3]

For housing prisoners of war they were indeed convenient. At the start of hostilities the Royal Navy had a large store of old warships in ordinary from which were chosen suitable vessels, usually two- or three-deckers. Many of these ships had begun their life in the Royal Navy during the middle of the eighteenth century, such as the *Sandwich*. Captured vessels, if they were unfit for further active service, were adapted as prison ships such as the *Vryheid*, Admiral de Wynter's flagship at Camperdown in 1797. As the war progressed the British captured many enemy warships, a fortuitous situation as increasing numbers of victories generated ever increasing numbers of prisoners of war. While new land prisons were built to alleviate the burden, it was impossible to predict the future transport of prisoners into Britain. It was a relatively quick and simple matter to convert a hulk into a prison ship if large shipments of prisoners arrived. While a hulk was being converted many of the existing ships were overcrowded until the new vessel was ready for use and could accommodate the excess.[4]

The main disadvantage in using an old wooden warship was that with the passage of time the cost and practicality of maintenance became a problem. This was especially so in 1812–13, when a combination of the Peninsular Campaign, the Anglo-American War and the war against the Danes was producing a continuous flow of captives into the country who required accommodation. At the same time, many of the older vessels were beginning to rot at their moorings. New hulks were brought into service, but while they were being installed many of the older vessels suffered from overcrowding. When the French prisoners were released the following year they took home with them tales of overcrowding in damp and disintegrating ships. This was so, but only because of the large number of captives arriving in the country, not because of any official policy regarding these men.

Fifty-five prison ships were used during this period as detailed in the following tables.[5]

His Majesty's Prison Ship Depot, Chatham

Ship		Period of use	Nationality of prisoners
Bristol		1794–1801	French, Dutch, Danes
Hero		1794–1801	French, Dutch
Eagle		1796–1800	French, Dutch
Sandwich	{	1797–1801	Dutch
	{	1803–1809	French
Gelykheid		1798–1800	French, Dutch
Camperdown		1798–1801	French
Vryheid		1798–1801	French, Dutch
Bahama		1805–1813	French, Danes
Kron Prinds		1805–1813	French, American
Irresistable		1808–1813	French, Danes
Sampson		1808–1813	French, Danes
Glory		1809–1814	French
Canada		1810–1812	French, American
Brunswick		1812–1813	French
Fyen		1812–1814	Danes
Nassau		1812–1814	American
Belliqueux		1813–1814	French

His Majesty's Prison Ship Depot, Plymouth

Ship		Period of use	Nationality of Prisoners
Prudente		1794–1798	French
Commerce de Marseilles		1796–1810	French
Beinfaisant		1803–1814	French
Europe	{	1796–1801	French
	{	{1803–1814	French
Genereux		1805–1814	Dutch
Hector		1805–1814	French, American
San Isidro	{	1796–1801	French

	Period of use	Nationality of prisoners
	{ 1805–1814	French
El Firme	1807–1814	French
Bravo	1808–1814	French, Danes
Panther	1808–1811	French
San Nicholas	1809–1814	French
Ganges	1811–1814	French
Oiseau	1813–1814	French
St. George	1813–1814	French
Temeraire	1813–1814	French, Danes
Vanguard	1813–1814	French
Neptune	1814	French

His Majesty's Prison Ship Depot, Portsmouth

Ship	Period of use	Nationality of prisoners
Captivity	1796–1800	French
Vigilant {	1796–1801	French
{	1806–1814	French
Fame	1797–1801	French
Portland	1797–1802	French
Prothée {	1797–1801	French
{	1807–1814	French, Danes
Royal Oak	1797–1802	French
Sultan	1797–1802	French
Crown {	1798–1802	French, Dutch
{	1806–1813	French, Germans
Fortitude	1798–1802	French
San Damaso {	1798–1802	French, Dutch
{	1808–1814	French
Le Pegase {	1799–1802	Spanish
{	1803–1813	Hospital Ship
Guildford	1806–1814	French, Russian, Danes
Suffolk	1806–1814	French

Vengeance	1806–1814	French
Veteran	1806–1814	French
Waldemaar	1807–1814	French
San Antoine	1808–1814	Spanish, German, Italian
Marengo	1809–1811	French
Ave Princess	1810–1814	French
Assistance	1811–1814	French, Danes
Kron Princessa	1812–1814	French
Sophia Frederica	1813–1814	French

Note: The *Guildford* was formerly the *Fame*.

When the Peninsula campaign began to generate large numbers of French captives there was an increase in the number of hulks to accommodate them. The years 1812 to 1814 saw a peak in the hulk total in Britain as many Americans came to join the French and other nationalities incarcerated in these depots. The English translator of Dupin's report wrote:

> The long duration of hostilities, combined with our resplendent naval victories, and our almost constant success by land as well as by sea, increased the number of prisoners so much as to render the confinement of a great proportion of them in prison ships a matter of necessity rather than of choice.[6]

When a ship was converted to a prison hulk it had all masts, rigging and sails removed and various superstructures erected for the accommodation of prisoners, prison staff, garrison and stores. All the decks were stripped and extra beams inserted for the slinging of the prisoner's hammocks. Gun ports were barred but rarely glazed over. The only furniture in the ships were benches that ran along each side plus three or four in the centre of each deck, the prisoners having to squat on the deck at mess time or manufactured their own chairs and stools. Prisoners regarded the hulks as the worst means of confinement. Sergeant-Major Beaudouin was confined on board the *Bristol*. He wrote:

The difference in the land prisons and the hulks is very marked. There is no space for exercise, prisoners are crowded together, no visitors come to see them, and we are like forsaken people.

The hulks were dirty and shabby. One prisoner wrote of his prison ship home; 'In fog it was weird. In moonlight it was spectral'. Prisoners were crowded onto the decks, including the orlop, with up to 850 men confined at any one time on board the hulk. Occasionally some overcrowding was evident due to the increasing number of prisoners brought to England. The *Brunswick* at Chatham serves to illustrate this. The orlop deck of this vessel was 125 feet in length, the breadth 40 feet at the waist, and the height 4 feet 10 inches. At night 460 prisoners were crowded into this area, of which number only 431 had hammock space, the remainder sleeping on the deck board. Only 6 feet was allocated for each hammock.[7]

The public attitude of the authorities to the overcrowding was 'the most roomy and airy ships of two and three decks were selected to be fitted up as prison ships'.[8] Commissioner's reports occasionally drew notice to the lack of room such as that from Plymouth in 1801 which stated that 'on board the hospital ships there are ... in all 400 patients, although the ships are not calculated to contain with propriety more than 300'.[9] Other reports included statements such as 'the prisoners are very healthy and the ships upon the whole in tolerable good order'.[10]

The orlop deck of the *Brunswick* was ventilated by 14 gun ports each 17 inches square, barred but unglazed. The atmosphere in such an environment at night was stifling even in winter, while in summer the prisoners went about naked to obtain some relief from the heat. It was said that the guards who removed the hatch covers each morning were often overcome by the onrush of stench from below.[11] Many requests for wind pipes and trunking were made to the Transport Board, but not all were approved. However, a report dated 17 May 1801 described the *San Ysidro* and *Commerce de Marseilles* as being clean and well ventilated, this report being signed by three Commissioners.[12]

Into this environment were crowded prisoners of all nationalities and ages, often for many years. Nicolas Roux, a

French seaman captured at Trafalgar, was not released from the Portsmouth hulks until 1814.[13] In 1798 the *Fortitude* at Portsmouth was home to 750 negroes taken in the French service. The *San Damaso* held 812 Dutch prisoners. The *Prothée* contained 148 French naval officers who had refused, or been refused parole, and 264 boys captured on merchant vessels and privateers. Of these youngsters three were of nine years, five of ten years and thirty-two of eleven years of age. One can imagine the effect of this environment upon such youthful minds.[14]

All captives in the hulks and land prisons were issued the same ration of clothing, bedding and food. Prisoners were issued with a hammock, palliasse, blanket, jacket, waistcoat, trousers, two shirts, one pair of stockings and a hat, all made of a sulphur yellow material stamped with the letters 'T.O.' (Transport Office). This vivid colour was to deter the prisoners from selling their clothing and bedding to the local inhabitants. Yellow clothing and bedding appearing in the local village would suggest that prisoners (often aided by their guards) were financing their gambling addiction by selling naval property!

The Food Ration

Prisoners were fed regularly both in the hulks and the land prisons. The table shows the food ration issued to all prisoners in confinement.[15]

Daily food ration issued to prisoners of war

	Bread	Beef	Fish	Cabbage	Potatoes	Scotch Barley	Salt	Onions	Beer
Sunday	1½ lbs.	½ lb.		½ lb.		1 oz.	⅓ oz.	¼ oz.	2 pints
Monday	1½ lbs.	½ lb.		½ lb.		1 oz.	⅓ oz.	¼ oz.	2 pints
Tuesday	1½ lbs.	½ lb.		½ lb.		1 oz.	⅓ oz.	¼ oz.	2 pints
Wednesday	1½ lbs.		1 lb.		1 lb.		⅓ oz.		2 pints
Thursday	1½ lbs.	½ lb.		½ lb.		1 oz.	⅓ oz.	¼ oz.	2 pints
Friday	1½ lbs.		1 lb.		1 lb.		⅓ oz.		2 pints
Saturday	1½ lbs.	½ lb.		½ lb.		1 oz.	⅓ oz.	¼ oz.	2 pints

Other vegetables such as peas or turnips were substituted when cabbage was not available, and fish (salted herring or cod) was issued twice a week in place of the beef. Breakfast consisted of dry bread, the midday meal was soup with a little bread in it, and supper was boiled meat or gruel. Six men formed a mess, but no spoons, knives or forks were issued, only bowls and pannikins. If the men wanted the refinements of cutlery they had to make or purchase it themselves, though knives were discouraged.

While the fish was ordered to be of 'good, sound quality' Louis Garneray described it as frequently being unpleasant and unfit for consumption, the salted herring especially often being in a rotten state. According to Garneray the prisoners sold the fish back to the contractors at 1d per ration, who in turn sold it back to the hulks at 2d per ration. With the money the prisoners purchased butter and cheese from the contractors via private transactions. Garneray wrote: 'I am convinced that some of those herrings saw ten years service with the Navy'! The cod was supposedly just as nauseating but could be rendered just edible when boiled for a long time.[16] Admittedly Garneray was writing for a French audience many years later, and may have embellished his memory of captivity to make his story more entertaining.

The official contracting regulations issued by the Transport Office in 1797 described the quality of food to be purchased from local contractors and issued to all prisoners:

Beer   to be equal in quality to that issued on His Majesty's
        ships.
Beef   to be good and wholesome fresh beef, and delivered in
        clean quarters.
Cheese to be good Gloucester or Wiltshire, or equal in quality.
Peas   to be of the white sort and good boilers.
Green   to be stripped of outside leaves and fit for the copper.
Bread   to be equal in quality to that served on His Majesty's
        ships.[17]

As much of the meat issued to the Royal Navy was salted and stored in casks, and the bread issued in the form of weevil-infested hardtack, the fare given to prisoners of war was good when judged by the standards of the time. The quantity received by the prisoners was similar to that issued to seamen who were expected to perform hard work at sea. The only difference was in the quantity of beer issued, a seaman receiving one gallon per day, a prisoner one quart.

By 1800 the price of food in Britain was rising dramatically. The price of wheat per Imperial quarter was 69s in 1799, 113s 10d in 1800, and 119s 6d in 1801. Contractors were allowed 5d per prisoner per day, and this increase in the price of flour resulted in many cheaper alternatives being sought for the prisoners' diet, such as using foreign imports of wheat, or poor quality or damaged flour. An official alternative was to use potatoes for making bread, but the prisoners complained and this idea was dropped. Dishonest contractors used mixtures of good and lean grain, and weed seeds.[18]

Beaudouin had this to say about the rations:

...half the time they gave us provisions which the very dogs refuse. Half the time the bread is not baked, and is only good to bang against a wall; the meat looks as if it has been dragged in the mud for miles. Twice a week we get putrid salt food, that is to say, herrings on Wednesday, cod-fish on Saturday. We have several times refused to eat it, and as a result got nothing in its place, and at the same time are told that anything is good enough for a Frenchman. Therein lies the motive of their barbarity.[19]

Beaudouin's account was written some years after the event, when memory and his target audience may have influenced his views. At the time the Board made strenuous attempts to monitor the rations given to prisoners and maintain an acceptable standard. A general directive sent to all Agents in 1804 stated that 'you will immediately forward to this office by coach a loaf taken indiscriminately from the bread issued to the prisoners'. The mountain of bread that resulted contained numerous loaves declared unfit for consumption, and the Board sent to all depots an example of the type and quality of the bread to be served out to prisoners 'made of whole wheaten bread actually and bona fide dressed through an eleven shilling cloth'.[20]

The Board and its Commissioners were kept busy investigating the many complaints relating to poor provisions supplied to the prisoners. The letters received, both from the prisoners and the Agents, stated that provisions were withheld from the prisoners, that the contractors were using salt water in the manufacture of bread instead of salt, and that clothing was rotten, of thin material and did not survive the first wet weather. The offending contractors were prosecuted.

In a letter dated May 1796 and signed by one Coquet and fifty other prisoners, a complaint was conveyed to the Board regarding the treatment experienced by the prisoners on the *Hero* at Chatham. They alleged that they should have received 1½lb bread daily, but the Agent only issued 1lb, occasionally substituting ½lb potatoes instead of the missing ½lb bread; and also some of the meat ration was withheld from them. The Board explained to them that due to a shortage of bread since late 1795 the allowance had been officially reduced from 1½lb to 1lb per day. This reduction was supposed to be made up with additional pulse or vegetables, but to satisfy themselves that there were no irregularities at the Chatham depot, an investigation of the situation was ordered.[21]

While prisoners of war complained about the food issued to them, their views have to be placed in context. Many civilians in the country did not eat meat on a daily basis. Prisoners received food every day, while their counterparts on campaign often received erratic supplies. In many cases the food given to prisoners in Britain was better than these men had received in France. In 1797 Ambrose Searle toured the Land Prison depots in the West Country. He noted that the 155 French prisoners held at Pembroke boiled their meat and vegetable ration into a strong broth which was 'a better diet than many of the local inhabitants can procure and better than received in France'. The small prison at Kergilliack (near Falmouth) housed prisoners he described as 'for the most part, hardy and robust seamen taken in Privateers'. He noted that 'there is reason to believe that their fare, as to food, is to most of them very superior to what they have been accustomed to obtain in their own country'.[22]

On board all vessels a committee of prisoners was allowed to inspect the provisions delivered, to see them weighed and to reject any they considered poor quality. The prisoners occasionally complained that these committees were not selected fairly, whereupon the commissioners would direct that they be chosen afresh each day. Regular visits by the commissioners kept any dishonesty to a minimum. Any contractor who was found to be giving short measure was mulcted of amounts varying from £50 to £100, with repeated abuse of the contracts resulting in legal action and supplies being purchased elsewhere. Any contractor disputing the matter with the Board found that payments to him were withheld until the matter was resolved. Any employee of the Transport Board found to be dishonest was dismissed from his post.

Overall the Agents were usually diligent in monitoring the quality of the food and clothing ration issued. The Board wrote to Captain Woodriff at Portsmouth in January 1810 '... we approve of your having rejected the red herrings of an inferior quality offered to be issued, and having received white herrings in lieu of a proper quality'.[23]

Commissioner Towry reported from Chatham in 1806 that the provisions were good in quality and that there were no complaints from the prisoners. He found that fresh milk and vegetables were given to the sick, who also received a gruel made from Scotch barley, rice, sugar and pimento.[24]

It was widely believed (especially amongst the prisoners themselves) that the food and clothing issued by the authorities was responsible for ill health on board the hulks. Boiling was a standard method of preparing the vegetable ration, and undoubtedly this would have destroyed some of the vitamin content. While their diet did contain the necessary vitamins and minerals for health, the quantities of these essential items would have varied from one batch of rations to another, and it was only the fact that additional food could be purchased that kept many of these prisoners in good health. Equally so this concept could be applied to men at sea and to a limited extent to men fighting on land.

The Health of the Prisoners

The quality and quantity of the rations also affected morale on board the hulks, and this in turn would have affected the general state of health of those prisoners. When Sir Rupert George visited the *Sandwich* in September 1807 he reported that the vessel was 'in the most perfect state of cleanliness ... the provisions of good quality'. This was born out by the sickness rate on board the vessel at that time. Out of 708 men only 18 were in the sick berth.[25]

Each ship had a sick berth and in each depot at least one vessel was designated a Hospital Ship for the treatment of more serious ailments. The *Renown* hospital ship at Plymouth had a staff (in February 1814) consisting of two surgeons, one assistant-surgeon, one matron, one interpreter, one cook, one barber, one mattress-maker, one tailor, one washerwoman and ten nurses.[26] Often French surgeons from amongst the prison population volunteered to serve in the hospitals, and the nurses were frequently from amongst the prisoner population.

The Board paid much attention to the health of prisoners of war. Commissioners reported any improvements that, in their opinion, could and should be made to the hulks to reduce the incidence of sickness. In 1806 Commissioner Towry noted that the hulks at Chatham were deficient in air funnels, needed to aerate the lower decks. He observed that on the *Rochester* the decks were washed on alternate days, which he considered too frequent, as the lower deck was always very wet.[27]

The French surgeon Dr Fontana was captured in Portugal in 1812 and confined at first on board the *Brunswick*. He took notes about the health of prisoners in his care and later wrote that the most prevalent illnesses were chest complaints, brought about by:

... moral despair caused by humiliations and cruelties, and deprivations inflicted by low-born uneducated brutes, miserable accommodation, the foul exhalations from the mud shores at low water, and the cruel treatment by doctors who practiced severe bleedings, prescribed no dieting except an occasional mixture, the result being extreme weakness. When the patient was far-gone in disease he was sent to hospital, where more bleeding was performed, a most injudicious use of mercury made, and his end hastened.[28]

It should be noted that consumption (tuberculosis) was common in society at the time and readily spread amongst people in close confinement, such as prisons, town dwellings, barracks and ships, including the hulks. Damp conditions would have exacerbated respiratory ailments.

Some surgeons may have been less than enthusiastic about their work on the hulks. Others were hardworking conscientious men who did their best for all the patients in their care. Commissioners' reports detail the attitude of surgeons to their work. In 1801 the health of the prisoners on the *Bristol* at Chatham was in the hands of Mr Young who resided on board and paid great attention to his duties. Between January 1800 and May 1801 he treated 1,602 patients of whom only 42 died. Mr Kent on the *Buckingham* was also regarded as an attentive surgeon with a very clean and orderly hospital. It is evident that those surgeons who resided on board the hospital ships were the most conscientious and their hospitals were invariably clean and efficient. In April 1801 it was discovered that most of the surgeons on the Portsmouth hulks spent much of their time residing and practicing on shore, and not attending to their duties amongst the prisoners. An order from the Board put a stop to this. It was evident however, that some surgeons were not suitable for their profession, no matter whom they were treating. Commissioner Otway, reporting from Plymouth in December 1796, discovered instances of neglect of duty by Mr Cooban the surgeon at Mill Prison. He had no control over his staff and the hospital while 'the Dispensary was a scene of riot and drunkenness' resulting from his assistants drinking the wine intended for the patients.[29]

Even with a positive attitude the number of prisoners arriving on board was bound to cause difficulties with health care. Many were in poor health before they arrived having suffered disease and wounds whilst on campaign, and many of these unfortunates succumbed whilst in captivity. Prisoners of war held by Britain's allies tended to suffer, as often these countries had no provision for looking after prisoners. The army of General

Dupont that capitulated to the Spanish in 1808 spent 18 months rotting in the hulks at Cadiz or in the prison on the island of Cabréra. Of the 17,635 men who originally surrendered, 2,500 survived and were transferred in batches to the Plymouth hulks in 1810. It was observed that one of these unlucky men simply lay down on the beach in the Hamoaze and 'died of dirt'. The majority of the others had to be admitted to the hospital ship, where many died despite medical care.[30]

The *Renown* received a batch of prisoners from Spain in 1814 whose condition was similarly dire:

> Fever and dysentery have been the prevalent complaints among the prisoners from Pampelune, whose deplorable state the Board of Inspection are in full possession of. .... pneumonia has recently attacked many of these ill-conditioned men termed Romans, many of whom were sent here literally in a state of nudity, an old hammock in the boat to cover them being excepted.[31]

Epidemics of consumption, pneumonia, dysentery, measles, smallpox and typhus frequently occurred. These diseases were prevalent amongst the civilian population throughout Europe at this time, but spread quickly in the crowded mass of humanity that was common to all prisons, including the hulks. Respiratory ailments were constantly in evidence, frequently leading to extensive outbreaks and numerous deaths. Some vessels no sooner got over one epidemic before another surfaced. The *Crown Prince* (*Kron Prinds*), home to Americans and French, suffered an outbreak of smallpox towards the end of 1813 that was successfully contained by the use of vaccination.

In April of the following year typhus emerged on board. Benjamin Waterhouse wrote:

> From four to six were taken down with it every day. We have about nine hundred men on board this ship; eight hundred of us wretched prisoners, and one hundred Englishmen [crew and garrison]. We are more crowded than is consistent with health or comfort. Our hammocks are slung one above the other. It is warm and offensive in the middle of our habitation; those who

have hammocks near the ports are unwilling to have them open at night. All this impedes the needful circulation of air.

The epidemic spread throughout the depot. Waterhouse continued:

As the appropriate hospital ship is now crowded with sick, we are obliged to retain a number in the *Crown Prince*. The sick bay of this ship is now arranged like a hospital ship; and the hospital allowance is served out; and the chief surgeon visits us every week. Our Committee, composed of the oldest and most respectable men among us, do everything in their power to keep the ship and the prisoners clean.

The worst affected was the *Bahama*:

One hundred and sixty Americans were put on board her in the month of January. She had been used as a prison for Danish sailors, many of whom were sick of typhus fever. These Americans came, like the rest of us, from Halifax; being weak, weary, fatigued and half-starved, their dejected spirits and debilitated bodies were aptly disposed to imbibe the contagion. Accordingly, soon after they went on board, they were attacked with it. All of the Danes were sent out of her; and her upper deck is converted into a hospital; the surgeon has declared the ship to be infectious, and no one communicates with her but such as supply the ship and attend the sick ... Out of three hundred and sixty-one Americans who came last on board, eighty-four were, in the course of three months, buried in the surrounding marshes, the burying place of the prison ships.[32]

Prisoners died of other causes. Those captured in tropical climes often succumbed to illnesses acquired there, and were recorded as dying of 'fever', a general medical term, the causes of which also occurred in Britain. Dropsy, scurvy, cholic and enteritis were other causes of death. Gunshot wounds were sometimes entered in the 'Accounts of Prisoners of War who Died' in the depots acquired either in battle or during escape attempts. The latter also resulted in the occasional drowning. Some ships recorded 'assassinations' amongst the prisoners; these were either the result of dueling or murder.[33]

The authorities did their best to improve the health of the prisoners. While the hulks may have had a poor reputation health wise, in some instances they were better than some of the land prisons. In December 1796 Commissioner Otway reported that:

> We have directed all the Blacks and People of Colour in health at Portsmouth to be removed into the *Captivity* and *Vigilant* prison ships, being the only ones now ready, the warmth and comfortable situation of the spaces allotted for their accommodation between the different decks we trust will prevent the effect the cold had hitherto on them at the prison [Portchester Castle].

Otway had discovered that the situation of the West Indian prisoners, mulattos and blacks:

> ... is truly melancholy, being rendered cripples for life by the loss of toes, fingers etc., some are even deprived of both feet ... many others I apprehend will meet a similar fate if detained in this country, as it is absolutely impossible to guard people of that description from the effects of a climate so very different from their own.[34]

The hulks may have been warmer than the stone enclosure of Portchester Castle, but it is debatable whether they were healthier in other respects. Some hulk commanders attempted to improve the conditions of their charges. Lieutenant Gardiner wrote to the Admiralty in 1796:

> I beg to state for their Lordship's information the wretched situation of at least 300 of the prisoners now on board of the *Europe* under my command, they are destitute of almost every article of clothing, and all that many have is a miserable piece of dirty old hammock sewed around their bodies, without shoes, stockings, shirts, without so much as a covering to the head or

a handkerchief to the neck and to complete their misery they have not an ounce of soap issued to them these three weeks and upwards. The Surgeon of the *Europe* has represented to me that he is apprehensive that some serious disorders may ensue if clothing is not issued to them at this inclement season of the year; and also hopes that their proportion of soap might be continued to keep them clean.[35]

The health and well being of the prisoners was not only in the hands of the Transport Board, their employees and the contractors. The prisoners themselves contributed to their environment in either a positive or a detrimental way. The official line was that the food ration was sufficient to keep a prisoner in good health when 'fairly and regularly consumed by him' and provided he took proper care of himself.

Social life on the hulks

The prisoners brought much misery upon themselves by their passion for gambling, with many of them gambling away their food and clothing. This was common knowledge in Britain and often cited as the cause of the poor conditions on board the hulks. This activity may have been instinctive in men whose leisure time in peace revolved around drink, women and the thrill of the dice. On board the prison ships there was a lot of time to fill and very little to fill it with. There was a roll call each day and a few prisoners had minor work duties to perform; the remainder occupied their day as best they could.

Many prisoners were regarded as being of low social standing, and not only by the authorities. Baron de Bonnefoux wrote:

There existed neither fear, reserve, nor self-respect among that class which could not claim the benefits of education. Among them reigned openly the most perverse immorality, the most shameful outrages to modesty, the most revolting of actions, the most unblushing cynicism, and, in the midst of the general misery, one added misery greater than can be conceived.

Waterhouse agreed with this view: 'Such a sink of vice I never saw, or ever dreamt of, as I have seen here'. Colonel Lebertre recalled that 'life on them is the touchstone of a man's character'.

Amongst the French there were three social classes of prisoner on board the hulks. *Les Raffalés* were the lowest, with the *Manteaux Impériaux* being the lowest of this group. They wore rags that swarmed with lice, and so their nickname facetiously referred to the bees of Napoleon's Imperial Mantle. They gambled away their food and clothing, and begged, borrowed and often stole from their fellows in their pursuit of gaming.

Les Messieurs en Bourgeois were the prisoners with enterprise, who earned money by working for other prisoners, by producing handicrafts, or by trading in food, drink and tobacco. They made enough to improve their own conditions on board, and some even returned home as quite wealthy men.

At the top of the social scale were *Les Officiers*. These were officers who had refused to give, or had broken, their parole, and who had money to improve their lot even to the extent of employing servants from amongst the other prisoners. It was not until 1811–12 that officers were separated from the men on board the hulks, either being confined in one vessel in a depot, or on one deck in each ship.[36]

There were so many troublemakers on the hulks that special vessels were allocated for the confinement of these hard cases. The appropriately named *Vengeance* at Portsmouth was one such vessel. The records for this ship describe the prisoners and their crimes. One individual was 'a very great thief', while another was stated to have been 'sent from Stapleton as been suspected to be concerned in forgeries and other ways of known bad character ... very troublesome and turbulent ... frequently threatened the life of the Sentinelle [sic] and Sergeant when sent to take him into custody ... has been confined several times'. One Jacques Silvester was sent to the *Vengeance* 'for beating a man and occasioning his death', and was noted as being a very troublesome man, often threatening both garrison and prisoners alike.[37]

To control such men, security on board the hulks was very tight. The *Prothée* was a typical vessel in that the guard during the day consisted of three sentries on the gallery (a walk-way running all round the ship, just above the waterline), one on the ladder leading to the old gun deck, one on the forecastle and one on each gangway. On the poop deck were a dozen armed men ready for instant action. At night were seven sentries on the gallery and one on the gun deck ladder, with an officer, sergeant, corporal and a dozen sailors continually moving around. Every fifteen minutes the cry 'All's Well!' could be heard. The ship's boats were slung ten feet above the water, and one was secured to the gallery. At least once a day the guards and turnkeys would sound every wall and grating with iron bars, and the prisoners were mustered on deck and counted.[38]

The vessels at each prison ship depot were mutually supporting in the event of trouble. If prisoners escaped from one ship then signals were made requesting assistance from the other hulks. At night signal lanterns were hoisted to the top of the masts to alert the other ships and to warn people on land. An entry in the log of the *Bahama* for 6 October 1809 reads 'Signal made from *Irresistable* that prisoners had made their escape. Sent armed boats in search of them'. On 29 December of that year the log records 'a signal being made by the *Buckingham* that the prisoners were riotous. Sent an armed boat to their assisistance'.[39]

Some prisoners attempted to encourage their colleagues in the pursuit of the more wholesome activities available on board, and were helped in their endeavours by the authorities, who supported anything that would make the prisoners less troublesome. Bonnefoux had some success on the *Bahama* by promoting education and handicrafts, while the Americans on the *Crown Prince* launched a crusade against the gaming tables that eventually succeeded. The elected Committees that monitored the rations also functioned to make 'wholesome laws and define crimes and award punishments'. This rough code of justice did go some way to controlling the large numbers of men confined together in such a small space. Offenders were tried before a 'court of justice' of fellow prisoners. One man found guilty of stealing money from a neighbour was sentenced to thirty lashes with a ropes end. Other crimes included violence and murder, the latter being a matter for the Assizes to deal with. Some of the prisoners even acted as paid informers for the authorities, with serious consequences if their compatriots discovered them.[40]

With large numbers of men of widely varied backgrounds and characters confined together, it was inevitable that tempers would flare and relatively minor disagreements explode into violence. The *San Damaso* had a reputation for its stabbing cases. In 1808 one Cabezas killed a fellow prisoner in a duel with knives, while in October of the following year a Spaniard was killed by being stabbed in seventeen places, and any one of these wounds would have been fatal according to the surgeon's report. This was the fourth stabbing affair on this vessel in that month. Those prisoners who were unable to obtain swords for their 'affairs of honour' resorted to using scissor blades or homemade knives bound tightly onto a stick to serve as rapiers.[41]

The less honourable amongst them resorted to plain and simple murder at the first opportunity. Luis Herquiada, a Spaniard, murdered a fellow prisoner on the *San Damaso* and was sentenced to hang in March 1808. Local newspapers always had room for a story about French prisoners of war and anything that happened on board the hulks, and this unfortunate individual provided good copy for the *Hampshire Telegraph*.

A most melancholy circumstance took place at putting the sentence into execution, owing to the hangman not understanding his duty. The rope was put around the malefactor's neck, and the cart moving away, he fell suspended; but, shocking to relate, in the convulsive agonies of death his feet were partly on the ground, and he underwent a most violent strangulation. His dying groans were awful beyond description. He remained in that situation for some time, and then spoke in great anguish, requesting to be put out of his misery. One of the javelin men, out of compassion for the unhappy sufferer, took him round the body, and lifted him up, in order to remove the rope, which was under his chin, to his left ear, he was again thrown off, and it was then some time before death put a period to his great sufferings. His body, after hanging the usual time, was delivered to the surgeons to be anatomised.[42]

As many prisoners of war were able to obtain newspapers – smuggled in at a price – this incident must have had a sobering effect on them when they read about it.

The inmates of the hulks were able to trade their handicrafts with the local populace, many of whom were ferried out to the ships to watch the prisoners wandering around the upper deck, known as the *Parc*. If they obtained permission from the Commanding Officer of that vessel, these civilians could board and view their erstwhile enemies from close quarter. Many of the visitors were women who purchased bone models as souvenirs of their visit, displaying a callous attitude to the manufacturers of their purchases. Colonel Lebertre noted:

> Even the women displayed an indifference absolutely horrifying. They would stay for hours together with their eyes fixed on the *Parc*, where the prisoners were, and without this spectacle of misery, which would so sensibly affect a Frenchwoman, starting a single tear. On the contrary, an insulting laugh was on their lips. The prisoners have known only one instance of a woman who fainted at the sight of the *Parc*.[43]

The reputation of the hulks was such that men dreaded being sent to them, and these vessels were well known to the French. Indeed, on the eve of Waterloo, Napoleon exhorted his troops with the words:

> Soldiers! Let those among you who have been prisoners of the English, describe to you the hulks, and detail the frightful miseries they have endured.[44]

The first impression of a hulk was a demoralising experience. Louis Garneray wrote, albeit for a French audience many years later:

> I can still remember vividly my dismay at the first sight of the *Prothée* as she lay at anchor in line with eight other floating prisons at the mouth of Portchester River. In the distance her monstrous black shape made me think of some vast tomb. ... I imagined the

haggard faces of the prisoners behind the thick wooden walls, but far worse than anything I could imagine was the reality when, a few moments later, the escort party led us up on deck and flung us without warning into the midst of the pitiful, horrifying inhabitants of the *Prothée*. Picture an army of corpses emerging from the grave, hollow-eyed, bent, unshaven, their faces wan and grey, their bones half-covered with yellow rags. Picture this, and you will still have only a feeble impression of what met my eyes when I saw my future companions.[45]

Those who were incarcerated on board could apply to the authorities for transfer to a Land Depot, or to a parole depot in the case of officers, and many such requests were granted. The Transport Board was well aware of the reputation of these vessels and sent persistent escapees and other troublemakers on board, both as a punishment and to keep a more secure eye on them.

In Britain these vessels were better than those experienced by convicts and comparable with the few such vessels used by the French for housing prisoners of war during the early years of the Revolutionary War. The English prison hulks were certainly better than those used by the Spanish in Cadiz harbour. Despite this, one French prisoner, and his views were typical, thought that the hulks in England were 'hell upon water'.

Notes

[1] Dupin p4.

[2] Abell, p54.

[3] Branch Johnson, p1–8. This work describes the hulks used for convicts and prisoners of war. The two categories of prisoner were kept separate, and were administered by civilian and naval authorities respectively. The two types of prisoner did not come into contact with each other.

[4] Hulks were used for many purposes, not just for housing convicts and prisoners of war. Many old vessels were placed in ordinary (ie. they had their masts, rigging and ordnance removed) at the naval bases of Britain. If they were still seaworthy they might be refitted

and sent to sea, or they could be used as receiving vessels for newly pressed men; storeships; guardships and dockyard vessels. For a detailed account of the uses to which ships of the Napoleonic period could be put see Lavery, Brian. *Nelson's Navy: the Ships, Men and Organisation 1793–1815* (London, 1989).

[5] This data has been collated from the records in the PRO, ADM103.

[6] *The Quarterly Review* Volume XXVI, Number LI, October 1821, p.7.

[7] Branch Johnson, p45-58.

[8] *The Quarterly Review*, p.9.

[9] TNA:PRO ADM105/44. Commissioner's Report, 7 May 1801.

[10] ibid. 29 August 1798.

[11] Branch Johnson, p.51.

[12] TNA:PRO ADM105/44, 7 May 1801.

[13] TNA:PRO ADM103/85. General Entry Book of French prisoners of war on board the Crown, Portsmouth.

[14] TNA:PRO ADM105/44, 29 August 1798.

[15] ibid. 27 April 1801.

[16] Garneray, Louis. *The French Prisoner*. (London, 1957) p.9.

[17] NMM ADM/MT/417. Admiralty Letters, January – June 1797.

[18] Seaman, p.372.

[19] Branch-Johnson p.82-83.

[20] TNA:PRO ADM105/44.

[21] NMM ADM/MT/415. Admiralty Letters, May 1796.

[22] TNA:PRO ADM105/44, 17 July 1797.

[23] TNA:PRO ADM98/261. Letters relating to Prisoners of War at Portsmouth, 18 January 1810.

[24] TNA:PRO ADM105/44, 17 September 1806.

[25] TNA:PRO ADM105/44, 14 September 1807.

[26] Abell, p.99.

[27] TNA:PRO ADM105/44, 17 September 1806.

[28] Abell, p51.

[29] TNA:PRO ADM105/44. Commissioners reports 23 May 1801, 27 April 1801 and 25 December 1796.

[30] The Pescott Frost Collection, Volume 1, p61.

[31] Abell, p.99.

[32] Waterhouse, p.102–103.

[33] TNA:PRO ADM103/646, Accounts of prisoners of war who died at Portsmouth 1799–1814.

34 TNA:PRO ADM105/44, 19 December 1796.
35 NMM ADM/MT/416, 23 November 1796.
36 Abell, p.59-60.
37 TNA:PRO ADM103/439. General Entry Book of French prisoners of war at Portsmouth on board the *Vengeance* 1806–12.
38 Garneray, p.7.
39 TNA:PRO ADM51/2183 Log of the *Bahama* 1 July 1809–30 June 1811.
40 Waterhouse, p.64 and 111.
41 TNA:PRO ADM103/646.
42 *Hampshire Telegraph*, 21 March 1808.
43 Abell, p.75.
44 Abell, p.98.
45 Garneray, p.5.

CHAPTER 4

The Finest Thing of its Kind

While the nature of the hulks inspired dread amongst prisoners of war, the land prisons did not have such an ominous reputation. The inmates of these places of confinement had more room to exercise and the larger population meant a bigger community in which to relate. There was also more communication with local civilians via the prison markets, at which the prisoners could sell their bone models and purchase extra food.

Those on board a hulk could apply for transfer to a land establishment and many requests were granted, especially if the prisoner had been on board for some years, or more especially if the request was accompanied by a testimonial from a surgeon that transfer would benefit the man's health. Prison ships did not last forever, and when such a vessel was condemned the inmates were often transferred to a land prison en masse, particularly when there was room for a large batch of men in the prison barracks.

The first land prisons used in the early 1790s were buildings that had been utilised for that purpose during earlier conflicts of the eighteenth century, and were convenient for the quick and easy transfer from the transports to a place of confinement, such as Portchester Castle and Forton Prison near the naval port of Portsmouth, and Mill Prison at Plymouth. The ever-increasing prisoner of war population generated fears over the security of these naval bases. When new prisons were built they were sited further inland, where security was easier (e.g. Norman Cross and Dartmoor). A further reason for constructing new land prisons was that they were cheaper to maintain than hulks for the same number of prisoners.

The table below details the land prison depots in use during this period. Of these only three were purpose-built during the Napoleonic period namely, Dartmoor, Norman Cross and Perth; the others had been in use as prisons during the eighteenth century, or were converted from old mills to alleviate the pressure on the system as the wars progressed. As prisoners were classified according to the army in which they were captured, the term 'French' included the many Germans, Dutch, Italians and Polish soldiers taken whilst serving Napoleon.

Land Prison Depots in Britain 1793–1815

Depot		Period of Use	Capacity	Nationality of POWs
Forton	{	1793–1801	3000	French
	{	1807–1814	3000	French, Spanish
Liverpool		1793–1801	4000	French
Mill Prison	{	1793–1801	3000	French, Dutch, Danish,
	{	1803–1814	3000	French, American
Stapleton	{	1793–1801	3000	French, Spanish
	{	1803–1814	3000	French, American
Portchester	{	1794–1801	7000	French, Dutch, Spanish
	{	1810–1814	7000	French
Norman Cross	{	1797–1801	7000	French, Dutch
	{	1803–1814	7000	French
Dartmoor		1809–1815	7000	French, American
Edinburgh	{	1796–1801	200	French, Spanish, Dutch
	{	1804–1814	1000	French
Esk Mills		1811	3000	French
Greenlaw		1803–1814	1000	French, Spanish
Valleyfield		1811–1814	3000	French
Perth		1812–1814	7000	French

The land used for each depot was usually leased from local landowners for the duration of the conflict. Such a contract was drawn up between the Prince of Wales and the Transport Board dated 10 March 1806, for land on Dartmoor to be used as a war prison.[1] Once the wars were over a site reverted to its original owner and often the wooden structures and all fixtures and fittings of the depot were dismantled and sold (as was the case with Norman Cross in 1816, and the wooden barracks in Portchester Castle the same year). Stone structures such as Dartmoor and Perth remained empty until a suitable use could be found for them.

Other sites were used for housing prisoners of war, but not on a permanent basis. These buildings have often entered local folklore as being constructed to house such captives, whereas in reality they were used to hold these men until sufficient guards could be obtained to convey them to more secure accommodation, or until space could be found for them in the depots. Many such prisons were a legacy of the system under the Sick and Hurt Board and were deemed unfit for use when the Transport Board took over the care of prisoners of war. There were usually no more than 200 men confined at these sites at any one time and such temporary prisons could be found at Deal, Dover Castle, Yarmouth, North Shields, Pembroke and Harwich. Falmouth was used as a temporary parole depot during the years 1793–1797, to accommodate French officers landed there from captured vessels, until they were either exchanged or transferred to depots inland.[2] As prisoners were marched to a depot, they were often quartered in a barn overnight along the route, and these buildings have entered local mythology as being 'French Prisons' during the period. They were, but only for prisoners in transit.

As the wars progressed new prisons were built or existing civilian buildings adapted for such use. Each depot will be described in detail, to allow an understanding of how it was part of the war prison system in Britain during the long war with France.

Prison Depots in England

Forton Prison

This place of confinement was constructed in early 1777 for the confinement of Americans taken in the War of Independence, and was originally called Fortune Prison. Initially constructed of wood, it consisted of two large, spacious buildings, between which was an airing ground. A shed was erected in the middle of this area that was 'open on all sides to admit the free circulation of air under which were seats for accommodation when the weather was hot and sultry'. In mid-1777 a hospital building was constructed while a wooden fence bordered the prison area eight feet in height. Americans occupied this depot until 1783.[3]

On the outbreak of war ten years later, Forton was immediately brought back into service for the confinement of French prisoners, although it was in a dilapidated state. During the 1790s the population consisted of French until the closure of the prison in 1801. It was reopened in 1807 to house both French and Spanish seamen, and 1813 it saw the return of American prisoners of war.[4]

Throughout its history it had an unhealthy reputation, and the records indicate that there were many outbreaks of disease at this depot. From 9 August 1793 to 31 July 1796, 1,093 prisoners died here, mainly from fevers but also from wounds received in battle. The year 1794 saw an epidemic of enteric fever cause the deaths of 200 prisoners in the space of one month.[5] Two years later it was noted that many West Indian women and children were there whose menfolk were incarcerated at Portchester Castle, and these unfortunates 'suffered greatly from the climate'. The unhealthy nature of the prison is evident from the accommodation available in the prison hospital. In 1796 there was provision for '8-900 patients in cradles at two feet distance from each other' and the hospital staff consisted of one surgeon, seven Assistant-Surgeons, one Dispenser, and five Assistant Dispensers; a large staff for any depot but especially so for a relatively small depot such as Forton.[6]

The sickness rate did not improve after 1807, the fact that the buildings were in a very poor state of repair not helping the situation. The depot underwent repair in the summer of that year, and whilst this work was in progress a serious fire broke out caused by the boiling over of a quantity of pitch in the workshop. The French prisoners helped to put out the conflagration, none taking advantage of the confusion to attempt escape.[7] The fire destroyed part of the old wooden barracks, which was no real loss as a more healthy structure was erected in its place. Even so, the depot was not a healthy place, with 800 prisoners on the sick list in November 1810 alone.

At the end of the Napoleonic Wars the building was used as a military barracks, until in 1836 the wooden structures were pulled down and sold to make room for a large military hospital that was built on the site. Towards the end of the nineteenth century the site became HMS *St. Vincent*, the shore establishment for the training of naval cadets. It is highly likely that the remains of the prisoners who died at Forton still lie buried on the site.

Liverpool Prison

Liverpool has had a history of housing prisoners of war. Frenchmen taken during the conflicts between 1740 and 1763 were lodged in the Old Tower, Water Street, and mixed with felons and debtors, both men and women. This prison was a very insecure cluster of buildings, and so when further prisoners were taken during the American Revolution they were housed in an old powder magazine on Brownlow Hill, which was demolished at the end of the war.[8]

In 1793 it was necessary to find a new prison, as the Tower was in a very dilapidated state. In the meantime, during 1786 the Corporation of Liverpool had erected a new Borough Gaol (according to plans submitted by John Howard, the prison reformer), and at the start of the Revolutionary War there were three buildings ready for use. The Transport Board was glad to find a ready-built prison on a convenient site and leased it from the Corporation. The Borough Gaol became known locally as 'The French Prison', and stood near Leeds Canal in Mile-House Lane.

To confirm that all was well with the accommodation of prisoners there, Sir Rupert George visited Liverpool in September
1797. His detailed report described the depot as:

> A most complete and substantial prison, in a detached situation to
> the northward of the town, and commands a beautiful prospect;
> it consists of six large detached buildings in which prisoners are
> confined, exclusive of a large building in the centre, two stories
> of which are appropriated to the purpose of a hospital, and the
> lower storey to an Agent's offices, Officer's guardroom, store
> rooms etc.
>
> The prisoners do not sleep on the ground floor in any of the
> buildings; they are lodged in the second and third stories, which
> principally consist of a number of cells, each nine feet by seven
> and ten feet high, on average about five inhabit each cell. At the
> end of three buildings there are six large rooms fitted with ham-
> mock posts and rails, these rooms are 11 feet high and contain two
> heights of hammocks. There are six courtyards, which are used by
> the prisoners for airing ground, and also another separate from
> the rest for airing ground for the sick.
>
> The prison has a plentiful supply of good spring water, raised
> by six pumps and is surrounded by a stone wall 20 feet high, one
> hundred and thirty seven yards long from north to south, 124
> yards from east to west, and 455 yards in circumference. ... the
> prisoners are indulged with an oven of their own ... to bake bread,
> as well as a space or ground in cultivation as a kitchen garden.[9]

The prison cost £70,000 to construct, a sum that many in the
country found unjustifiable. Further building work was not
completed until 1812, with the entire structure being demolished in 1856.

Mill Prison, Plymouth

To the west of Plymouth Hoe can be found Mill Bay, an area taking its name from a medieval water powered corn mill. The shel-
tered anchorage of Millbay gave rise to a large naval base, and as
this site was developed from the seventeenth century onwards

it was only natural that some facility would be given over to the housing of prisoners of war taken by the Navy. In about 1695 a prison with a capacity for 300 captives was opened on the shore, possibly built utilizing the existing old mill building. By 1718 there was a further prison building in use northeast of Millbay, known as the 'French' or 'Mill' prison. A fire at the prison in 1745 curtailed its use for prisoners of war but by 1758 it was back in operation. During the American Revolution it was home to both French and American captives, and during the early years of the French Revolutionary War it was expanded to hold 3,000 prisoners, becoming known as Millbay.

During the Napoleonic War Mill Prison was used to house French prisoners, alongside the prison ship depot nearby. The prison was square, with the barrack buildings bordering two of the sides, the remaining perimeter being bounded by a brick wall. The main barrack was a two-storey brick building. A Commissioner's report of August 1806 describes the depot as consisting of 'The Grand Prison' housing 1,000 men; the 'Cachot Prison' with 650 men; and 'The American Prison', so called from its use during the American Revolution and at this time empty.[10] By 1812 the buildings were in desperate need of refurbishment and were then improved. The depot closed in 1814, only being used again for Russian prisoners taken in the Crimean War.[11]

Stapleton Prison

This depot was situated in Bristol, and originated during the American Revolution when many captured French, Spanish and Dutch seamen were entering the country via this port. The story of this depot illustrates the problems faced by the authorities in finding suitable prison sites.

A small prison existed in Redcliffe Back, and this was re-opened in 1778. The Mayor and the local Militia condemned the site as it was insecure and within the town perimeter, and they suggested that an old prison at Knowle should be used again. This depot had housed 1,700 prisoners of war in 1763, but by the 1770s its water supply had failed and so the idea was dropped. The Admiralty was therefore compelled to advertise for a large building 'not nearer than twenty miles from the coast, with a good water supply and a large airing-ground, walled and fenced'. One Nehemiah Bartley, a Bristol distiller, offered a site in Stapleton Parish, three miles southwest of Bristol near the banks of the River Frome at a rent of £75 per annum.

The prison had been constructed by 1779 and covered an area of five and a half acres being built of stone and costing £3,000. The main building was 256 feet in length and 45 feet in width with two floors partitioned lengthways, thus being divided into four separate and narrow rooms. To the east of this main structure was built a hospital, about a third of the size of the prison building. Some old farm buildings were left standing to act as storerooms and stables while a perimeter wall on which stood sentry boxes in pairs facing each other surrounded the site.[12]

Stapleton Prison was in use from 1779 until 1783, after which it remained empty, but Nehemiah Bartley did sell the site outright to the Admiralty instead of leasing it to them. In 1785 some members of the Marine Society asked the Admiralty for the use of the hospital building as a school for the education and subsequent apprenticeship of 'poor boys, young vagrants and criminals to the Sea Service'. This early form of training of naval cadets continued, albeit with varying success, until 1796, when a combination of dwindling numbers of applicants for the school and ever-increasing numbers of prisoners of war arriving in the country forced the Admiralty to again use the entire prison, dissolving the school in the process.[13] By this year it must have ceased actually being used as a school anyway, for French prisoners of war had arrived at the depot in 1793.

The depot was in use from 1793 until 1801, and during this period was home to French and Spanish, mainly seamen, although in 1798 some French troops captured in Ireland were sent there. This year brought forth the suggestion that in the event of a French invasion of England, the prisoners at Stapleton should be confined in some local coal pits, to reduce the number of troops necessary to guard them![14] The years 1803 to 1814 saw French prisoners at the depot again, but in 1813 a number of Americans also arrived there, taken on privateers in the Atlantic and disembarked at Bristol. In the early years of the war with

Revolutionary France the prison was described as being in a somewhat dilapidated state, the perimeter wall being only six feet in height, instead of the original fifteen, and in a very fragile condition. By 1800 it was felt necessary to increase the accommodation at the depot, and so a new building was erected between the existing structure and the hospital, with some prisoners of war being employed as unskilled labour in the construction work. In 1804 further buildings were erected, and the depot could now hold 3,000 captives. By this year the perimeter wall had been restored to its original height and a ditch 18 feet in width had been added outside.[15]

Of all the depots in Britain at the time, Stapleton had an unsavoury reputation based on overcrowding, poorly ventilated buildings, and wells that occasionally ran dry. On the cessation of hostilities in 1814, 2,000 prisoners of war were sent home, including many sick. A few months later the buildings became an Ordnance Store and were used in this capacity until 1832. An outbreak of cholera in that year resulted in the old prison depot being used as a workhouse, to alleviate overcrowding at the local hospital, while five years later the site was purchased to shelter 1,100 paupers. The old buildings were demolished during the period 1861–1865 and a new workhouse erected, becoming an institution for workshop training of the mentally ill. In 1948 it was converted into Stapleton Hospital. However, even by this year the site was still referred to as 'The Old French Prison'.[16]

Portchester Castle

Those visitors energetic enough to climb to the top of the keep at Portchester Castle will see, as they reach the end of their ascent, numerous names carved into the stonework at the top of the stairwell. Many of these names are accompanied by dates, such as 'P. Caborit 1745' and 'Lezac 1797', reflecting the long history of the castle as a war prison.

The outer walls and towers date from the third century and were part of a Roman coastal defence system. The Normans built the keep and throughout the medieval period the castle was strengthened and made more comfortable for the inhabitants. The buildings around the keep include the remains of the palace of Richard II, other living accommodation and the ruins of a seventeenth century mansion.

The military significance of Portchester Castle declined as Portsmouth and the naval dockyard expanded. Various plans were proposed to use the site as a store or a military hospital, but nothing came of these projects. However, during the Second Dutch War (1665–67) the Board for Sick and Wounded Seamen leased the castle for housing prisoners of war.

It was ideal for this purpose, for although many of the buildings were in a state of disrepair, the castle was still a solid, secure building, with walls up to 30 feet in height and six to ten feet thick. It was situated near the naval base of Portsmouth and so was convenient for the transport of prisoners from abroad. Its situation near the Channel would, on first impression, seem to have favoured escape attempts, but throughout the history of this depot successful escapes were few, due to the tight security around the castle, in the surrounding area and at sea.

Portchester Castle as a War Prison and Military Depot

Conflict	Period as Prison	Nationality of Prisoners
Dutch War	1665–67	Dutch
War of Spanish Succession	1702–12	French, Spanish
War of Austrian Succession	1745–49	French, Spanish, Polish
Navy Store	1749–56	
Seven Years War	1756–63	French
Revolutionary War	1794–1802	French, Dutch
Army Store & Depot for King's German Legion	1803–10	
Napoleonic War	1810–14	French[17]

The castle was used throughout the seventeenth and eighteenth centuries as a war prison. The War of the Spanish Succession saw French officers and Spanish soldiers housed in the medieval castle, while during the War of the Austrian Succession a number of Spanish soldiers found themselves alongside French and Polish sailors there. However, these numbers were small compared to the 4,000 Frenchmen sent to Portchester during the Seven Years War. This conflict established Portchester Castle as an important prisoner of war depot.

The American Revolution brought Americans to Forton Prison nearby. As the war in the erstwhile colonies expanded to involve France, Holland and Spain, the Admiralty gave some thought to the problem of housing the undoubted number of these nationalities who would enter Britain as captives. In 1784 the castle was properly fitted up as a war prison; the moat was cleared and filled with water and the keep was divided into five storeys. Plans were drawn up to build further accommodation so that the castle could hold 8,000 prisoners. The war in America ended before the castle was used for its intended purpose, but the ideals propounded by the American colonists were soon to have a bloodier impact in Europe, and ultimately to elevate Portchester Castle to the height of its war prison existence.

When France declared war on Britain in 1793 it soon became apparent that this conflict would be fought on a far greater scale than ever before. This was reflected in the large number of French prisoners brought to Britain throughout the 1790s. In 1794 the castle was again established as a war prison, with further wooden buildings being constructed for the prisoners and garrison. It remained as such until 1802, when it reverted to a military store.[18] From 1803 it was decided not to use the depot for prisoners of war as during the previous decade there had been many concerns voiced over the wisdom of having so many enemy nationals next to the country's major naval base. The keep was used to store gunpowder and the military barracks to the north of the castle were home to the artillery of the newly formed King's German Legion. The brick powder store for the garrison is the only barrack building to survive.

90

The Peninsular War necessitated the use of the castle for prisoners of war again from 1810, in which role it remained until 1814. It was then suggested that the barracks be used to house sick and wounded British soldiers from the Peninsula Campaign, but while the depot was possibly fitted out for this purpose, there is no evidence that it was actually used as a hospital. The numbers of prisoners of war housed here varied from 4,769 in 1795 to some 7,000 in 1814.[19]

Norman Cross

By February 1796 the matter of accommodation for prisoners of war in the country had become most urgent. The year 1795 had seen Holland overrun by the French and forced to become a satellite republic of France. The country was now at war not only with the French, but also the Batavian Republic, as Holland was now known. The North Sea fleet based along the eastern coast of England would bear the brunt of the fight against the Dutch, and there was no substantial prison accommodation available to support this fleet and its forthcoming haul of captives.

The Transport Board rapidly searched for a site on which to build a new prison. The Board had several requirements to consider. Any new prison had to be within easy reach of a port so that prisoners could be disembarked and conveyed rapidly and at minimal cost to their place of confinement. The site was not to be too near an unfortified port as this would facilitate escapes, and possible enemy intervention to release and arm the thousands of prisoners of war in England. The site had to be healthy, with a good water supply and near to local markets for provisions. It also had to be near trunk roads, not only for ease of administration but also so that in the event of a rising a sufficient number of troops could be rushed to the spot.

Norman Cross was built on a site that possessed all these advantages. On the Great North Road it was seventy-six miles from London. Prisoners landed at Yarmouth or Lynn could be marched to the depot, or first transported by water to Yaxley, Stanground or Peterborough, from where it was only a short march to the depot. Deep wells were sunk to supply water, and provisions could be obtained readily from the towns in the sur-rounding fertile countryside.[20]

Plans were drawn up in December 1796 and work began almost immediately. It was decided to build the prison out of wood as rapidity of construction was an important requirement. The work was under the direction of William Adams, Master Carpenter to the Board of Ordnance, and the original plans were modified and expanded as the building work progressed.

The framework was constructed in London and conveyed to Norman Cross where 500 carpenters and labourers were employed day and night, seven days a week. The work pro-ceeded rapidly and on 13 February 1797 it was reported that the prison would be ready in about three weeks for the recep-tion of prisoners. This estimate proved to be somewhat pre-mature despite the work being performed as fast as possible. That same month the decision was made to adapt some of the prison barracks then being constructed into a hospital. In the following month plans were altered to increase the prisoner accommodation by adding an extra storey to each block then being erected.

By 25 March progress was such that a staff could be employed, and it was reported that part of the prison was ready for the reception of 1,848 prisoners. A portion of the military barracks had been garrisoned by a detachment of troops ready to mount guard over the expected inmates, who eventually arrived on 7 April, just four months after building had commenced.

The prison covered a total area of 42 acres and was octagonal in shape. The outer boundary was originally a strong stockade fence but this was replaced in 1805 with a brick wall bordered on the inside with a ditch, nine yards wide and five feet deep, known as the walk for the 'silent sentries'.

The prison barracks were in the form of four quadrangular courts each of about 3½ acres. Half of this area was used as an airing ground for the prisoners, while the remainder contained four wooden two-storey barracks (or caserns as they were some-times referred to) each 100 feet long and 22 feet wide, and roofed with red tiles. Each of the floors in the barracks was divided by partitions into three chambers; each barrack housed 500 prisoners who slept in rows of hammocks, arranged in tiers one above the other. The northeast quadrangle was eventually used as a hospital and accommodation for the medical staff, plus barrack accommodation for boys, and for officers who had refused to give their parole. The quadrangles were surrounded by high stockade fences, and separated from each other by roads 20 feet wide. At the centre of the prison was an octagonal blockhouse in which were mounted cannon.[21]

The prison was designed for maximum security, both to prevent prisoners escaping and to deter any attempts at a general uprising amongst the prison population. The blockhouse and a liberal number of sentry boxes and high fences surrounding the barracks all served to keep the prisoners secured and deterred from any organised insurrection. Outside the prison wall at each gate was a guardhouse, while the arrangement of military barracks ensured that troops could be quickly rushed to any trouble spot.

The depot at Norman Cross cost £34,581 11s 3d, which was expensive compared to other establishments at the time. The prison served until 1814, and in 1816 it was sold by auction, the barracks being dismantled and used for building materials.[22] Some of the administrative buildings remained (the Agent's house in particular) and were strengthened with brick and altered to form larger country houses, in which condition some of them remain today. All that remains of the rest of the depot is part of the brick perimeter wall and some of the wells.

Dartmoor Prison

Of all the war prisons, Dartmoor stands out because it was on a desolate site, constructed of sombre granite. It is a miserable place to be, even on a bright sunny day. But why build it there?

During the early years of the Napoleonic War Portchester Castle remained empty of prisoners as it was too near the naval base and dockyard of Portsmouth. The period 1803–05 was a time of great anxiety for Britain as Napoleon amassed an invasion armada across the Channel, and for reasons of security in the Portsmouth area it was decided not to use the castle as a war prison. By 1805 there was considerable pressure on the

Transport Office due to the ever-increasing number of prisoners of war entering Britain, many of whom were captured because of French invasion preparations. It was decided to build a new land prison somewhere away from the naval ports at which there were increasing number of prison hulks. In a wave of patriotic generosity the Prince of Wales granted the Transport Board permission to lease some land within the Duchy of Devon and Cornwall for the construction of such a building. Sir Thomas Tyrwitt, Lord Warden of the Stanneries of Devon and Cornwall and Secretary to the Duchy, also a close friend of the Prince, suggested that the Board might like to view a prospective site on Dartmoor.

Sir Thomas had dreamed of using the moorland for agriculture but had been thwarted in his ambitions by the weather. A small population who lived in the specially constructed village of Princetown, named after his Royal friend, tended the few sheep that he managed to raise.

The site that Sir Thomas suggested was next to the village, and after copiously entertaining Mr Daniel Alexander, an Agent from the Admiralty, and Mr E. Bouveries, an architect, these gentlemen returned to London in July 1805, suitably refreshed and firmly convinced that the site was the best available. Their reasons were set out in a report dated 20 July 1805, and were listed as:

1. The water supply is good and plentiful.
2. The soil is gravel and good for building on. The peat is two feet deep in places and would thus provide plenty of fuel.
3. The turnpike road runs near the site chosen and will facilitate the transport of provisions.
4. It is suggested that goods may be sold cheaply to the Prison from the surrounding towns, rather than incur the expense of taking them from Plymouth.
5. There is plenty of stone on the spot for building the Prison and granite for paving it.
6. His Royal Highness the Prince of Wales gives as many acres of land to the Board as they want. Therefore the prisoners may have a garden, which is better for their health.

7. When the Prison is finished it will save the expense of prison ships.
8. It will have the advantage of being a roomy and airy prison, compared with the hulks.[23]

Space, good communications and a healthy site were thus the criteria that the Board accepted. Sir Thomas's political opponents pointed out that communications to anywhere on Dartmoor were often non-existent during winter, and the locally available building material would undoubtedly be acquired from Sir Thomas's own granite quarries, but these words went unheeded.[24]

Work began on the prison in March 1806 and proceeded unusually slowly, delays being caused by the weather and by the civilian labour force making frequent demands for extra pay. Cornish masons were employed to construct the prison, and their labour costs rose by 20% during the course of construction. Further problems arose from the scarcity of timber, due in part to the blockade of Prussian ports.

When supplies did become available, the price rose from £5 per load to £8 in 1806. Rising labour costs and increases in prices for building materials made the building contractor cut costs wherever possible, and some of the building work was found to be very poor indeed. It was hoped that the depot would be ready for use by the end of 1807, but an inspection that year found that the prison and barracks were nowhere near ready for occupation. The first buildings were not ready for the reception of prisoners until May 1809.[25]

The prison covered 30 acres enclosed by stone walls, the outer wall being sixteen feet high and separated from the inner wall by a broad military way in which bells hung on wires connected with all the sentry boxes along its length. Initially there were five large barrack blocks for the prisoners, described as stone barns, sixty feet in length, with windows two feet square and unglazed. There was no provision for heating, and no chimneys. In 1812 two additional barracks were built, each housing one thousand men on two floors. On each floor the prisoners slept in a treble tier of hammocks slung upon cast iron pillars. Above the top floor ran an attic designed to be used as an exercise area in bad weather, but eventually even this was used to accommodate prisoners. The barracks had their own airing grounds and supply of running water with outside shelters for inclement weather. Other buildings were erected for the accommodation of the prison staff and the garrison of five hundred troops.[26]

The prison cost £135,000 to build and was described by a contemporary writer as 'probably the finest thing of its kind and worthy of the humanity and renown of Great Britain'. The prisoners incarcerated within its walls did not share these sentiments. They regarded Dartmoor as the most detestable of all the British war prisons, being on a desolate site with no heating in the barracks and unglazed windows exposing them to the Dartmoor weather. One prisoner, Louis Catel, described Dartmoor as being a 'little Siberia' for seven months of the year, often covered with unmelting snow. Escape from the prison was difficult because of its site and the inhospitable moors.[27]

The first French prisoners marched up from Plymouth and arrived on 24 May 1809. Within a month the total was doubled to 5,000 individuals, increasing to 9,000 in 1812. From April 1813 there arrived numerous drafts of American prisoners, and between that month and March 1815, 6,473 American citizens were incarcerated in Dartmoor Prison. There were still Americans there in June 1815, as 5,000 French troops taken during the Waterloo campaign were arriving. These soldiers remained at Dartmoor until February 1816, when they were finally returned to their homeland.[28] The depot officially ceased to be a war prison on 20 February of that year and remained empty until 1850. It was then refurbished and used as a convict prison and is still in use today as one of Her Majesty's Prisons, administered by the Home Office. The present Prince of Wales still collects a rent for the lease of the land on which the prison is situated.

Prison Depots in Scotland

In 1799 there were proposals to construct prison depots in Scotland to alleviate the pressure on the depots south of the border, and to place captives further away from the channel coast. Ambrose Searle suggested three potential sites; Nedpath Castle near Peebles, Inchkeith Island in the Firth of Forth, and Linlithgow Palace.

No decision was made on these proposals before the war ended.[29] Other sites were used in Scotland however, especially when in 1810 it was felt that there were too many prisoners held in the southern half of the country, posing problems of security. In that year it was decided to send more of them to the north of England and to Scotland.[30]

Edinburgh Castle

There is scant information relating to prisoners of war held at this site. Prisoners, mainly Spanish and Dutch but including a few French privateer officers, were held in the cells under the Castle from 1796 to 1801. A Commissioner's report dated 10 July 1799 comments that the cells were not very well ventilated, and this may account for the closure of this depot in 1801.[31] However, the depot was utilized again from 1804 until August 1811, although the prisoner population was numbered in the hundreds. Prisoners of war convicted of forging or uttering banknotes were often transferred there where the security was tighter.

Esk Mills

An old Cotton Mill at Esk Mills, nine miles from Edinburgh and part of the prison depot area around Penicuick, was leased to the Transport Board in October 1810. This site was cramped by the steep banks of the River Esk which prevented expansion of the depot. This site was opened in response to the influx of prisoners from the Peninsula campaign, the first prisoners arriving on 4 February 1811, when 2,817 French soldiers and seamen arrived via Greenlaw. There was accommodation for 3,000 prisoners, but there were problems in housing the necessary troops to guard them. It would appear that this prison depot was hurriedly brought into service, and it was not suitable for the rapid influx of prisoners.

On 19 February 1811, just two weeks after it began operation as war prison, there was a mass escape of prisoners. The
Edinburgh Evening Courant of 21 February reported the story:

> An attempt was made by the French prisoners to escape from
> the depot at Penicuick [Esk Mills]. Twenty seven effected their
> purpose, but we hear that they have almost all been retaken.
> Four of them are stated to have been shot by the soldiers and one
> drowned attempting the cross the Esk.

Events such as this provided an exciting story for the newspaper.
The report described how the escape was made.

> By raising the floor of the room in which they were confined,
> they opened a communication with the mill lead [lade, or water
> course], dug through an arch with which it had recently been cov-
> ered and came out on a narrow strip of ground, where three sen-
> tinels were stationed between it and the river. The first sentinel's
> piece missed fire, the shot of the second did not take effect, but by
> that of the third one of the prisoners fell. They are all Frenchmen
> and among them are several officers.[32]

The dead prisoner was Lieutenant Nicolas Boulet of the privateer *Le Vengeur*. There was evidence that all the other prisoners
may have tried to help the escapers win time to get clear. The
Transport Board ordered that all the other prisoners should be
placed on short allowance for three days for not answering their
names at roll call, and for a further period until the damage done
to the prison was made good. This did not please the prisoners
who became very troublesome and insolent towards the guards
and the Agent. As a precautionary measure 500 of them were
removed to Edinburgh Castle in March.

On the 11th of that month there was a serious disturbance at
the prison in which two prisoners died. On investigation it was
discovered that the commotion was due to parts of the building
collapsing! It was decided that it would be too costly to make
the depot a secure prison, and so all prisoners were moved to

Valleyfield and Edinburgh Castle. Esk Mills had only been open as a prison depot for one month.[33]

Greenlaw

Greenlaw House was leased in 1803 from the Trotter family, who no longer had any use for this tall square mansion of three storeys, nine miles south of Edinburgh. Philippe Baudouin, a French soldier held there, described the prison in his memoirs:

> This prison is a country house. Two miles away where is billeted the detachment that guards us is Penicuick. This country house is surrounded by two rows of palisades with sentries all around them; to our side is situated a little wood which sometimes facilitates escapes.

There was accommodation for 1,000 prisoners who lived in rooms 20 feet square with 30 hammocks in two tiers one above the other. The rooms had windows with shutters, and the doors were stout wooden affairs with heavy iron bolts. There was evidence of slackness in the administration of the depot by 1808 on the part of the Agent, Malcolm Wright, a solicitor, and amongst the soldiers on duty there. Rear Admiral Vernon at Leith complained of 'irregularities' there in April 1808, while in October the following year Lord Cathcart complained to the Board of the 'serious abuses prevalent at the depot'. In December 1810 the efficiency of the depot was improved by the appointment of Lieutenant Joseph Priest RN as Agent. The prison closed in 1814.[34]

In November 1812 the Transport Board purchased the Greenlaw estate from the widowed owner Mrs Trotter for the sum of £10,000 with the intention of expanding the depot. This expansion did not materialize, but the Board gave it further serious consideration in 1815. When Napoleon landed in the south of France on 1 March 1815 and all Europe united their efforts to defeat him, the Transport Board made plans for the continuation of the long wars against France. As far as these gentlemen were concerned they could expect many thousands of captives to arrive in England, and so plans were devised to expand the war prison establishment. Greenlaw was to have been enlarged to accommodate 5,000 prisoners in eight barracks, built to a similar design as at Dartmoor.[35] Other depots were to have been enlarged, but the Battle of Waterloo ensured that these plans remained in the archives.

Valleyfield

This depot was rapidly opened in March 1811 to accommodate the many prisoners arriving from Spain, and further building work to enlarge the depot occurred in response to the closure of Esk Mills. Valleyfields was situated half a mile upstream from Esk Mills, and 1½ miles from Greenlaw. From 1709 the buildings were part of a paper mill owned by the Cowan family who sold the site to the Transport Board for £10,000 in December 1810. The depot was overlooked by the village of Penicuick on the slope above it, and was the largest prison in Scotland until Perth was built in 1812. Prisoners were lodged in the large buildings formerly used for paper manufacture, while the Agent and his staff lived in houses at the top of the hill formerly belonging to the Cowan family. Charles Cowan described the depot in his memoirs:

> The new prisons added at Valleyfield were about six in number, from 80 to 120 feet in length, chiefly of wood, and of 3 storeys; they had no glass in the openings for light and air which were closed at night by very strong wooden shutters, and secured by strong iron stanchions, nor were there any fireplaces or artificial heat, for it was expected that animal heat would suffice for their comfort, the prisoners having been stowed away as close almost as herrings in a barrel ... The prisons and level ground on which they were erected were surrounded by a strong wooden stockade or palisade, with a carriage road outside and guarded by military.

There was accommodation at the depot for 3,000 prisoners, and by the time the depot closed in 1814 about 7,500 prisoners had passed through its doors.[36]

Perth Prison

A new depot was planned at Perth in 1810 to accommodate the large influx of captives from the Iberian Peninsula, and construction began in the autumn of that year. Work was carried on even during the severe winter of 1810–11, when fires had to be lit to thaw the lime. The construction brought work for 1,500 labourers, and resulted in new stone quarries being opened in the locality to provide the raw material for the buildings.[37]

The depot consisted of five three-storey buildings, each 130 by 30 feet, with outside stairs, and each having its own airing ground surrounded by a palisade. A barrack had accommodation for 1,140 men. These buildings surrounded an area known as the Market Place, while south of this ground was a building for 1,100 petty officer prisoners. To the north of the barracks was a hospital block. Around the interior of the prison perimeter was a moat 10 feet in width, bordered by an iron palisade, with the outer stone wall being 13 feet in height, on top of which was a sentry-walk.

By August 1812 part of the barracks was ready for the reception of prisoners of war, and 400 French men and a few women arrived from Plymouth via Dundee. Transports of prisoners arrived at Leith from Lisbon almost on a daily basis, and by September the population had reached 4,000 and by the following January the depot was at its maximum of 7,000 inmates. Here they remained until June 1814, when they were rapidly returned to France. The depot officially closed on 31 July 1814.

From 1815 until 1833 Perth Prison was used as a store for military clothing, with many local people advocating its use as a convict prison, in which capacity it is now employed.[38]

Life in the Land Prisons

The Land Prisons did not inspire the dread and foreboding that was associated with the hulks. Prison ships were a very restricted means of incarceration, while the prisons ashore afforded more space in which to roam. While each deck of a prison ship had its own committee and social hierarchy, each barrack in the land depots had its own class system and means of imposing some sort of order and discipline upon its occupants.

At Dartmoor there were five distinct classes amongst the French population. *Les Lords* were people with money or officers who had broken, or refused to give, their parole. These men were able to live a relatively comfortable life within the confines of the prison, often employing servants from amongst the other prisoners. They often had their own messes with meals specially procured and prepared by their own cooks. Next in the social scale were *Les Labourers*, the clever, industrious men who lived comfortably by their endeavours, such as the manufacture and sale of bone models. They saved money and, it was said, many of them left the prisons in 1814 wealthier than when they had first arrived. The class below them was *Les Indifférents*; loafers and idlers but not troublemakers. These formed the bulk of the prison population. The lowest groupings at Dartmoor were *Les Misérables* and *Les Romains* (or Romans; the equivalent of *Les Raffalés* on board the hulks). The former were the troublemakers – always plotting and planning some mischief – while the latter were so called because they lived in the cock-loft of one of the barracks, which became known as the *Capitole*, and gave them their sobriquet of Romans. They were the scum of the prison society, wandering about virtually naked as they were all inveterate gamblers. Their violence and thieving made them a terror to the other prisoners, and Commissioner's reports make frequent reference to the problems of issuing them with clothing and bedding. As far as the authorities were concerned both these lower classes were the troublesome groups. Each depot had its share of Romans.[39]

Commissioner Towry, visiting Norman Cross in the summer of 1807, reported that the clothing issued to each prisoner should last him eighteen months. *Les Misérables* were causing a problem at the depot by selling their clothing, and so it was noted with approval that the Agent, Captain Pressland, was issuing these captives with old, worn-out items.[40] This observation is a recurrent theme throughout the Commissioners' reports of the period. While it was noted that many of the prisoners sold their food and clothing to support their gambling habits, it is often the two lowest classes who are mentioned in connection with this.

The food and clothing ration in the land depots was identical to that issued on board the hulks, with only slight variations in quantity and type, according to the supply situation. In addition, some of the depots (such as Norman Cross) had areas set aside as vegetable gardens so that the prisoners could produce some of their own food. The menu at Portchester in April 1801 comprised a soup made of the beef and pea ration, together with bread that on occasion was found to be only partially baked. Sick prisoners were given an additional ration consisting of a gruel containing Scotch barley, rice, sugar and pimento, the whole boiled for four hours.[41] When certain food items were scarce, gruel was issued to all prisoners. This meal was not to everyone's taste. An American at Dartmoor wrote in 1814 of this dietary replacement:

> It is made of oatmeal which we Americans very generally detest. Our people consider ground oats is only fit for cattle and it is never eaten by the human species in the United States. It is said that this oatmeal porridge was introduced to the prisoners of war by Scotch influence, and we think that none but hogs and Scotchmen ought to eat it. A mess more repellent to the Yankee's stomach could not well be contrived.[42]

In early 1815 there was a shortage of bread at Dartmoor, and so biscuit was issued to the Americans there. The Board took a tough line with the prisoners, ordering that any prisoner who refused the substitute was not to be issued anything in its place.[43] One consolation for the Americans however, was the somewhat copious supply of spirits finding their way into the depot via the soldiers of the garrison. The regulation issue of two quarts of small beer per day, sold in the prison canteen, was the only alcohol allowed. When the Board heard of a number of cases of drunkenness amongst the prisoners they instructed the Agent to 'make timely application to the Commanding Officer, whenever [he] has reason to believe that the soldiers are concerned in introducing spirits'. Strong beer and spirits were very definitely forbidden.[44]

The quality of food supplied by the contractors was often a problem. While the Board attempted to monitor the rations issued at all the depots, and fine those suppliers found to be giving short measure or poor quality items, bad food still entered the system. If the Board's own employees did not notice the poor quality rations supplied, then there were philanthropic civilians who took it upon themselves to report any deficiencies in this area. Stapleton had some kind souls in the area looking after the interests of the prisoners there. Lord Bateman, writing to the Board in 1797, reported that:

> ... the bread is scandalously bad. The beef given out for two sick prisoners is hardly fit for dogs and humanity obliges me to represent this.[45]

Two Bristol merchants visited the depot in 1795 and found some of the prisoners 'pale and emaciated, two appearing to be dying of famine', with the bread being mouldy and the meat ration of the poorest quality. Commissioner Rupert George was sent to investigate and reported that 'the beef and vegetables are boiled in a very good soup, seven quarts to each mess of six men', but even he had to admit reluctantly that 'in a few instances the prisoners have seized dogs within the prison and made soup of them'.[46]

The disposal of the food and clothing ration to finance gambling could have serious consequences for the health of such prisoners as Commissioner Searle noted at Stapleton:

> Some ... French have died from a deficiency of food as well as clothing ... that the want of food has been occasioned by the prisoners parting with the rations of several days together by gaming, as well as their clothes ... and thus have brought upon themselves ... the complicated miseries of hunger and cold, underwhich many have sunk into their graves.[47]

Searle concluded that the food ration was adequate for health. Even the French Agent, Baron Otto, was inclined to agree with the view that the lowest class of prisoner brought much misery upon himself.

Many prisoners sold their clothing, often aided by soldiers of the garrison. Portchester Castle was a unique prison in that it had within its grounds the local parish church. This was open to the inhabitants of Portchester village each Sunday, during which many prisoners sold some of their clothing to the 'worshipers' attending the service. To counter this the Board ordered that the prisoners be locked up on Sundays, although it was noted that the Dutch prisoners then confined in the keep did not sell any of their food or clothing ration, unlike the French.

When the French had sold all their own rations, and especially if they always seemed to be on a losing streak in games of chance, they often resorted to robbery to fuel their gambling addiction. During the Revolutionary War the large number of West Indians at Portchester were 'robbed and plundered by the European prisoners ... they considering themselves as a superior race of beings to the unfortunate Blacks'.[48]

All depots had a gambling problem, and even re-clothing prisoners who had sold their garments did not stop these men indulging in this vice. Guillaume Ferraud was held at Norman Cross and in 1807 it was recorded that he was issued 'three times clothes, twice with old and once with new, has received three suits of bedding ... has now nothing'. This man was but one of 113 prisoners in the depot without clothes or bedding on that date.[49] It was often suggested that such offenders might best be punished by confinement in a prison ship, and this was the punishment (aside from the Black Hole), that was applied to the more persistent individuals.

The attitude to the sale of their rations does illustrate some of the differences between the various nationalities, of which the authorities were very much aware. As far as possible the nationalities were segregated, and not only for administrative reasons. On the hulks this was by separate decks, while in the land prisons it was by separate barracks although the different nations could mingle in the exercise areas. During the 1790s the French were housed in the wooden buildings at Portchester, while the Dutch and West Indians resided in the keep. The Spanish were housed in Assheton's Tower (the northeast corner of the medieval castle). While the governments of France and Spain may have been allies, the common soldiers and seamen did not find it so easy to unite in a common cause. An animosity between the two frequently erupted into quarrels and duels, especially when the Spanish were sent home in 1808; many Frenchmen tried to pass themselves off as Spaniards but were exposed by prisoners whose country was now allied to Britain. The Dutch were noted as being well-behaved compared with the French, but quite happy to fraternize with their ally.

Of all the nationalities within the British war prisons, the Americans were regarded as the most troublesome. They also had the strongest views regarding the other nations represented within the depots! Upon capture in 1813 one American was housed in the prison on Melville Island (Halifax, Nova Scotia) sharing this abode with about 200 Frenchmen. However, many of these French lived and worked amongst the local inhabitants and were;

> ... everywhere favoured for their complaisance, obedience and good humour ... and had the character of behaving better towards the British officers and inhabitants than the Americans ... for our men seem to take a delight in plaguing, embarrassing and alarming those who were set over them.

This captive noted that a Frenchman always tried to please, while many Americans seemed to take an equal delight in letting the Nova Scotians know that they longed to be at liberty to fight them again![50]

When Benjamin Palmer and his colleagues were disembarked at Plymouth they were marched up to Dartmoor Prison. Along the way they acquired some extra food, despite the efforts of the guards to prevent this:

> We meets a turnip cart and here's for land privateering ... they all rush upon the cart and get some turnips ... the farmer stops and gazes with downcast eyes but we tell him the King pays for all.

Whether His Majesty received a bill for a cartload of turnips is not recorded, but this does illustrate the problems often posed by the Americans. When these men were in residence at Dartmoor they liked to celebrate the 4 July by flying the Stars and Stripes over their barracks, much to the annoyance of the Agent! In early 1815 some English officers visited the depot to watch the American prisoners at work and play, so the band formed in No.4 barrack struck up a loud rendition of 'Yankee Doodle Dandy'. Apparently this was the favourite tune for annoying the Agent and the guards. As Palmer recorded: 'O it galls them!'[51]

Benjamin Waterhouse noted in his journal the differing characters of the prisoners with whom he was incarcerated. Danes were described as thick-skulled and plodding; a Dutchman as 'lazily stowed away in some corner with his pipe, surrounded with smoke and steeping his senses in forgetfulness.'; lively, singing Frenchmen; and of the Portuguese and Spaniards (of which there were a few in the prisons), Waterhouse wrote 'they are rattlesnakes; shining, glossy, malignant and revengeful beyond any fellows I ever met with'. Of the Irish he noted that they 'appear to have more spirit than brains'.[52]

The Americans had their equivalent of the *Romans* in the form of the 'Rough Alleys'. If the standard American prisoner of war was not troublesome enough, these men were worse, often stealing from the stores and breaking open the prison gates. The Americans formed a number of small shops and stalls at Dartmoor, selling tobacco, lemonade and hot potatoes. Any shop-owner found guilty of swindling was invariably beaten and his premises destroyed by a vigilante group of 'Rough Alleys'. The negroes at Dartmoor formed a class of their own, presided over by a seven foot tall individual known as 'Big Dick'.[53]

There was a daily routine within the land prisons as typified by Portchester Castle. At 6.00am in summer and 7.00am in winter a bell announced the arrival of the turnkeys and their escort of soldiers who opened the barrack doors and counted the prisoners. At 9.00am the market bell was rung, opening the market to both the prisoners and local civilians and at the same time the distribution of bread was made. Prisoners were divided into messes of twelve, with one soup-pot issued per three men. The bell announced the closing of the market to English sellers at 12.00 noon, and after this the prisoners were allowed to trade only amongst themselves. At the same time the soup and meat ration was distributed. Sunset heard the bell yet again, as the turnkeys and guards went through the evening count. All prisoners had to be inside their barracks at this time, and all lights were extinguished.

Occasionally there was a general airing of the barracks and hammocks, and the prisoners were obliged to stay outdoors until midday. During this airing session the turnkeys took the opportunity of sounding all walls and floors to discover if any escape attempts were being engineered. The Surgeon would visit all rooms each day to examine their state of cleanliness.[54]

Prisoners of war regarded the land prisons as being infinitely better places to be confined than the hulks. A greater chance for exercise, a larger space in which to move about, and a larger community were all factors that made those on board the hulks yearn for transfer to a land establishment. However, this larger community was fodder for epidemic disease. While the hulks produced many suffering from respiratory ailments, and had the occasional outbreak of diseases such as smallpox and typhus, the outbreaks in the land prisons tended to involve a larger proportion of the prisoner population. Deaths occurred all the time from a variety of complaints; pneumonia, phthisis and bowel infections were all common causes of mortality. All the prisons suffered extensive outbreaks of infectious disease that made no distinction between prisoners and garrison.

During the nineteen years of its existence there were 1,770 deaths amongst the prisoners at Norman Cross, of which about 1,000 occurred during an epidemic of enteric fever (probably typhoid) during 1800–1801. The remaining deaths were spread over the other years. As this disease is spread via contaminated food or water, it is quite possible that the wells in the depot were infected and responsible for prolonging the disease. The outbreak even took its toll of the garrison.[55]

With a prison housing up to 7,000 captives, guarded by 500 troops, the adequate disposal of sewage was always going to be a problem. Cesspits were used to accumulate the waste until it could be removed, usually by prisoners employed at a rate of 3d per day and supplied with wheelbarrows. All the land prisons obtained their water from wells dug within the grounds, and so it was inevitable that these would be contaminated at some time in the depot's history. Portchester Castle had a novel method of disposing of its waste. The moat around the medieval castle was used as the cesspit; this being connected to an outer moat that flowed into the harbour. The action of the tides each day was supposed to flush the system. However, a Commissioner visiting Portchester during the summer of 1810 commented that he could smell the depot while in the village about half a mile away, and authorised the employment of some of the Frenchmen to ensure that the drainage system was free of blockages.[56] On board the hulks it was a simple matter to throw waste over the side.

Epidemics occurred in all the depots. From November 1809 until the following April, Dartmoor Prison was in the grip of an outbreak of measles. Four hundred prisoners succumbed to the disease, and were buried without ceremony on the moor outside the depot.[57] Smallpox took its toll of the American prisoner population at Dartmoor, beginning its ravages in January 1815 and accounting for 72 deaths until it was brought under control in the Spring, the Board specifically ordering a supply of 'Vaccine Matter' to be sent to Dr George Magrath, the conscientious and devoted surgeon at the depot. Indeed, so impressed were the Americans with the medical service they received from this hardworking man, they wrote to the President of the United States of America in April, as a 'testimony of their gratitude to Mr Magrath for his treatment of them during their confinement'. The Board noted this testimonial with approval in their correspondence with the Agent at Dartmoor.[58]

It is very easy to condemn the treatment of prisoners of war in Britain as being brutal and conducive to sending many of them to their graves after contracting an infectious disease. This is the picture generated by later historians with the benefit of hindsight, comfortable in the knowledge that they can call upon the services of a much improved medical science. Prisoners of war were looked after as well as the Transport Board could achieve. The main problem for health was one of a crowded mass of humanity being conducive to epidemics of disease, whether these infections came into the depots with the captives, or were spread by contact with the garrison and local civilians. Smallpox, enteric fever, measles and other infections were common amongst the civilian populations of the time. Many of the depots had hard-working and devoted men such as Dr Magrath in charge of the hospitals, and the correspondence between the Agents and the Board contains frequent instructions about the acquisition of medical supplies and the correct treatment of various categories of sick prisoner. The health of such captives was an important issue with the Admiralty, and the many thousands of prisoners had access to the best medical care available at that time.

So what was the mortality rate of the land depots compared with that on board the hulks? Various writers have attempted to give figures for this, but this author believes that it is impossible to arrive at an accurate assessment. The official death toll was 10,341 for the period 1803–1814, but this does not distinguish between the different depots.

Some prisoners arrived in the land prisons and on the hulks in a poor state of health, either because of their treatment on campaign or whilst in the hands of other gaolers such as the Spanish. Some of these men died from their infections, some died while attempting to escape, and others at the hands of their colleagues. Men in poor health on board the hulks could apply for transfer to a land establishment, and many such requests were granted if the surgeon recommended that this would be in the best interest of the prisoner concerned. Some of these men would die on land; some would later be sent home sick. How many of these died in their homeland as a consequence of their captivity is impossible to say. Likewise, many of those who returned home at the end of the wars in reasonably good health may have had their lives shortened by their spell in captivity, especially if they had been captive for a long period.

Undoubtedly the land prisons and hulks did affect the health of prisoners of war who spent many years within them. Which hulk or land prison was the unhealthiest is difficult to state with any degree of accuracy, although sickness problems are mentioned more frequently in the records in relation to Stapleton Prison. This book will not attempt to place a figure on the mortality rate for any depot, as this is too complex a subject for an accurate assessment to be made. However, after reading many hundreds of Commissioners' reports, Board minutes and Agents' letters it is evident that the Admiralty consisted not of callous, unfeeling and remote men, but men dedicated and sympathetic to the needs of individuals who were in the unfortunate position of having been captured.

Prisoners of war died in the depots, but many more would have died had it not been for the dedication of the naval and civilian officials who administered the system.

Notes

1   TNA:PRO ADM7/877. An abstract of the title deeds and documents relating to Estates and property occupied for the custody of prisoners of war.
2   TNA:PRO ADM103/103, 104, 105 and 128. General Entry Books for prisoners of war.
3   Alexander, John K., *Forton Prison during the American Revolution: A case study of British prisoner of war policy and the American prisoner response to that policy.* Essex Institute Historical Collections 103 (October 1967) p.365–389.
4   TNA:PRO ADM103/349-368. General Entry Books for prisoners of war at Forton 1807–14.
5   TNA:PRO ADM103/641. Death Certificates, Forton Prison 1793–1814.
6   TNA:PRO ADM105/44, 19 December 1796.
7   Grover, G.W.M. (Ed.). *History of the Royal Marine Divisions* (Portsmouth, 1931) p21.
8   de Curzon, Alfred. *Dr James Currie and the French Prisoners of War in Liverpool 1800–1801,* (Liverpool 1926) p.15–17.
9   TNA:PRO ADM105/44, 20 September 1797.
10 TNA:PRO ADM105/44, 2 August 1806.
11 www.plymouth.gov.uk/military-docks
12 Vinter, Dorothy. 'The Old French Prison, Stapleton', Transactions of the Bristol and Gloucestershire Archaeological Society Volume 75, (Bristol 1956) p.134–135.
13 Vinter, p.139–140.
14 Latimer, John. *The Annals of Bristol in the Eighteenth Century,* (Bristol 1893) p.521.

15 Vinter, p143–144.
16 Vinter, p168.
17 Abell, p166.
18 TNA:PRO WO40/16. War Office Unnumbered Papers, 14 September and 5 October 1802.
19 TNA:PRO ADM98/252. Admiralty Letters to Agent, Portchester Castle 1810.
20 Walker, Thomas James. *The Depot for Prisoners of War at Norman Cross Huntingdonshire, 1796–1816,* (London 1913) p.10–11.
21 Walker p.17–46.
22 *Sale By Auction of Norman Cross Barracks* (Auction Catalogue) September 1816 (Peterborough Museum File Code E529).
23 TNA/PRO ADM105/44, 20 July 1805.
24 Endle, Rufus. *Dartmoor Prison,* (Bodmin, 1979) p.6.
25 Joy, p.18-28.
26 Abell, p.235-40.
27 Trafford, Dr P.A. *Dartmoor Prison and its American Prisoners 1813–15,* Journal of the Prison Medical Association, 1985 p.9–11.
28 TNA/PRO ADM98/228. General Entry Book for Prisoners of War at Dartmoor Prison.
29 TNA:PRO ADM105/44 10 July 1799.
30 NAM 7412-28 Letter 5. Lord Cathcart to Horse Guards, 1 October 1810.
31 TNA:PRO ADM105/44 10 July 1799.
32 *Edinburgh Evening Courant* 21 February 1811.
33 MacDougall, Ian. *The Prisoners at Penicuick.* (Midlothian District Council 1989), p.17–19.
34 ibid. p.6–14.
35 TNA/PRO T62/94 . Proposed plan for the prison at Greenlaw 31 March 1815.
36 MacDougall p.23.
37 Penny, G. *Traditions of Perth,* (Perth 1836) p.91.
38 Abell, p.155–158.
39 Endle, p.9–10.
40 TNA:PRO ADM105/44, 10 July 1807.
41 ibid. 2 January 1801.
42 Trafford, p.10.
43 TNA:PRO ADM98/228, 7 April 1815.

[44] ibid. 14 December 1814.

[45] TNA:PRO ADM98/213, November 1797.

[46] TNA:PRO ADM105/44, 19 December 1796.

[47] ibid. 2 January 1801.

[48] ibid. 19 December 1796.

[49] TNA:PRO ADM105/44, 10 September 1807.

[50] Waterhouse, p.22.

[51] Palmer, p.102 and 127.

[52] Waterhouse, p.68 and 109.

[53] Palmer, 130–141.

[54] Abell, p.173–175.

[55] Walker, p.163–165.

[56] TNA:PRO ADM98/252, Admiralty Letters to Agent, Portchester Castle. 21 July 1810.

[57] Abell, p.246.

[58] TNA:PRO ADM98/228, April 1815.

CHAPTER 5

Prisoners of Honour

On the morning of Saturday 15 July 1815, Napoleon Bonaparte surrendered to the captain of HMS *Bellerophon*, thus becoming the most famous prisoner of war of the Napoleonic era, if not of all time. His gamble to regain power had met its end on the muddy slopes of Waterloo.

There were many soldiers who followed the great man through the mud of that final conflict including Francois Guidon, a lieu-tenant in the 46eme de Ligne, part of the Corps d'Armée of General D'Erlon. It is not recorded at what stage of the battle this officer was taken prisoner, but General Picton's Division and the British Heavy Cavalry escorted a large number of captives to the rear of the allied line after the repulse of D'Erlon's force. Guidon was brought to England and sent on parole to Ashburton, Devon. He is still there, for he died on 18 July 1815 aged 22 years, and was buried in the churchyard. Later in the nineteenth century a willow tree was planted over the grave, reputedly grown from a cutting taken from the tree growing over Napoleon's grave on St. Helena.[1]

There are many such graves around Britain, the last resting places of officers captured in the battles of the period. Many other officers on returning to France left behind some memento to remind the local inhabitants of their temporary presence.

On 19 April 1812 Wellington's army successfully stormed the citadel of Badajoz in Spain. The bloody assault and sub-sequent orgy of plunder and rape by the British troops did not prevent the capture of many of the French garrison, who entered captivity with souvenirs of their stay in the citadel. In the Lady Chapel of St. Mary's Church in Launceston, Cornwall, there hangs a wooden crucifix looted from a church in Badajoz by a French officer. This soldier was billeted upon Abraham Shepherd, a hat maker in the town, to whom the crucifix was given as a mark of appreciation for his hospitality. The relic passed down through the Shepherd family until it was presented to the church.[2]

These are just two stories linking French prisoners of war with British towns and villages. However, many such places have some reminder of this aspect of the prisoner of war story.

While the majority of prisoners remained incarcerated in hulks or Land Prisons, those captives of a certain rank and above were offered their parole. They were required to give their word of honour in writing not to attempt to escape, and to abide by certain regulations, if allowed to reside in one of the towns or villages designated as parole depots. The 'word of a gentleman' was a solemn bond, not to be given lightly, and overall the system worked well, with both British and French officers keeping their word. As the wars dragged on and many officers on both sides of the Channel could see no end to their confinement, breaches of parole became more frequent, although involving a relatively small proportion of the total number of officers residing in parole depots.

These depots were places where the inhabitants were happy to have enemy officers billeted upon them; where there was ample accommodation available for the purpose; and where the local squire or magistrate (often the same person) would agree to oversee the security of the prisoners. The local populace very rarely raised any objection as an influx of parole prisoners brought welcome business to the area. The local magistrate would have to work closely with the appointed Agent, and often the former was an officer in the local Yeomanry, and so could quickly call upon troops in the event of a disturbance.

A town could be designated a parole depot after a request for such recognition was sent to the Transport Board. If the influx of prisoners into the country warranted an increase in the prison establishment, a Commissioner would be sent to view a prospective site for such a depot. The Board, prior to any decision being made, would discuss his opinions and those of the inhabitants.

Commissioner Ambrose Searle, writing in 1807, recommended that parole depots should not be too near each other as French prisoners had been known to send clandestine correspondence from town to town via travelling civilians.[3]

Many towns and villages throughout Britain were used as depots. One of the misconceptions relating to the subject of prisoners of war on parole has been the notion that a town designated as a parole depot remained so throughout the long period of the wars. Not all those used during the Revolutionary Wars were used again after 1803, and indeed the Napoleonic period saw the greater use of such depots. During the 1790s an officer could expect to be exchanged rapidly, usually after no more than a year in captivity. Hence there was no requirement for a large number of parole depots. Exchange was not so frequent after 1803 for French officers, and so the parole prisoner population increased, requiring a larger number of depots. Scotland had a number of towns designated as depots, especially after 1810 when more captives were moved to the north of the country.

Parole Depots

Depot	Period of Use	Nationality
England		
Alresford	1795–97	French
	1809–12	French
Andover	1810–11	French, Russian
Ashbourne	1803–12	French
Ashburton	1794–98	French
	1815	French
Ashby-de-la-Zouch	1804–11	French
Ashford, Kent	1794–98	French, Dutch, Spanish
Beccles	1795–98	French

Bishops Castle	1811–12	French
Bishops Waltham	1803–11	French, Spanish
Bodmin	1794–98	French
Bridgenorth	1812–14	French
Callington	1795–1800	French
Chatham	1811–14	French
Chesterfield	1803–11	French
Chippenham	1795-98	French
Crediton	1805–11	French
Dartmouth	1796–98	French
	1813–15	American
Falmouth	1793–97	French, Spanish
Hambledon	1796–1801	Dutch, Spanish
Launceston	1805–12	French, Prussian
Leek	1803–12	French
Lichfield	1795–1800	French
	1803–11	French
Moreton-Hampstead	1807–14	French
Northampton	1809–12	French
North Tawton	1809–11	French
Odiham	1803–15	French, American
Okehampton	1809–11	French
	1815	
Peebles	1795–1800	French
Peterborough	1797–1800	Dutch
Petersfield	1795–97	French
Reading	1805–12	French, Danish
South Molton	1803–05	French
Tavistock, Devon	1794–98	French
Tenterden	1803–11	
Tiverton	1794–98	French

	1803–11	French
Thame	1804–14	French
Wantage	1808–10	French
Weymouth	1796–97	French
Wincanton	1805–11	French
Wales		
Abergavenny	1812–14	French
Brecon	1806–12	French
Llanfyllin	1812–13	French
Montgomery	1805–11	French
Newtown	1812–14	French
Oswestry	1809–12	French
Welshpool	1811–12	French
Scotland		
Biggar	1811–14	French
Cupar	1811	French
Edinburgh	1795–1800	French
Dumfries	1815	French
Forfar	1796–1801	French
Greenlaw	1812	French
Hawick	1812–14	French
Jedburgh	1812–14	French
Kelso	1810–12	French
Lanark	1812–14	French
Lauder	1811–13	French
Lockerbie	1815	French
Lochmaben	1815	French
Melrose	1812–14	French
Ormskirk	1796–98	French

Peebles	1795–1800	French
	1803–11	French
Sanquhar	1812	French
Selkirk	1811–14	French
Ireland		
Cork	1795–98	French
Dunmanway	1795–98	French
Kinsale	1793–98	French[4]

A parole depot would see many hundreds of officers during its period as a place of confinement, but usually there were no more than 120 to 130 at any one time. Between 1803 and 1811 Tiverton was home to 667 prisoners, while Thame saw 422 'foreign gentlemen' during the period 1803–14.[5] It was also the practice to keep batches of officer prisoners together, as this made it administratively easier to deal with these men, many of who were of the same ship or regiment. The town of Alresford received a number of officers and their wives in the summer of 1810, all of whom were captured on the island of Guadeloupe earlier that year.[6]

Those prisoners granted parole were commissioned officers of the rank of sous-lieutenant in the army and gardes-marine in the navy and above. Civilians captured while performing political duties were also paroled, as were captains and second officers of merchantmen over 50 tons, and captains and the next two officers of privateers carrying 100 men and armed with 14 four-pounder guns and over.[7] Many of these men were allowed to take their servants with them provided they took responsibility for their behaviour. Allowing a common soldier or seaman the liberty of a parole depot was a privilege that the Board would rapidly withdraw if it were abused. Captain Recar, on parole at Wantage, lost one servant but was allowed another. The Board contacted the Agent at Portsmouth informing him that; 'Marc Rideau, servant to Captain Recar ... has been ordered, in consequence of his improper conduct, to be sent into your custody'. Before Recar was allowed another servant, the Board required information on a possible substitute; they wrote; 'You will report to us the case of Jean Baptiste Bellette ... for whom Captain Recar has applied to have as a servant in the room of the former'.[8]

If an officer was granted parole, he signed an undertaking to abide by the parole regulations and not attempt to escape. He was issued with a passport to his town of residence, with instructions to travel to the town upon a certain date and by a specific route, with the journey being made at his own expense. On arrival at the depot he reported to the Agent.

Certificate issued to Parole Prisoners
No.....By the Commissioners for conducting His Majesty's Transport Service, for the care of Sick and Wounded Seamen, and for the Care and Custody of Prisoners of War.
These are to certify, to all His Majesty's Officers, Civil and Military, and whom else it may concern, that the Bearer...........
.... as described on the back hereof, is a detained Prisoner of War, on Parole at .... and that he has liberty to walk on the Great Turnpike Road, within the distance of one mile from the extremities of the town; but that he must not go into any field or cross-road, nor be absent from his lodgings after five o'clock in the afternoon, during the months of November, December, and January; and after seven o'clock in the months of February, March, April, September, and October; or after eight o'clock in the months of May, June, and July; nor quit his lodgings in the morning until the bell rings at six o'clock; wherefore You, and every of You, are hereby desired and required to suffer him the said .... to pass and repass accordingly, without any hindrance or molestation whatever, he keeping himself within the said limits, and behaving according to the law.
Given under our Hands and Seal of Office
at London, this .... Day of .... 181..[9]

Upon signing his parole certificate, the prisoner agreed to obey the laws of the country; not to carry on any clandestine correspondence; nor to violate the parole regulations. These regulations restricted the prisoner to remaining within one mile of the town limits along the turnpike roads. The help of the locals was enlisted to observe this rule, in that notices were posted around the depot stating that prisoners were permitted to walk or ride on the turnpike road within the prescribed mile, but that exceeding the limit or going into a field rendered them liable to arrest, the taker receiving a reward of 10 shillings.

To mark the limits of their parole, milestones were erected around the depot (when they did not already exist), and where these coincided with some natural feature such as a tree, the object became an additional mark of the limits. In Hampshire on the Odiham-Winchfield Road there stands an old oak tree next to the milestone, and this is known locally as 'Frenchman's Oak'. There is also a similar tree at Whitchurch, one mile from Tavistock, known as the 'Honour Oak'. At Ashbourne in Derbyshire, a line of white posts extends along the Derby Road and is known as 'Frenchman's Mile'. A local legend in Ashburton has it that a milestone was sited on the Broadhampston road just before a sharp bend. The officers on parole in the town heard that there was an impressive view just around the bend, outside their parole limits. One day they stealthily carried the stone around the corner so they would not break their parole when admiring the Devon countryside. There the stone has remained. An apocryphal story perhaps, but one in keeping with the prisoners' character and attitude![10]

Many local people welcomed parole prisoners into their homes as it generated useful income via charges for food and lodgings. Several houses in a depot would be used as billets for the prisoners. Odiham, a little village in Hampshire, had more than thirty cottages occupied by French and American officers, a significant proportion of the accommodation available. Two houses in the High Street possess a legacy of their early nineteenth century occupants in the form of names – 'Frenchman's' and 'Frenchman's Cottage'. If a road was known locally for its foreign prisoner population, then its name would often change to reflect this fact. One road in Petersfield was used for French officers during the Revolutionary War, and became known locally as 'Frenchman's Lane', later in the nineteenth century becoming known as 'Frenchman's Road' by which name it is known today.[11]

The number of officers billeted in houses depended upon the rooms available. In Reading, Mr Joseph Restall of London Street had as paying guests a M. le Nesle and one Marc Claro. Mr Bowdens of East Street had four officers in his house, while Mr Cox of the Feathers Inn supplied accommodation for six French gentlemen.[12] All parole prisoners had to remain in their lodgings between set times throughout the year. If they violated this curfew they were liable to arrest and punishment. The Agent was instructed to employ someone to ring a bell at the prescribed times to warn the prisoners to be back in their lodgings.[13]

The officers were given an allowance of 1s 6d per day, while civilians on parole received 1s 0d, and from this they had to pay for their lodgings, food and clothing. The Agent paid this money in advance twice a week, and personal attendance was necessary to collect it, except in the case of serious illness. Those officers with private means could have money sent from home via the French Agent in London, but those without such extra finances often found it hard to subsist. A constant complaint from the parole prisoners was the high rent they were often charged. Lodgings cost from between three and five shillings per week for the room alone, a large proportion of the weekly allowance of 10s 6d. Many officers petitioned the Transport Board for an increase in their allowance. This happened with some Russian officers on parole at Andover in October 1809, who were informed that their existing allowance was the same as that given to the French, and so no special increase could be awarded to them.[14]

The financial hardship experienced by parole prisoners was greater if they had their wives and children with them. Until 1810 the Transport Board did not regard these dependants as prisoners of war and declared that they were free to return home whenever they wished. If they elected to remain with their menfolk that was their concern, but no extra allowance would be given to them. By 1810 the system for exchanging French prisoners of war had all but collapsed, and this had the added effect of hindering the remittance of money from France. Many prisoners were now suffering real poverty, especially those with family. The Board therefore granted a payment of one shilling per day to each woman and child over 12 months, except for English women who married parole prisoners and any resultant children. While this eased the prisoners' situation, many still insisted that the allowance was too meagre.

Some prisoners raised extra funds by giving lessons to the locals in dancing, swordplay and languages. These activities increased the chances of romantic liaisons occurring, often resulting in marriages and births. The parish register of Launceston in Cornwall records eleven marriages of French officers with English women. The records for Odiham record that Adelaide was born to Anne Webb and her lover, Henri Barré de St. Lau in 1805, while Jean Marie Pasquire married Sophie Brookes in 1811.[15] Many officers found their financial situation in serious trouble from these affairs of the heart.

Those officers with wives back home in France were able to arrange for their partners to join them in the parole depots, at their own expense. As was only natural, these families had in common their language, nationality and enforced captivity that linked them together in close-knit communities. While the social life of the English community was open to them, they also organised their own social functions, often to celebrate an Imperial event or personal anniversary.

The authorities frowned upon the celebration of Imperial events, although the French on parole often organised these functions under the guise of personal commemorations. The Board obtained news of a forthcoming function and wrote to John Dunn, the Agent at Alresford, enjoining him to forbid the prisoners to assemble at the Swan Inn to celebrate the marriage of Napoleon to Marie-Louise of Austria in April 1810.

An intercepted letter of 1812 (intercepted because it was sent without permission), signed by 'Henrietta', who was apparently the daughter of one of the parole prisoners, contains many items of personal news and outright gossip about the French families at Alresford. She appears to have been thoroughly enjoying life, with social events among English and French friends and a description of the arrangements for a ball that her parents were giving to celebrate their Silver Wedding anniversary.[16]

At the wars' end, many of the English wives of French officers followed their loved ones home even though the British
Government warned that they would have no rights in France.
Some decided that England was more of an attraction than their
husbands, and chose to remain while their partners returned
home.

Charles Aubertin was a French officer paroled to Andover
where he developed an infatuation for a seventeen-year-old girl
by the name of Harriet Sedgley. This young lady persuaded him
to stay in the town after peace was declared in 1814, and the
following January they were married. They lived in Andover
until 1817 when Charles, homesick for his native land, returned
to France having unsuccessfully attempted to persuade her to
return with him. They maintained a regular correspondence
and Charles sent her remittances until 1820, when he returned
to his wife and again tried to persuade her to go to France. These
efforts were also fruitless, whereupon he left Andover and was
never heard of again. Harriet set up a loom for silk weaving and
died in 1829 at the comparatively early age of 31.[17]

While the constriction of their parole regulations was of major
concern to the prisoners, probably the greatest test was accepting a relatively small area in which to live that invariably became
of little interest after a while, and of being accepted by the local
inhabitants who after all, were at war with them. Many of these
prisoners accepted their lot and waited until they were either
exchanged or the war ended. Some officers attempted escape,
and their stories will be related in a later chapter. Those who
accepted their fate made the best of their situation and led lives
of 'comparative gaiety', as one eyewitness recalled at Ashburton.
Another inhabitant of that town related that the French officers
there were 'very nice and gentlemanly and taught French and
dancing'.[18] Most parole prisoners occupied their time by walking, riding, fishing and gambling. Some made bone and wood
models to sell to the local inhabitants, and many parole depots
had thriving Masonic Lodges formed by the prisoners.

Prisoners violating the regulations were liable to arrest,
and the reward offered to civilians if they assisted in such an
arrest ensured that watchful eyes were about. Many civilians

encouraged parole violations so they could claim the reward. Agents often warned prisoners not to exceed the one-mile limit and to stay on the main roads, and some Agents benevolently overlooked minor trespasses. However, these often led to complaints from the public or assaults on the prisoners by bounty hunters. Messengers sent in pursuit by the Agent searched for any prisoners at Thame who were not in their lodgings by the proper hour, and the runner who caught them was rewarded with one shilling. One David Edwards earned regular pocket money in this way by good-naturedly reminding the Frenchmen of their parole obligations.[19]

While prisoners were arrested for violating their parole, the Transport Board was very firm in dealing with locals who abused the captives. One such incident concerned a French officer residing at Montgomery.

At the last Quarter Sessions for Montgomery a farmer of the neighbourhood of Montgomery was prosecuted by order of the Commissioners of the Transport Board for assaulting one of the French prisoners of war on parole in that town, and pleading guilty to the indictment was fined £10, and ordered to find sureties for keeping the peace for 12 months. This is the second prosecution which that Board has ordered: it being determined that the prisoners shall be protected by Government from insult while they remain in their unfortunate situation as prisoners of war.[20]

Mr Jones, the Agent at Bishops Waltham in 1796, informed the Board of an incident concerning William Nash, the constable. One of the prisoners had thrown a stone at Nash, striking him on the leg. Obviously Nash deserved this treatment, for Jones observed that Nash was very troublesome to the French prisoners as he made a point of arresting any officer he found on the streets only a few minutes after the curfew hour. Nash received a severe reprimand from the Board via the local magistrate.[21] The Comte de Gramont claimed that on occasion he was hissed and spat at as he walked the streets of Ashburton, a result of the hooligan element present in any town. Local boys pelted prisoners with dirt and mocked their appearance and language. Occasionally adults attacked them, jeering French defeats and celebrating British victories. News of the British victory of Vittoria in June 1813 arrived in Oswestry late one evening, the cheers of the inhabitants brought out some French officers playing billiards, and a brawl occurred. The locals later dressed a dummy as Napoleon, paraded it through the town on a donkey, and then hanged and burnt it under the window of General Vielande, taken prisoner at Badajoz.[22]

Ambrose Searle visited Thame in September 1807 and found the principal officers to be content but noted that:

> some of the inferior officers complained of the insults to which they were exposed from the lower orders of the people, though it did not seem that they could fix upon any individual.

Searle asked the Postmaster, Surgeon and some of the prominent inhabitants of the town if the prisoners were abiding by the regulations. These people all confirmed that the prisoners were quiet and orderly.[23]

When Searle visited the town in July of the following year he discovered that a Mr Wykham had been employed by the Agent to patrol the one-mile limit and report any trespass of prisoners. This he considered to be unfair and unnecessary, and prompted him to enquire of 'seven respectable persons' about the Agent and his employees, and their relationship with the parole prisoners. He also recommended that clearer marks be made at the one-mile limit from the extremities of the town, so that there could be no confusion amongst the prisoners as to the extent of their parole. He noted that most officers there were well behaved, and the few escapes had been effected by prisoners who were 'chiefly of the lower orders'.[24]

The local gentry often entertained officers on parole and while deploring any verbal or physical abuse suffered by these foreign gentlemen, could often be equally insensitive. The Marquis d'Hautpol, on parole at Bridgnorth, received an invitation to dine at the home of Lord Malville. On this occasion there were many English officers present who, without regard for his position, began to express (in French) their very negative views of

Napoleon and the French Army. D'Hautpol was a 24-year-old captain in the 59th Regiment de Ligne, captured at Salamanca in July 1812, and at the time was still suffering from a bayonet wound in the right arm and a musket ball in the leg. He indignantly demanded permission to withdraw from the table and the house, and accepted no further invitations there.[25]

Some parole officers elicited sympathy and respect from all levels of the society upon which they were thrust. Admiral Villeneuve was described as 'a most melancholy gentleman' when he briefly resided at Bishops Waltham, Hampshire; the locals looking upon the unfortunate victim of Trafalgar with both pity and respect. In the aftermath of Britain's greatest naval victory and the loss of the much-loved Nelson, perhaps the inhabitants of the village felt they could be magnanimous. He was on parole there for a few weeks alongside other senior officers of the French navy taken in that engagement; Captain Majendie of the *Bucentaure* (Villeneuve's flagship), Captain Lucas of the *Redoutable* (from which the musket shot was fired that killed Admiral Nelson) and Captain Infernet of the *Intrépide*. Villeneuve was bound by the parole regulations except that he had his limits extended to three miles outside the town. Officers had to lodge their swords with the Agent until released, but the French Admiral was allowed to retain, but not to wear, his arms. He requested that he might be allowed to reside in London with his twenty-year old mulatto servant, Jean Baque, but this request was denied. Instead, he was allowed to choose any parole town for his residence, his choice being Reading, arriving there on 30 December 1805 along with the officers named above. In January 1806 he and Majendie attended Nelson's funeral at St Paul's Cathedral. While Villeneuve was willing to show respect for his dead adversary in this way, it cannot have been a comfortable situation for him to see the British display a universal grief for their fallen hero. He had lost a fleet and failed Napoleon, who was not likely to be sympathetic towards his naval commander. In March of that year Villeneuve was exchanged for four British Post-Captains and returned to France, where his Emperor refused him permission to travel to Paris, and so he stayed in Rennes where one day he was found stabbed. It is thought he took his own life, although some suspected that he was murdered on the orders of Napoleon; the price for his failure to destroy the British fleet. However, given the situation he found himself in and his demeanour whilst a prisoner, it would not be surprising if he had resorted to suicide.[26]

Admiral Jan Willem de Winter, commanding the Dutch fleet at the Battle of Camperdown in October 1797, was captured on board his flagship the *Vrijheid* and sent to England on parole. He was impressed with his treatment, and did not seem to display the melancholy and despair that his French counterpart later adopted. On his release from his parole obligations in December 1798 (although he had returned to Holland in November 1797), de Winter stated in a public address in Amsterdam:

> The fortune of war previously forced me to live abroad, and being since then for the first time vanquished by the enemy, I have experienced a second state of exile. However mortifying to the feelings of a man who loves his country, the satisfactory treatment I met with on the part of the enemy, the English, and the humane and faithful support and assistance they evinced towards my worthy countrymen and fellow sufferers, have considerably softened the horrors of my situation ... the noble liberality of the English nation since this bloody contest justly entitles them to your admiration.[27]

Admiral de Winter's flagship became a prison hulk moored at Chatham. This fact obviously did not affect his opinion of the English people!

While the most senior officers usually commanded respect from amongst their enemies, certain categories of officer did not. Perhaps their actions did not endear themselves to the local authorities, or an ingrained prejudice in English society had something to do with it. When some black prisoners arrived from the West Indies in 1796, to reside in Portchester Castle, Portsmouth's Governor Sir William Pitt did not allow the black officers their parole. He wrote to the War Office to justify his decision:

> The Blacks, who were called the officers, many of which were violent in their behaviour and savage in their disposition, and

1 *An English prison ship, from a French print dated 1846.*

2 *The military barracks along the north wall of Portchester Castle. The only building that survives today is the garrison's brick-built powder store. (Captain Durrant, reproduced with permission of Hampshire Museums Service)*

3 *The Landgate at Portchester Castle circa 1813. The guard house to the left survived until the 1960s. (painting by Captain Durrant, reproduced with permission of Hampshire Museums Service)*

4 *Interior of Portchester Castle showing the stockade that separated the northern half of the outer bailey and the medieval buildings where prisoners were housed. (Captain Durrant, reproduced with permission of Hampshire Museums Service)*

5 *Stapleton Prison, Bristol. (From an engraving by J.P. Malcolm;* Gentleman's Magazine, *May 1814)*

6 *One of the original barrack buildings at Dartmoor Prison. (Author)*

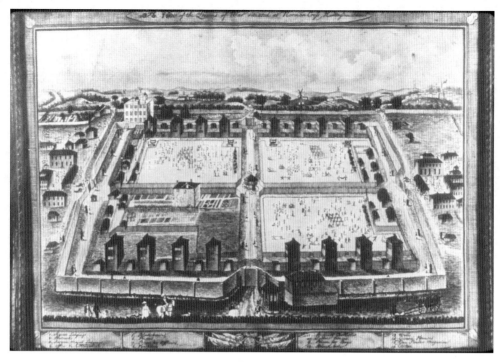

7 Painting of the depot at Norman Cross. (Peterborough Museum and Art Gallery)

8 The Blockhouse at the centre of Norman Cross prison depot. Note the alarm bell, 3-pounder swivel guns, and numerous musket slits that could direct fire into any of the prison courtyards. (Captain Durrant, reproduced with permission of Hampshire Museums Service)

9 One of the courtyards of Norman Cross prison, showing the open-air ovens the prisoners were allowed to bake bread. (Captain Durrant, reproduced with permission of Hampshire Museums Service)

HONOUR OAK TREE

MARKED BOUNDARY OF FRENCH PRISONERS ON PAROLE
IN TAVISTOCK FROM PRINCETOWN
DURING THE NAPOLEONIC WAR. (1803 – 14).
ALSO WHERE MONEY WAS DEPOSITED
IN EXCHANGE FOR FOOD
DURING A CHOLERA OUTBREAK IN 1832.

10 The Honour Oak Tree that marked the parole limit of prisoners at Tavistock, Devon. (Author)

11 *The crucifix from Badajoz, given to Abraham Shepherd and now in St Mary's Church, Launceston, Cornwall.* (*Author*)

12 *The grave of Francois Guidon, Ashburton, Devon. The wreath was laid as part of the twinning ceremony with Cleder, France, in 1985.* (*Author*)

13 The gravestone of *Géneral de Brigade Charles de Proux, captured in Spain in August 1812 and 'Discharged Dead' on 29 May 1813 aged 76 years, whilst on parole at Bridgnorth. (Author)*

14 *Louis Ambroise Quantain died at Moreton Hampstead on 29 April 1810. He was 'interred with Masonic honours, he being a Freemason. One hundred and four French and Danish officers that were on parole here, as well as most of the respectable inhabitants of this place attended his funeral'. (Author)*

CY GIT
PIERE FERON,
CAPITAINE AU
66⁵ REG¹ DE LIGNE,
CHEVALIER DE L'EMPIRE
FRANCAIS. NE A RHEIMS
DEPART¹ DE LA MARNE
LE 15 AOUT 1766,
DECEDE A ODIHAM
LE 8 MAI 1810.

PIERRE JULIAN JOUNEAU
Son of
IEAN JOSEPHE JOUNEAU
DE DAURE and of MARIE
CHARLOTTE FRANQUINY
DE FEUX
Officer in the adminiftration
of the French Navy
BORN IN THE ISLE OF RHE
Died at ODIHAM Sept⁴ 4ᵗʰ 1809
in the 29ᵗʰ year of his age.
He was a prifoner of War
Death hath made him free

15 Captain Pierre Feron of the 66ᵗʰ Regiment was captured on Guadeloupe in February 1810, and died at Odiham on 7 April. He was buried alongside Pierre Jouneau who had been taken at sea in 1805 and died 4 September 1809 on parole. (Author)

Ici eft le Corps
de MARIE LOUISE Vᵉ FOURNIER
Epoufe de Fᵒⁱˢ Bertet
Capitaine au Corps Impérial
de L'artillerie Francaife
decedée le 11 Avril 1812
agée de 44 ans

16 Marie Louis Fournier was the wife of Captain Francois Bertet. After his capture on Guadeloupe in February 1810 she elected to accompany him on parole to Alresford, Hampshire, where she died on 11 April 1812. (Author)

17 *The Council House, Llanfyllin, Wales. The interior decorating was performed by Lieutenant Pierre Augeraud, who was captured in Spain in 1812. (Author)*

18 *The market stalls at Forton Prison. (Captain Durrant, reproduced with permission of Hampshire Museums Service)*

19 A prisoner making a model of bone saved from his meat ration. This is part of a display telling the story of the prison hulks, in the Guildhall Museum Rochester. (Author)

20 Intricately carved stern of bone ship model in the Science Museum, London. (Science Museum)

21 Bone ship made by American prisoners at Dartmoor and now in the Watermen's Hall, Billingsgate. This is the largest model known at 7 feet in length. The plinth on which it stands is of wood from HMS Temeraire. (Author)

22 The prisoners made models of anything their imagination and ingenuity could devise. This cockerel stands about 9 inches high, and each feather is a separately carved strip of bone. It is on display in the Norman Cross Collection, Peterborough Museum and Art Gallery. (Author)

23 *Many of the models had working mechanisms. When a handle is turned on this model the spinning wheel rotates and the figures move. (Peterborough Museum and Art Gallery)*

24 *The dice and dominos in this box reflect the serious problem that gambling posed in all the depots. This domino box is on display in Southsea Castle, Portsmouth. (Author)*

25 Straw marquetry trinket box in Plymouth Museum. (Author)

26 Straw marquetry box in the form of a writing desk in Plymouth Museum. (Author)

27 A Night View of the Prison Ships Lying in Gillingham near Chatham *by Francois St. Jean. Note the alarm lanterns at the top of the masts, and the musket flashes of the guards firing at prisoners escaping from the* Sampson *in the bottom right corner of the picture. (Guildhall Museum Rochester)*

28 Straw Plait Merchants trading with prisoners of war at Norman Cross. *This is artistic licence as the activity was illegal and would not have occurred so openly as this (Painting by A.C. Cooke, reproduced with permission of Luton Museums Service)*

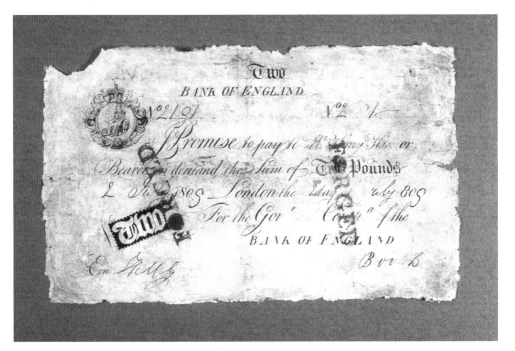

29 Forged £2 banknote found on board a prison ship and officially declared a forgery by the Bank of England. (Bank of England Museum)

30 The memorial to prisoners of war at Chatham. (Author)

31 In April 2005 His Grace the Duke of Wellington inaugurated the restored eagle memorial at Norman Cross. This memorial is a tangible reminder that the final resting place of 1,770 French and Dutch prisoners of war is near the site of this depot. (The Norman Cross Eagle Appeal)

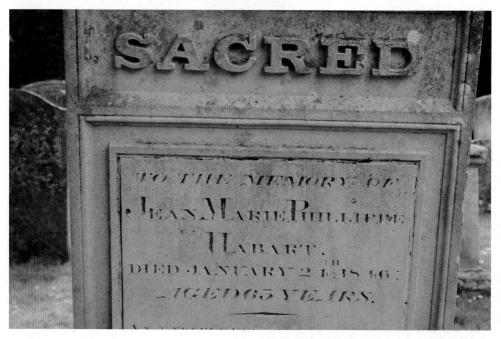

32 The gravestone of Jean Marie Philippe Habart in Stilton churchyard. Habart had been held in Norman Cross and was one of the few prisoners who stayed in England after the war. He married Elizabeth Snow of Stilton, set up in business as a baker and corn merchant, and was robbed and murdered in 1846. (Author)

doubtless many of them had been placed in that situation from having been conspicuously eminent in acts of rebellion and barbarity.

Sir William thought these people very improper persons to be turned loose in any country:

... but particularly so in this neighbourhood, where principles subversive to the Government have already been disseminated by the French on parole, which officers possess less dishonourable principles than the prisoners of colour. The greatest care should be taken to watch over the conduct of these prisoners, for though they are considered as officers by the present French constitution, it is impossible to look upon them as gentlemen, many of them have risen to high officer from the meanest extraction, void of education and principles, consequently very little respect can be paid to their assertions [to be allowed parole as officers].[28]

Occasionally some parole prisoners would render a service to the local inhabitants that would invariably be brought to the attention of the Board. This service was often looked upon favourably for the purpose of exchange.

Joseph Maudet, on parole at Oswestry, rescued a four-year-old child from the jaws of a lion. His mother had taken the child to see *Gillman and Atkins Menagerie of Wild Beasts* in March 1814. The child incautiously approached too near a cage in which two lions were confined and was dragged against the bars by one of the beasts. Maudet 'rushed forward, extricated the child by main force from the animal's grasp and happily restored him to the arms of his mother'. A local petition to the Transport Board stated that 'the action speaks for itself and requires no comment' and was signed by the Mayor of Oswestry, his deputy, the coroner, town clerk, the vicar and rectors of three neighbouring parishes. They urged the Board to release Maudet and this request was readily granted.[29]

While some prisoners were well behaved and respected especially if they contributed to the community, others were a positive nuisance. In 1814 American prisoners at Reading were so unruly and troublesome that the authorities were forced to remove them to Dartmoor. Occasionally parole prisoners would cause a serious disturbance that warranted prompt local action. One such case concerned Generals Rochambeau and Boyé at Wincanton. The official report, penned by Ambrose Searle, describes the affair in detail and is reproduced here in its entirety:

> General Rochambeau, with about six or seven French officers taking with them several dogs, left Wincanton to the distance of between four and five miles, and came upon the lands of a farmer, who knowing them to be prisoners of war and far out of bounds, warned them off, threatening to have them seized if they did not immediately retire. Possibly no great delicacy of language was used by such a person on the occasion; but, however, the General and his party were so much irritated that they fell upon the man and treated him roughly. Some haymakers at a distance, observing the contest, hastened to the farmer's assistance, attacked the Frenchmen, and beat them, especially Rochambeau himself, very severely. Upon their return to the town, they exasperated their countrymen in their behalf to such a degree, that they threatened vengeance, procured clubs and such sort of weapons as they could find, declared they would burn the town, and seemed determined upon the utmost measures of revenge. They were headed by Rochambeau and Boyé, with some few others of the most violent among them. The Agent, who is a captain in the Volunteer Corps of the district, exceedingly alarmed at these proceedings, found himself obliged, after some unavailing endeavours to pacify the uproar, to call out his men for the public safety, and to make known his situation to the Board. The neighbouring Gentlemen and principal inhabitants at last succeeded in stilling the outrage, but not in quieting the apprehension of the inhabitants, till, upon the representations made to the Board, the two Generals above named and nearly twenty others were separately removed to other depots.

Searle later visited the area to see how these particular prisoners were faring. He wrote:

> The town has since been, and is now, perfectly quiet and easy. The prisoners too, finding that they must submit to the inconvenience

of removal in case of disturbance, and their passionate dem-
onstrations of joy upon Bonaparte's successes having subsided,
which appear to have had some influence upon the insolence
of their conduct on the occasion, are now orderly and decent as
before. The removal of the ringleaders was really necessary, and
led to the desirable effect.

General Rochambeau was transferred to Moreton Hampstead
where he caused no trouble, whilst Boyé was sent to Crediton
where he 'conducted himself with propriety'.[30]

While many prisoners on parole rendered some service to the
community in which they were temporary residents, and earned
the approbation of their English neighbours, many such captives
were willing to express their gratitude for kindnesses bestowed
upon them. In 1814 there were a number of Norwegians on parole
in Reading. Norway had been ruled by Denmark until the Treaty
of Kiel on 14 January 1814, when the country had been ceded to
Sweden. Denmark had supported Napoleon, while Sweden had
been persuaded (with the offer of Norway) to enter the coalition
against France. The Norwegian people had rebelled and formed
their own government, whereupon Swedish forces invaded the
country, supported by a blockade of Norwegian ports by ships of
the Royal Navy.[31]

The Member of Parliament for Reading, Mr J.B. Monck, made a
public speech against the British Government's attitude towards
Norway, expressing his view that 'if the blockade of that country
was persisted in, it would be petitioned against by every county
and every town in England'. The Norwegians in Reading sent
him a letter full of praise and thanks for his support of their
people, and for his concern for their welfare. They informed him
that liberty had been offered to all Norwegians in the prison
depots (approximately 800, both on parole and in the hulks) if
they would acknowledge the sovereignty of Sweden, which they
unanimously refused to do.[32]

There is much to remind us of the sojourn of foreign prisoners of war in the towns and villages of Great Britain. The names
given to houses and roads are all part of the local history of such
areas, but it is the graves of the prisoners that remain a perma-

nent reminder of their story. Many Local History Societies take pride in the fact that they have a French prisoner buried in their churchyard, and ensure that the grave is well kept, not only as part of their local heritage, but also out of respect for such unfortunate men and women who remained here long after the war with France was over.

Alresford, in Hampshire, was home to 375 parole prisoners between 1809 and 1812. They were taken prisoner on board privateers, gunboats, and frigates; on Guadeloupe, Sicily, Naples, and in Spain and Portugal. Pierre Garnier was a second lieutenant in the 66éme de Ligne, captured on Guadeloupe in February 1810. He arrived at Alresford (via Portchester Castle) on 19 June in the company of 54 other officers from the island, one judge and his secretary, 13 wives and children, and 13 servants (some black). He became ill the following April and died there on 31 July 1811, and was buried in the churchyard where his gravestone may be seen. His exact cause of death is not recorded in the Admiralty records (he has the annotation 'DD' entered by his name, signifying that he was 'discharged dead'), but it is possible he succumbed to ill health acquired while stationed in the West Indies. Also at Alresford can be seen the gravestone of Marie Louise Fournier, wife of Captain Francois Bertet, both of whom were part of the French garrison on Guadeloupe. Other graves in this town belong to Cypryen Lavau, a privateer officer, and Joseph Hypolite Riouffe, a frigate officer.[33]

Two French officers are buried at Odiham, Hampshire. Pierre Feron was a captain in the 66éme de Ligne taken prisoner on Guadeloupe alongside Pierre Garnier. He arrived on parole on 7 April 1810, and died exactly one month later. His grave is next to that of M. Jouneau, a naval officer captured in August 1805, and who died in September 1809.[34] When a parole prisoner died his effects were sent to the Agent's office, either to be sold to pay any debts incurred by the deceased, or to be eventually sent to his family on the Continent. In the case of Jouneau, his effects were sent to his brother who was residing on parole at Launceston. When the Agent at Odiham, Mr Charles Shebbeare, asked who was to pay Jouneau's funeral expenses of two guineas, he was instructed to send the bill to Launceston as well! The regulations stated that the funeral should cost no more than two guineas unless the other prisoners wished to contribute. In this case the Board took the opportunity to reclaim some of the costs of running a parole depot.[35]

Many other gravestones remain to remind us of the parole prisoners. At Moreton Hampstead one Ambroise Quantain, a French artillery lieutenant, died and was buried in the graveyard. His headstone has since been transferred to the wall of the church entrance, but is particularly interesting in that it has the Masonic device carved on the stone. Not all prisoner-graves are still marked by gravestones. Some headstones have been removed over the years, if indeed they existed at all, to make room for those of the local populace, while others have been eroded by the elements and are thus difficult to locate. Joseph Delette was a civilian passenger in *Le Furet* merchant vessel, captured in June 1809. He was taken with his wife and sent on parole to Okehampton, and on 19 April 1812 his wife died in childbirth and was buried alongside the dead infant.[36] Their graves still exist, and it is only local knowledge that directs the visitor to two small and badly eroded headstones beside the church. Little of the inscriptions can be discerned on these particular monuments.

Disease and ill health took their toll of the prisoners on parole, but some died of old age. General of Brigade Charles de Preiux, captured in Spain in August 1812, was 'discharged dead' on 29 May 1813. The records give us a description of a 74-year-old man, of slender build, with grey hair and grey eyes who ended his military career in England.[37]

Many thousands of enemy officers and civilians resided on parole in the depots of Britain. However, it was also the practice to allow some captives to go back to their country of origin on parole, as long as they signed an agreement not to serve against Britain until they had been 'fairly and regularly exchanged'. This method was frequently adopted during the Revolutionary Wars, when Exchange Cartels were often organised between Britain and France, Spain and Holland. The officer concerned signed an official document:

Form of the Engagement subscribed by all Prisoners of War,
    permitted to return to France, On Parole.

Whereas the Commissioners for conducting His Britannic
Majesty's Transport Service, and for the care and custody of
prisoners of war, have been pleased to grant me, the undersigned
[prisoner's name] as described on the back hereof, late [his rank;
regiment or ship] and now a prisoner of war at [his Parole depot],
leave to return to France, upon my entering into an engagement
not to serve against Great Britain, or any of the Powers in alliance
with that Kingdom, until I shall be regularly exchanged for a
British prisoner of war, of equal rank; and upon my also engaging,
that immediately after my arrival in France, I shall make known
the place of my residence there, to the British Agent for Prisoners
in Paris, and shall not change the same on any account, without
first intimating my intention to the said Agent; and moreover, that
at the expiration of every two months, until my exchange shall
be effected, I shall regularly and punctually transmit to the said
Agent a certificate of my residence, signed by the magistrates or
Municipal Officers of the place.

Now in consideration of my enlargement, I do hereby declare
that I have given my Parole of Honour accordingly, and that I will
keep it inviolably.

Given under my hand at [his place of residence as a prisoner]
this day of [date].[38]

Comprehensive lists were compiled by the Transport Office giving full descriptions of all officers who had given their parole
and been permitted to return to their own country. These lists
were updated every three months, and a reward of one guinea
was paid to anyone who discovered a named prisoner serving
without having been exchanged. Separate lists were published
for French, Spanish and Dutch prisoners who had given this
undertaking. These nations also adopted this approach with
British officers, and the system worked well during the 1790s but
after 1803 the system was not employed so extensively.

This method of parole had distinct advantages over the procedure for keeping the officer on parole in Britain. First, the
Admiralty did not have the expense of looking after the officer,

and second, it speeded up the exchange process. Officers sent home could apply to their own governments for an enemy officer to be released in exchange for themselves, thus releasing that officer from their parole obligations. The more superior an officer sent home on parole, the more likely it was they had some influence in government circles, or had connections with senior military officials. Admiral de Winter was sent home to Holland in November 1797, having spent only a month on parole in England. He was able to use his influence to secure his release the following year.[39] Jacques Durvial was an officer on parole in France, being released from his parole obligations in 1799, in exchange for Major Matthew Jenner of the 39th Foot who had arrived as a prisoner in France that year.[40] When an officer was taken captive by someone who had a friend or relative held prisoner of war, it was common practice for the officer to be released on parole on the promise he would use his influence to secure the release of his counterpart. Provided the details of the transaction were sent to the Transport Office, there was no objection to this procedure, and in fact it was actively encouraged. To break the parole obligations was a slur on a man's honour, so any officer who could not secure the release of a prisoner held by his own side was obliged to return to his captor's country to reside there on parole until he was exchanged.

However, most officers taken prisoner had to endure periods of captivity, though not perhaps as arduous as their men, in the parole depots of Britain.

Notes

[1] Pilkington, Francis. *Ashburton: The Dartmoor Town* (Devon, 1981) p.43

[2] Rendle, Joan. *Gateway to Cornwall* (Bodmin 1981), p.88.

[3] TNA:PRO ADM105/44, Commissioner's Report 2 October 1807.

[4] TNA:PRO ADM103 passim. General Entry Books for Parole Depots.

[5] TNA:PRO ADM103/572, 601, 606, 607, 608. General Entry Books for Parole Depots.

6   TNA:PRO ADM103/552, General Entry Book of French prisoners on parole at Alresford.

7   TNA:PRO ADM98/200. Letters relating to prisoners of war on parole 1809.

8   TNA:PRO ADM98/261, 9 January 1810.

9   TNA:PRO ADM105/62.

10   Pilkington, p.74.

11   'Petersfield Place Names' in Petersfield Papers No.1, Petersfield Area Historical Society, 1976.

12   TNA:PRO ADM103/598. General Entry Book of French prisoners of war on parole at Reading.

13   TNA:PRO ADM105/93. Instructions to Agents for prisoners of war on parole, 14 September 1808.

14   TNA:PRO ADM98/200, 10 October 1809.

15   Parish Records of Odiham, Hampshire 1800–1811.

16   TNA:PRO ADM105/61.

17   The *Andover Advertiser,* 21 June 1918.

18   Pilkington, p.74.

19   Brown, J. Howard & Guest, W. *A History of Thame* (Thame, 1935), p.171–172.

20   Chapman, Murray. *Napoleonic Prisoners of War in Llanfyllin.*

21   TNA:PRO ADM99/96. Board Minutes 31 August 1796.

22   Crimmin, P.K. 'French prisoners of war on parole 1793–1815: the Welsh border towns'. Paper delivered at Guerres et Paix 1660–1815 (Rochefort 1986) p.68.

23   TNA:PRO ADM105/44. 12 September 1807.

24   ibid. 26 July 1808.

25   de Goutel, E.Hennet. *Mémoires du Général Marquis Alphonse D'Hautpol* (Paris 1906), p.84.

26   For details of Admiral Villeneuve and his life whilst on parole, plus an account of his last days in France see Abell, p445–446; TNA: PRO ADM103/598 General Entry Book of French Prisoners of War on Parole at Reading; Jenkins, E.H., *A History of the French Navy* (London, 1973), p.264.

27   Abell, p.446. Admiral de Winter entered the Dutch Navy in 1762 and rose to the rank of lieutenant. Politically he was a republican politically and joined the French Army, serving with it as a General in Holland in 1795. He was appointed Admiral and given command

of a Dutch fleet, even though he had never commanded a ship. For details of his abilities, or otherwise, whilst afloat, see Parkinson, C. Northcote, *Britannia Rules: The Classic Age of Naval History 1793–1815* (Alan Sutton, Stroud, 1994) p.46–49.

[28] TNA:PRO WO 40/8, War Office Unnumbered Papers, 20 October 1796.

[29] Crimmin, p69-70.

[30] TNA:PRO ADM105/44, 2 October 1806.

[31] Haythornthwaite, *The Napoleonic Source Book* p.246.

[32] Ditchfield, P.H. *Reading Seventy Years Ago: A Record of Events from 1813–1819* (Reading, 1887) p.101–102.

[33] TNA:PRO ADM103/552, General Entry Book of French prisoners of war on parole at Alresford.

[34] TNA:PRO ADM103/563, General Entry Book of French prisoners of war on parole at Odiham.

[35] TNA:PRO ADM98/200, Letters relating to prisoners on parole, 4 October 1809.

[36] TNA:PRO ADM103/594, General Entry Book of French prisoners of war on parole at Okehampton.

[37] TNA:PRO ADM103/565, General Entry Book of French prisoners on parole in Bridgnorth.

[38] TNA:PRO ADM103/495, 1 July 1799.

[39] TNA:PRO ADM103/615, General Entry Book of prisoners of war sent to Holland on parole 1796–99.

[40] TNA:PRO ADM103/506, French exchanges effected 1798–1801.

CHAPTER 6

All Kinds of Little Works

The most demoralising aspect of captivity for a Napoleonic prisoner of war was the enforced idleness. For the inmates of the Land Prisons and Hulks there was official work for only a few prisoners, and this often only on an occasional basis. Parole prisoners had the delights of their town or village with which to occupy them, but even these lost their appeal after a while.

To alleviate this boredom and to prevent it being channeled into escape attempts and other troublesome behaviour, the authorities encouraged any activity that kept busy the minds and hands of the prisoners; any legal, wholesome activity that is. The activities adopted by the prisoners were many and varied, some official, some approved, and some most definitely not condoned.

There was some official work available to a few prisoners, although the British did not employ their captives on work outside the prison walls, as foreign prisoners were so employed in France. When the pool of French labour was depleted due to the conscription of the adult male population, the French Government gladly availed itself of its large prisoner of war workforce. This situation did not apply in Britain where there was an ample supply of civilian labour.

When convict hulks were first created during the late eighteenth century it was envisaged that the convicts would provide a cheap source of labour for various projects such as fortifications and dockyard construction. The use of this cheap labour was resented by the civilian workforce, because of which convict labour was never used fully. The imposition of prisoners of war as workers in the community would have resulted in civil unrest and so was a domestic impossibility. The Transport Board was always diligent in preventing prisoners of war from working outside the depots in any great number. Parole prisoners at Tavistock were employed assisting with the harvest until Lord Lennox, a local landowner, complained to the Board, whereupon orders were given to the Agent there to prevent this practice.[1] Occasionally a few prisoners might be employed as casual labour to assist in repairs to the exterior of a prison, but only under the supervision of civilian labourers, and only if they could be properly guarded.

Life in a land prison or onboard a hulk could be one of unremitting monotony. There was a roll call each day, and the Surgeon would visit the barracks daily to inspect the general conditions and listen to any health-related requests or complaints. One prisoner from each mess would attend the cookhouse and collect the ration for his colleagues. Part of the routine would be the daily ablutions including laundry, at the wooden troughs stationed in the courtyards, or on the upper deck of the hulks. The prisoners would also use these areas for their amusements and such sports as they could organise.

Conversation was a preoccupation of many, with main topics of discussion invariably being the prospect of liberation, and the course of the war, as far as they could ascertain from the gossip of the turnkeys and guards and from what little they could hear in the market. New arrivals at the prison would bring news of other depots, events in Europe, and prospects (or otherwise) for exchange. Some of the news was based upon truth, much on fabrication and rumour. Certain prisoners received letters from home, after these had passed through the Transport Office for censorship. Newspapers were not officially allowed, but many were smuggled into the depots, often with the connivance of the guards and turnkeys. According to Benjamin Waterhouse, the inmates on the *Crown Prince* had access to a number of newspapers, for which they paid 16 shillings per month to have them smuggled on board. The *Whig* and *Bell's Weekly Messenger* were popular amongst the Americans, while the French took the *Star*. The *Statesman* was popular with the more educated prisoners, but they were charged 28 shillings per month for this publication, the expense of which was defrayed by the sale of green fish to the contractor, caught in the River Medway. No doubt the authorities were pleased to see the prisoners quietly fishing to augment their rations![2]

Some prisoners were appointed to attend with the prison authorities and inspect the bread, meat and vegetables as they were delivered. However, for the majority of the men, how they filled their time was their affair. If their activities were legal then they received approval from the prison staff. Illegal occupations were quelled upon the authorities discovering the perpetrators.

Many prisoners were conscripts and came from all walks of life, be they of practical or intellectual disposition. The war prisons contained skilled artisans including jewelers, watch-makers, teachers and Government officials who could put their education and training to good use. Industrious prisoners who had artistic talents could find work within the prison as actors, authors, artists and teachers.

Portchester Castle had a typical range of activities adopted by the prisoners, and was a veritable hive of industry. Within the depot could be found manufacturers of straw hats, stock-ings, gloves, purses and braces. There were tailors, shoemak-ers, caterers (selling home-made sweets and biscuits), lemonade sellers, comedians (Punch and Judy-type puppet shows, and marionettes), and even, according to one prisoner, goldsmiths. Education was not neglected; there were self-styled professors of mathematics, drawing, languages (English, French and Latin), writing, fencing and dancing. St. Aubin, a French officer held at the depot for a while, stated that many prisoners arrived at Portchester unable to read or write, but left with a good versing in these skills.[3]

A Parliamentary report dated 25 July 1800 stated that:

... the prisoners in all the depots in the country are at full liberty to exercise their industry within the prisons, in manufacturing and selling any articles they may think proper excepting those which would affect the Revenue in opposition to the Laws, obscene toys and drawings, or articles made from their clothing or the prison stores, and by means of this privilege some of them have been known to carry off upon their release more than 100 guineas each.[4]

When these manufacturing activities conflicted with the local civilian industry they were stopped. The objection was that the prisoners, supported out of the tax revenue paid by the local inhabitants, were allowed to undersell the latter in their own local industries. Thus in some parole depots in Wales the Frenchmen were stopped from making pastry and confectionery, and straw plait manufacture was banned at Norman Cross and Portchester Castle.

All the prisons had a market, and on board the hulks civilians were allowed to trade with the prisoners. Prisoner vendors would erect stalls or simply display their wares on the ground, and sell to the locals or to each other. Dealers from outside the prison would bring with them the produce of the neighbourhood, such as clothing, feeding utensils, tools and materials the prisoners could use for their work and foodstuffs. The prisoners could sell items they had made, both to civilian sightseers who looked upon the prisons as curiosities, and to locals who acted as agents for the sale of manufactured work.

In 1797 Captain Fremantle RN and his wife Betsey visited Portchester Castle and saw three thousand French prisoners. Betsey wrote that 'they are very industrious and make all kinds of little works. We bought a Guillotine neatly done in bone'.[5]

Private George Farmer, on garrison duty at Portchester wrote this of the market.

Every possible encouragement was given to the exercise of ingenuity among the prisoners themselves by the throwing open of the Castle yard once or twice a week, when their wares were exhibited for sale, amid numerous groups of jugglers, tumblers, and musicians, all of whom followed their respective callings, if not invariably with skill, always with most praiseworthy perseverance. Moreover, the ingenuity of the captives taught them how on these occasions to set up stalls on which all manner of trinkets were set forth, as well as puppet shows and Punch's opera ... Then followed numerous purchases, particularly on the

part of the country people, of bone and ivory knickknacks, fabricated invariably with a common penknife, yet always neat, and
not infrequently elegant. Nor must I forget to mention the daily
market which the peasantry, particularly the women, were in the
habit of attending, and which usually gave scope for the exchange
of Jean Crapaud's manufacture for Nancy's eggs, or Joan's milk,
or home-baked loaf.[6]

The above officer, together with the Fremantles, would have
seen a strictly regulated market, constantly patrolled by the
guards and turnkeys. This was to ensure that neither vendors
nor buyers were cheated. Commissioner Searle, writing from
Bristol in 1808, described the market in Stapleton Prison, which
was allowed from 9.00am until 12.00 noon each day:

> The sale is carried on in a small enclosure, in view of the pris-
> oners, by parties delegated by them from among themselves
> assisted by the Turnkeys, whose business it is to prevent fraud
> and imposition on all sides, and to prevent the introduction and
> disposal of forbidden or improper articles. The indecencies found
> at Norman Cross are almost unknown here. The intervention of
> indifferent parties between buyers and sellers probably renders it
> too difficult without immediate detection.[7]

Every article made by the prisoners had its price attached, together
with the name of the individual who made it. Unfortunately the
name was only attached in a temporary fashion, so the majority
of prisoner of war work that survives is anonymous. A few items
however, have the maker's names inscribed upon them, such as
several beautiful pictures in straw marquetry made by Jean de la
Porte and preserved in Peterborough Museum.

Bone-work

Of all the manufacturing activities in the prisons, the most pro-
lific and that most associated with these prisoners of war was
the production of bone models of ships, houses, guillotines

– anything in fact that the prisoner's ingenuity and imagination could design and build. The models were also made of many other materials including wood, ivory, tortoise shell and metal (iron, brass, copper and even silver). Additional materials used in this work included glass, hair, paper, cloth, straw, dyes and pigments, although the most commonly used material was the bone saved from the meat ration, the best pieces becoming a negotiable commodity amongst the prisoners.

There was an almost unlimited supply of bone from the large weekly consumption of meat at the depots. A prisoner at Forton, Germain Lamy, related that:

> ... beef bones and mutton bones were kept on all sides, those that could not work selling them at good prices to those who could.[8]

Beef bone was the most common because of the greater quantity that was available. In some of the larger models whalebone was used.

The bone was first cleaned by boiling, and the resulting glue-forming substances saved for use in the model making. The bones used in all the models are always very white in colour; this bleaching was achieved by exposure to either sulphur (used in the prisons as a disinfectant), hydrogen peroxide (used to bleach straw for plait manufacture), or lime (which was also used in the prisons).

Ivory was occasionally used when it was made available to the prisoners, to be used for small items such as the feet and lid handles of trinket boxes. That this substance was in use is evident by the business card of a parole prisoner at Leek that reads 'James Francis Neau, Derby Street, Leek. Begs leave to inform the Public that he has on sale straw hats, Beautiful Straw, Ivory and Bone Fancy Articles, made by the French Prisoners'.[9] The wood used for modelling was also available in unlimited quantities, since much of this material was used in the construction, repair and heating of the prisons. The type of wood depended on the source. From within the prison would come oak and fir, while box, mahogany, lime and walnut were often supplied by civilians who actually commissioned specific items of work.

Many metals were used, again obtained from within and outside the depot. Iron, brass and copper were used in both sheet and wire form. Many ship models may be seen with the hull below the waterline covered in copper sheet, in imitation of the shipbuilding custom of the day to protect the hull from the depredations of the toredo worm. Gold and silver are sometimes to be found lining parts of a model. In the Merchants House Museum, Plymouth, there are some models of contemporary French artillery equipment made of bone with silver fittings. These precious metals came from the personal ornaments of the prisoners, and from the gold and silver coins that were in circulation. The coins were beaten out into thin sheet and then cut up for the models.

The rigging for these models was made of hair, either human or horse. The latter hair was also used to make such curious articles as hair bracelets, finger rings and necklaces. Paint was used to colour the ships, trinket boxes and straw marquetry, and came principally from the civilians in the markets. Many of the trinket boxes have pictures painted on or in them.[10]

Before fashioning any of this material into a model, the prisoners had to make or purchase the necessary tools. Tools were present amongst the prisoners in great abundance, ostensibly for manufacturing but also put to good use as offensive weapons and in escape attempts. In 1805, because of many escape attempts and some unrest, the Agent at Norman Cross impounded all implements and tools that were locked away during the night and reissued to the prisoners the next morning.

The tools were made from pieces of hoop iron (from casks used for food storage), bolts, nails and knives. These were converted into knives, chisels, gouges, saws and a wide selection of other tools, including fine engraving tools, and pens and brushes for forging banknotes.[11]

The ship models are of all types, from ships of the line to small rowing boats, and were produced with intricate detail. They vary in size from such ambitious efforts as the two-metre ship in the Watermen's Hall in London, made by American prisoners, to miniatures of about five centimetres in length. The majority however, are about sixty centimetres long. Many are mounted on bases of polished wood or straw marquetry, and some are enclosed in cabinets of wood or straw-work.

Usually a group of prisoners would combine their talents to produce such models, each individual making a certain part, to be assembled by yet another into the finished item. While many of the ships were based on actual vessels, the makers had to rely on their memory for the details, and it was here that they allowed their imaginations free rein. Almost every part of the model would be decorated with carved scrolls, leaves, flowers, or pierced filigree patterns, with ornate carving on the stern galleries and even carved deck furniture. It must be remembered that the prisoners were making these models for the local civilian market, as Betsey Fremantle recalled, and so any addition to the model would be utilized that would help it to sell. Some models have been set upon a base representing a dockyard slipway with naval items lying alongside. Many of the larger models have a pair of drawstrings protruding from under the transom, often tied to a bone head. When pulled they reveal a simple spring system that makes the guns disappear and run out; an ingenious broadside effect.[12] The smaller models are just as elaborate, with carved figureheads the size of a grain of wheat; gun ports a few millimetres square; and sails made of wood shavings or translucent ivory of tissue paper thickness.

It was not only ships that were modelled out of bone. Museum collections around the country contain working guillotines, musical instruments, chess sets and a wide variety of items produced by men with little to do but pander to their ingenuity. Peterborough Museum contains a working bone palace; by turning a handle the guards march, workmen saw wood, and civilians walk up and down. Many gaming items were manufactured, perhaps to be sold and used amongst the prisoners themselves. Domino sets, dice and pieces for the game 'Jack Straws' may all be seen in museum collections.

Many other items were made from bone, wood and straw. Peterborough Museum houses a fascinating collection of models of French military equipment made by French officers on parole at Oswestry, Shropshire, between 1811 and 1814. These were originally the property of Henry Tozer, the Agent for this parole depot. The models are made primarily of wood and include ship's guns, field artillery, caissons, mortars, tools, shear-hoists, shells and powder barrels.

Straw Work

Both Norman Cross and Portchester Castle had, for a while, thriving straw plait industries amongst the prisoner population. At Norman Cross this was initially in the manufacture of straw hats and bonnets, but this was forbidden by the authorities from the earliest years of the prison's existence. The manufacture of straw plait was not banned until later.

Straw plait was a staple industry of many English communities during the Napoleonic Wars, especially in the counties of Bedfordshire and Hertfordshire. During the 18th century fine straw hats had been imported in large quantities from Italy, but the war impeded supplies from abroad, and so the home industry became more important. The manufacture by the prisoners competed with that of the civilian population. Prisoners of war were fed by the State, and were supplying the English market with untaxed merchandise, in competition with the very people who contributed to their maintenance.

As the war continued, the Government found more and more articles to tax to raise the necessary funds to continue the conflict. Among these articles were straw hats and bonnets. The prisoners arranged for accomplices from amongst the guards and the civilians attending the markets to smuggle the straw in, and the manufactured hats out. Tax was avoided. Sir Rupert George wrote that it was evident that the prisoners did smuggle in:

> ... the straw manufactured for the purpose of being made into hats, bonnets etc. by which the Revenue of our country is injured, and the poor who exist by that branch of trade would be turned out of employ.[13]

The straw plait industry was very labour intensive and so the number of prisoners involved in the trade must have been considerable. It is assumed that some of the straw for this work came from the prisoner's bedding, but most was supplied to the depots by local merchants. When this straw was used for marquetry it was acceptable to the authorities, but when used in the manufacture of plait the trade in such material was stopped. Wheat at that time grew to a height of about three feet, and after harvesting the stalk was cut into lengths of about 10 inches. It was then sorted into different grades according to thickness. It was then ready to be split into very fine plait; the finer the plait the better the quality of the finished hat or basket.

Tools for splitting straw were made and used by the prisoners, and some of these unique items, first used at Norman Cross, were adopted by the straw plait industry in Luton, Bedfordshire. The museum at Peterborough has in its collection some straw splitters made of bone with wooded handles, and others made of bronze. Other inventions were used. A nineteenth-century historian wrote about the straw plait trade:

> At Norman Cross they revolutionised the straw plaiting trade. Up to their time the straw was plaited whole and called 'Dunstable', but it was a case of necessity being the mother of invention. Their supply not being equal to the demand, one of them invented the 'splitter'. This consists of a small wheel, inserted in a mahogany frame, and finished in the centre with small sharp divisions like spokes. From the axle a small spike protrudes, on which a straw pipe is placed and pushed through, the cutters or spokes dividing it into as many strips as required. By this contrivance the plait could be made much finer, the strips could be used alternately with the outside and inside, or even the inside alone, which is white, and is known in the trade as 'rice straw'.[14]

After being split the straw would be bleached; dyed various colours; plaited in various styles, and flattened. This raw plait was sold by plait dealers to those who made hats and baskets, and these would be sold in the prison markets, albeit clandestinely.[15]

Soldiers and civilians involved in this trade ran a great risk. Soldiers caught aiding this illegal activity received the lash for their participation, unless they were officers. In 1807 a Lieutenant Mortimer of the Militia garrison at Norman Cross was discovered to be involved in the selling of straw plait from the prison. The ensuing military enquiry forced him to leave the Militia service, but not before he had paid all money owing to the prisoners.[16] Civilians were awarded prison sentences. Three such participators were tried at Huntingdon in 1811; one was sentenced to twelve and the others to six months imprisonment.[17] However, the straw plait trade was a profitable one for both prisoners and their accomplices, and was extensive. It was estimated that at one time 3000 inmates were involved in the business at Portchester.

As long as all straw work was strictly confined to various ornamental items, on which there was no tax, then it was allowed. The production of straw plait for hats was prohibited by an order of June 1798. This did not stop the illicit manufacture of such materials. The Board wrote to the Agent at Norman Cross in November 1808:

> If the manufacture of plait could be effectually prevented, it is not our wish to prohibit the prisoners from making baskets, boxes, or such like articles of straw. The prisoners might purchase wool and make frocks, for their own use; if any should be sold, a stop is to be put to the manufacture.[18]

Straw was used to produce a wide variety of legal marquetry work, such as pictures, fans, tea-caddies, silk holders and trinket boxes, with each piece of straw being separately coloured and attached. Plymouth Museum Service possesses a number of fine examples of trinket boxes, each containing numerous drawers and compartments, and some including charming water colours on or in the box. In Luton Museum there is a fine example of a writing desk made from wood and covered with straw marquetry, the desk being 18 x 15 x 6 inches in size. On the lid is a harbour scene with a sailing ship and classical ruins. Inside the lid is a picture of a church and a windmill. The bottom of the desk has been embellished with a parlor scene of a lady and gentleman, and there are six drawers in which writing implements may be stored.

Art

Many prisoners took up art as an occupation. The more famous of these artists was Louis Garneray, incarcerated first in the *Prothée* hulk in Portsmouth Harbour, before being allowed his parole at Bishop's Waltham. While on the *Prothée* he taught French to the daughter of the ship's commander. With his earnings he purchased paint, brushes and canvas, and developed a talent for painting, especially for seascapes. He also produced portraits of the guards, for a price of 6*d* to a shilling.

Indeed, Garneray turned his captivity into a career opportunity, selling his work in Portsmouth, becoming a successful artist in France after the war, and publishing books during the 1840s on his adventures and captivity during the Napoleonic Wars. While his book entitled *The French Prisoner* is strongly Anglophobic, and contains many rather fanciful stories of prisoner of war life with himself as the central character, it does give us a flavour of what life in the hulks and parole depots was like, and makes for an interesting read. In this book he tells us of his success as an artist in Portsmouth Harbour, whilst on the *Prothée*:

One day I was visited by a little round man, who came uninvited into my humble studio and began to look at my pictures in the most brazen manner, without a word to me! 'These seascapes', he said at last, 'are not bad at all for a Frenchman. If you are inclined to be reasonable, perhaps we can come to some sort of agreement. I am a dealer in Portsea.'

As I was very short of money at that time I thought I saw heaven opening before me and I hastened to assure him that in matters of business I was not at all a difficult sort of person.

'My boy,' said the dealer, for it is the habit of the English to treat us with a contemptuous familiarity. 'My boy, you are wrong to speak in such a way. If it had been your fortune to fall in with a Jew instead of an honest man like me this admission would have cost you dear. But it was a good star that brought Abraham Curtis to you.' He spoke the name in such a way that I supposed him to be a person of some reputation and I did not dare admit that I had never heard the name before.

After a short discussion it was agreed that he would take all my pictures, on condition that they were of a certain size and finish, at one pound or twenty-five francs apiece. I was overjoyed at his offer, which I had not in the least expected. I received six pounds that very day for the pictures he found in my studio and took away with him.[19]

Many other prisoners painted the scenes around them and sold their work to the local inhabitants. In many museums around the country may be seen artwork attributed to prisoners of war. In Southsea Castle there is a picture of the hulks in Portsmouth Harbour, and was painted by an unknown prisoner of war on board one of them.

The Guildhall Museum at Rochester possesses two pictures by Francois St. Jean. One is of the hulks in the Medway showing the surrounding dockyard and other vessels in the harbour. The inscription at the base of the painting states that it was painted on board 'His Majesty's Ship Canada, May 12 1811'. Francois St. Jean also produced a painting of these vessels entitled *A Night View of the Prison Ships Lying in Gillingham near Chatham* with a view of prisoners endeavouring to escape from the Sampson. This is an unusual work, in which we can see the sentries firing at the escaping prisoners.

Officers on parole occasionally decorated their lodgings with pictures painted directly onto the wall. In a hardware shop in Newtown, Wales, there is a painting of a warship on the wall of the basement, carefully preserved by the proprietor. This picture is approximately 6 feet by 4 feet and is titled *Neptune 74*, being attributed to French officers residing there in 1812.[20]

One parole prisoner even took up interior decorating as a hobby. Pierre Augeraud was a lieutenant in the French Army, being captured in 1812. He was sent on parole to Llanfyllin in Wales, where he resided in what is now the chemist's shop. He divided his time between gazing longingly out of the window at the Rector's daughter across the road, and decorating his rooms on the first floor with wall murals, depicting imaginary scenes, but some of the detail is reminiscent of the countryside in Spain, where he was captured.[21]

Theatres

While many of these artists produced pictures or decorated bone and wood trinket boxes with their handiwork, there was another artistic outlet for such people, certainly in Portchester Castle and at Dartmoor Prison. In each of these depots the prisoners constructed a theatre in which they gave performances of comedies, tragedies and other theatrical displays that entertained both themselves and members of the garrison.

At Dartmoor the prisoners used No.4 Prison Barracks for their theatre. Benjamin Palmer went to see a play performed by the blacks in the depot entitled *Heir at Law*, the ticket costing him 6*d*. He commented that the scenery was very good and so was the performance, although he complained about having to sit behind a seven-foot-tall negro. After the play there was a grand dance.[22]

When Portchester Castle was reopened as a prison in 1810, the French prisoners arriving in that year requested permission to construct a theatre in the basement of the keep. This request was readily granted, and the Agent Captain Paterson was instructed to provide wood for the use of the prisoners. A stage was built and seating for 300 people installed.

This theatre would appear to be the most organised and active of such playhouses, with artists producing colourful scenery, musicians finding work in the twelve-piece orchestra, and amateur playwrights penning numerous works. Aside from the home-written works, scripts were obtained from France via the Agent in London. The theatre saw productions of tragedies such as *Mahomet* and *Les Templiers*; comedies such as *Les Deux Gendres*, *Le Barbier de Séville* and *Les Folies Amoureuses*; and operas such as *Pierre le Grand* and *Les Deux Journées*. Musical scores were either purchased or composed by such men who had been musicians in the French Army. This theatre was a great success, and visitors to the castle may see the remains of this story if they look up when they enter the basement of the keep. On the beams above they will see faded gold scrollwork, part of the decoration for the theatre.[23]

Banknotes

In 1797, William Pitt's government issued a general circulation of banknotes. This paper money was an effort to limit the circulation and depletion of the country's gold reserves, and thus aid the finance of Britain's war effort. Paper money only works if there is enough gold available to back all of the notes in circulation, and the system can be undermined by the production of large numbers of forged notes.[24] The French Government realised this and produced large numbers of forged British banknotes that were circulated in the West Indies and the United States of America, with smugglers bringing them over from Calais to Dover. For example, in 1801 a total of £15,549 worth of forged notes was discovered in circulation in Britain, half of which was attributable to the low denominations of £1 and £2 notes, while the remainder was mostly £5 notes.[25] Forged banknotes became a great problem, and the public developed a great mistrust of this paper money. The Bank of England's inspectors were kept busy examining both real and forged notes, and after 1803, these gentlemen were often called upon to visit the hulks and land prisons to examine notes found in the possession of prisoners of war.

Forged banknotes varied in their appearance, depending on the type of paper available and the skill of the counterfeiter. There were two ways of forging banknotes; either by engraving copper plates and printing money, or by the use of pen and ink. Some of the best examples of hand-drawn notes were made by prisoners of war, who had plenty of time on their hands with which to develop their skills. Forgery by prisoners of war was first detected at Norman Cross in 1804, and thereafter became a serious problem, especially as far as the Bank of England was concerned. The Bank pursued forgers wherever they might be, and found helpful allies in Their Lordships at the Admiralty, and the Commissioners of the Transport Board.

Anyone convicted of forging banknotes went to the gallows, while passing or uttering forged notes resulted in a term of imprisonment or transportation to Botany Bay. However, there was a serious problem in gaining enough evidence to convict an individual for forgery. The person concerned had to be caught in the act of forging, or had to be discovered with pen, ink and paper about their person. To convict someone of uttering forged notes, it had to be proved that the individual knew the note was forged. This was not always easy, as the forgeries were often far away from the forger when discovered. Prisoners of war acquired genuine banknotes when they sold their wares in the prison markets, and certainly many genuine notes were in circulation within the prison depots. An example of the problem facing the Bank of England occurred in January 1812.

Jean Faragos, a French prisoner, was apprehended uttering a forged £5 note in Portsmouth. He had offered it to a shopkeeper who, suspecting it was forged, apprehended Faragos. Faragos stated that he had received the note from one Louis Paraca, who admitted the fact and on whom was found another forged £5 note. Now Paraca claimed he received the two notes from a French prisoner named Barrié, on board the *Hector* prison ship at Plymouth, when he, Paraca, was confined there. Barrié owed Paraca for some clothes and straw-work he did for him. Paraca gave one of the notes to Faragos to buy some handkerchiefs for him when Faragos was allowed ashore on some errands.

The Bank's solicitors advised that the evidence would not be enough to convict, but recommended that Mr Buckley the Constable be rewarded for his diligence in helping to detect this business, and to encourage others to look out for forgeries.[26]

This system of rewards was used to catch a number of forgers in the war prisons. While many prisoners of war made money by literally manufacturing it, others could make even more by informing on these forgers, as was the case at Norman Cross in 1805.

Two of the clerks at the depot, Todd and Delapoux, acted as liaison between the Agent Captain Pressland and two prisoner informers, Alexander Coulon and Francois Raige. These men were involved in the discovery of a plan to produce forged notes at Norman Cross. The two clerks were able to converse without suspicion with the two informers. The information was passed to Captain Pressland. He in turn passed the information to the Bank of England. This went on for about a month, and resulted in two French prisoners being convicted of forgery and hanged. The Bank paid a reward to all concerned. Pressland was offered 50 guineas; the two clerks each received 20 guineas; while Coulon was given £30 and Raige £25. These two prisoners were released by order of the Transport Board, partly as a further reward for their services, and partly for their own safety.

Pressland however, being a public-spirited naval officer, declined his reward as he was only carrying out his duty. The Bank however, insisted that he accept a piece of plate if he would not take the 50 guineas. Pressland asked for 'a goblet with which to quaff the health of the Governor, Directors and success to the Bank.'[27]

This system of rewards became a very effective way of discovering forgeries within the prisons, and the Admiralty worked very closely with the Bank of England on this matter. These rewards could cause problems however.

In April 1812 the Governor of the Bank wrote to Lieutenant Lyte, commanding the *Glory* prison ship, offering him a piece of plate '... as a mark of their approbation of the important services rendered by you to the public and the Bank by the detection of French prisoners engaged in the fabrication and circulation of forged banknotes'.

This affair had indeed been a major operation, with a number of the officers and crew of the *Glory* being involved in detecting the forgers. In addition to Lieutenant Lyte, Lieutenant Campbell of the Royal Marines received a reward of £50; Robert Weir, Master of the *Glory*, was given £50; William Hay, Master's Mate, £50; Sergeant Thomas Lowe, Royal Marines, £20; Marine Privates Robert Needham and David Mead each received £25; Marine Privates John Prothero and John Perry, £20 each; John Martin, Ship's carpenter, £10; Marine Sergeant Thomas Turner, £10; and Marine Private Alexander Mayers, £10. This was an extensive and generous distribution of reward money, but not as generous as some of the recipients expected.

In late April, Sergeant Thomas Turner wrote to the Bank complaining of the distribution of the reward money. He had only received £10, while both Privates Mead and Perry were given more, although they had been under his direction at the time.

At the same time William Gifford wrote to the Governor of the Bank of England with a complaint. He was the Gunner on board the *Glory* and had been involved in the detection of forged notes in the past, yet had received no reward. The Ship's carpenter, John Martin, also wrote complaining of the distribution of the reward money. The Bank was having none of this! They wrote to Lieutenant Lyte explaining that rewards were only paid to the crew and garrison in the event of a conviction, and were given at the judgment of the Governor and Directors of the Bank; Gifford's case was a separate event. Lyte was asked to convey this information to all concerned. The Bank wrote that 'we cannot undertake to carry on a correspondence with every petty officer who may fancy rewards of this nature should be distributed like prize money'.[28]

Forged banknotes were used as currency between prisoners and with civilians who traded in the prison markets, and there was a considerable amount of forged currency in use by the prisoners, if one Robert Dolliver is to be believed. When he was convicted of uttering forgeries, he informed the Bank that when some French prisoners were sent on a transport to Scotland in October 1811 they took with them a total of £1,500 in forged Bank of England notes.[29]

The prisoners had an unusual means of transferring money from one ship to another. One day in 1812 a marine sentry patrolling the walkway around a hulk at Chatham was hit by a potato, thrown from another ship. On inspection, he discovered that it had been hollowed out and inside was a forged £2 note. Whether hitting a marine sentry was an added bonus in this form of credit transfer cannot be ascertained, but this event was noted in the minutes of one of the Bank's meetings.[30]

Many forged banknotes were found in the possession of soldiers and marines guarding prisoners of war, and their wives, who often ran errands for the captives. While many guards were enthusiastic in their detection of forgeries, when they knew that a reward would come their way, there were some who found it difficult to resist the temptation to accept forged notes for services rendered to the prisoners. In November 1810 four privates of the Nottinghamshire Militia on sentry duty at Dartmoor Prison were bribed with gold and forged notes to let some French prisoners escape. Both the escapees and the soldiers were detected and confined.[31] John Brabazon, a soldier of the Roscommon Militia on duty at the same depot in 1812, tried to pay for food and drink in a tavern with two forged £1 notes. The proprietor, Mrs Deacon, was suspicious of these notes and conveyed her concern to the local Constable, who arrested Brabazon and ascertained that the notes had been acquired from some French prisoners.[32]

Between 1804 and 1815, twenty eight prisoners of war were convicted of forgery and hanged, and this total included three Americans. 1812 was a good year for convictions with seven prisoners going to the gallows.[33] Julien Dubois, a French prisoner at Portchester Castle, was tried at the Lent Assizes in Winchester on 4 March 1812 and 'convicted of forging a £2 banknote and for uttering the same knowing it to be forged.' He was executed on 28 March.

The Bank of England was always determined to prosecute offenders, whoever they might be. Private Franklin of the Royal Marines was part of the guard on board the *Glory* prison ship. He was convicted of having 'received a note from a French prisoner and uttered it, knowing it to be forged.' The forger was discovered to be one Auguste Duboille. Both Franklin and Duboille went to the gallows.[34] In April 1812 the Transport Office asked the Bank for details of the French prisoners who had been executed for forgery so that a notice could be prepared and posted in all the depots as a deterrent.[35]

Conviction of forgery carried the death penalty. Conviction of uttering forged notes carried a term of imprisonment. But here was a problem! These men were already in prison. To overcome this somewhat significant obstacle, the Bank arranged with the Admiralty that those convicted of uttering forgeries would be confined in cells in Edinburgh Castle or at Newgate, and all expenses relating to their confinement would be paid for by the Bank.[36] In 1812 transportation to Botany Bay became a punishment for uttering forgeries. But even this sentence was not the punishment the Bank of England hoped. In that year one Nicholas Longueville, incarcerated in Portchester Castle, was convicted of coining Bank Tokens. He was sentenced to transportation. However, the Agent at Portchester informed the Bank that this sentence was, as far as Longueville was concerned, liberty and reward instead of punishment. To transport him to Botany Bay would be to give one Frenchman a new life away from prison depots, conscription in the French Army and life on campaign. The most suitable punishment was therefore to closely confine him at Portchester Castle and prevent him offending again.[37]

Pornography

Forging banknotes may have caused a few headaches for the Their Lordships at the Admiralty, the Transport Board, and the Bank of England, but there was one manufacturing activity that upset those people attempting to improve the morals of the nation.

From its inception in 1797, at the depot of Norman Cross the 'depraved taste of some of the British purchasers' resulted in the production by the prisoners of obscene pictures and carvings. Even by 1808, Norman Cross had a dubious reputation for the indecent material coming out of the depot, although other prisons did manufacture such items. The national output seemed to reach a peak in that year, so much so that in Bristol, the local secretary of the Society for the Suppression of Vice wrote to the Admiralty to complain about the amount of vulgar snuffboxes, toys and drawings emanating from Stapleton Prison. As a result, the entire prison market was closed until the actual culprits were informed upon by their colleagues. The guilty individuals were transferred to the hulks at Portsmouth.[38]

This was the most effective way of combating the problem, by closing the markets and thus affecting all the prisoners until the manufacturers of such material were discovered. The transfer of the culprits to the hulks helped to reduce the problem, but there are continual references to obscene material being manufactured in many depots in the Board's Minutes up to the end of the war in 1814. Certainly there was a lucrative trade in such articles, with many civilians acting as agents on the outside of the depots.

Religion

No official provision was made for the religious welfare of prisoners of war. Those who died were buried without ceremony in or around the depot grounds. Parole prisoners who ended their days in Britain were allowed to be buried in a corner of the local churchyard, with the parish priest officiating at the ceremony. Otherwise the only religious education and comfort afforded prisoners of war was that they administered themselves, or what was given to them by volunteers.

The majority of French prisoners were of the Catholic faith, while the country in which they were captive was Protestant, with small followings of the gradually increasing Methodist and Baptist sects. In the early years of the French Revolution, some 8,000 Roman Catholic priests and nuns were driven from the continent to find refuge in Britain, where they were given sanctuary and allowed to practice their faith, even though Catholic Emancipation for the British population would not be granted until 1829.[39] These émigrés provided some volunteers for the religious well-being of prisoners of war.

During the late 1790s a few Roman Catholic priests were allowed to administer to the inmates at Norman Cross, but this would appear to have been an occasional circumstance, depending on how well behaved and conscientious these gentlemen were. In 1807 the Bishop of Moulins attended the depot, having been given permission and paid a salary by the Transport Office to tend to the spiritual needs of the prisoners, especially within the prison hospital. The Bishop had been deported from France in 1791, finding employment with the Bourbons abroad until 1799, when he made his way to England. He would appear to have been respected by the authorities and prisoners alike, the only blemish on his career being when he was allowed a servant from amongst the prisoners in the depot. He acquired one Jean Baptiste David, a sixteen year old seaman, who was allowed to reside on parole with the Bishop at Stilton, near to the depot. David however, abused the trust placed in him by becoming involved in the illegal straw plait trade. This involvement was denied by the Bishop but the Board was adamant that they had evidence linking David with the activity. After petitioning people of influence in the vicinity, the Bishop was allowed to keep his servant but only on the condition he kept a strict eye on him in future. Aside from an inability to manage his own affairs (he was continually in debt), the Bishop of Moulins worked hard amongst the prisoners until 1814. He was described as:

> ... a noble Chaplain ... He walked up every day to Norman Cross, and acted very charitably to the prisoners, doing his utmost to stop their frequent duels.[40]

During the 18th century the preaching of John Wesley was gaining support amongst many. These Methodists eagerly took their religion to whoever would listen, and they found a ready congregation within the confines of the prison depots. While their brand of Christianity was not always condoned by the officers in command at the prisons, the Board was quick to realise that Methodist preaching also included the education of the flock; an activity that kept some of the prisoners away from any thoughts of mischief.

In 1810 Captain Simmons of the *Glory* prison ship invited William Toase, a Methodist Minister, to preach to the Frenchmen on board his ship. Initially Toase went to talk to the prisoners to find out how receptive they would be to his preaching, and at the same time he distributed some religious books. The following day he held a service on deck in which he sang a French hymn and gave prayer to a large congregation who expressed their gratitude for this act of Christian charity. Encouraged by this response, Toase preached on board at least once a week, distributing many copies of the New Testament and other religious tracts. Indeed, Toase was proud of his conversion of many on board to Methodism. He observed three distinct classes among the prisoners. The first consisted of a considerable number who were as careless as they were ignorant of true religion; the second were many more who were superstitiously attached to the rites of the Roman Catholic Church; while the third group was not an inconsiderable number who heard the unmixed truths of Christianity with deep feeling. Toase encountered the forging activities of the prisoners on board the *Glory* during the summer of 1811. On his arrival on the vessel he discovered that all the prisoners had been confined below;

> ...on account of a forgery that had been committed on the Bank of England, by one or more of them. The Commander was determined to keep them all under deck, until they delivered up the criminal, or criminals. When this was done, I was thankful to find that not one of those who had favoured our mission was found among the guilty persons.

Encouraged by this success in keeping his flock on the right path in life, he applied to Lord Liverpool for permission to visit the other ships in the Medway. This permission was granted via the Transport Office in October 1811, and it was then that Toase dramatically expanded his parish. He visited all the ships at that depot, and was allowed to visit other depots at Portsmouth, Plymouth, Dartmoor and Stapleton. The authorities realised that, aside from his religious teaching, he was keeping many prisoners gainfully employed. On board the hulks, small circulating libraries were formed in which were available books in the form of Bibles, Testaments and religious pamphlets, in French, German, Italian, Dutch and Spanish. These libraries were supervised by French officers, who also helped to run the schools set up to teach many of the prisoners to read and write.

To cope with the increased workload, Toase employed additional preachers. Monsieur Armand de Kerpezdron, a French émigré from Jersey, preached at Chatham until 1814. American and Danish prisoners were the responsibility of the Reverend Walter Griffith who also distributed religious tracts on board the cartel vessels sailing for France. Indeed, so respected were these men that the prisoners on the *Glory* included in their own laws an article that 'the Methodist Ministers be respected and encouraged'.

In late 1811 William Toase set off for Portsmouth in the company of another preacher, the Reverend William Beal, to introduce themselves to the inmates of Portchester Castle and Forton.

Their congregation at the latter was very attentive, and pleased with this reception they preached to the prisoners in the castle yard at Portchester. Toase recalled:

> A prisoner lent me a table on which I stood. The materials of the table being feeble, and much worse for wear, the poor man crept under it, and supported it with his back until I had done preaching.

Toase did note however, that when the dinner bell rang most of his congregation left him!

The conclusion of hostilities in 1814 resulted in the rapid release of all the prisoners of war in Britain. Toase attended the cartels sailing across the Channel and gave as many prisoners as possible a Bible, Testament or religious tract. William Toase and his colleagues earned the admiration and respect of many hundreds of prisoners of war. Many captives found comfort in religion through the services conducted by the Methodist ministers, and undoubtedly many of them received the rudiments of an education in learning to read the Scriptures. It is perhaps comforting to think that some captives died at peace with the support of such men as William Toase.[41]

Freemasons

Freemasonry was popular in the French military during the period 1797–1814, so it is not surprising to learn that many French prisoners of war were Freemasons, and that members of the English Craft helped to alleviate the distress of their French Brethren in the parole depots by subscribing sums of money for their relief. While many French Freemasons on parole were received as visitors at Masonic meetings in Britain, a number of them formed their own Lodges. This had also been the case during the earlier wars of the 18th Century, when officers on parole formed their own Masonic Lodges in Basingstoke, Petersfield, Leeds and York. During the period 1756–1814 a total of 26 Lodges and Chapters of Freemasons were established and conducted in Britain.[42]

As many Britons were Freemasons, there was a spirit of tolerance and mutual co-operation between the two nationalities if
they found that there was a Masonic bond between them. The
authorities had no objection to the French setting up Lodges
provided they were not a venue for violating their parole obligations. In 1810 there was a Lodge at Tiverton – the *Enfants de Mars*
- meeting in a room in Castle Street until two officers escaped
and the Board prohibited the meetings.[43]

In that year the British Lodge at Kelso received visits from
several French officers on parole in the town:

> The Right Worshipful in addressing them, expressed the wishes
> of himself and the Brethren to do anything in their power to
> promote the comfort and happiness of the exiles. After which
> he proposed the health of the Brethren who were strangers in a
> foreign land, which was drunk with enthusiastic applause.

This particular Lodge was host to these Frenchmen on a number
of occasions when the 'harmony was greatly increased by the
polite manners and the vocal power of our French Brethren'.[44]
In January 1813 the Lauder Lodge admitted eight Germans and
one Frenchmen who 'on the occasion of their induction, when
the time for refreshments after business came, the foreign members delighted the company with yarns of their military experiences'.[45]

Some of the French Lodges, such as the one at Wincanton,
admitted English members, and certainly had numerous visits
from their local counterparts. While these activities were allowed
by the Transport Board, the Agents were instructed to keep them
under observation to detect any subversive and troublesome
activities.

Notes

1 TNA:PRO ADM99/96. Minutes of the Transport Board September
1796.
2 Waterhouse, p.99.

3 Abell, p.166–185.
4 British Museum B.P.8/9. Correspondance with the French Government relative to prisoners of war 1801.
5 Kennedy, Ludovic. *Nelson and His Captains* (London 1975), p.103.
6 Gleig, G.R. *The Light Dragoon* (London, 1850), p.20.
7 TNA:PRO ADM105/44. 26 July 1808.
8 Freeston, Ewart C. *Prisoner of War Ship Models 1775–1825* (London 1987), p.43.
9 Bennett, Joan; Parrack, Colin; Poole, Ray; Walton, Cathryn. *French Connections: Napoleonic Prisoners of War on Parole in Leek 1803–1814* (Churnet Valley Books, Leek, 1995), p.101.
10 Freeston, p.40–54.
11 ibid., p.32–39.
12 Tatlow, Jonathan. *Restoring Prisoner of War Models*, Model Shipwright No.24, June 1978, p.19–24.
13 TNA:PRO ADM105/44. 26 July 1808.
14 Walker, p.138–139.
15 *The Straw Plait Pack*, Luton Museum Service, Luton, Bedfordshire.
16 E535, Order Day Book for Garrison at Norman Cross, June 1807. Peterborough City Museum.
17 Walker, p.140–141.
18 TNA:PRO ADM98/235. Transport Board to Agent Norman Cross 11 November 1808.
19 Garneray, p.54–55.
20 The venue in question is the Muradec DIY shop, on the corner of Brolic Street and Park Street, Newtown, Wales. The picture was uncovered when the wall was decorated, and is now carefully preserved by the proprietor.
21 Murray Ll. Chapman, *Napoleonic Prisoners of War in Llanfyllin*, p.70–85. The building in which the murals adorn the first floor walls is known as the Council House.
22 Palmer, p.108.
23 Abell, p.184–185.
24 For a detailed account of the history of British banknotes and the problem of forgeries see Byatt, Derrick, *Promises To Pay: The first three hundred years of Bank of England notes* (London, 1994).
25 ibid. p.43.
26 BoE AB87/1. Letter No.44, 24 January 1812.

27 BoE AB86/2. Letters No.8–12, October 1805.
28 BoE AB87/1. Letters No.172, 176, 177, 179 and 184, April 1812.
29 ibid. Letter No.183, 28 April 1812.
30 ibid. Letters No. 228 and 234, November 1812.
31 BoE AB86/2. Letter No.87, 24 November 1810.
32 BoE AB87/1. Letter No.196, 9 June 1812.
33 BoE *The Forging of Banknotes by French Prisoners of War*, unpublished manuscript 1963.
34 BoE AB87/1. Letter No.168, April 1812.
35 ibid. Letter No.170, 14 April 1812.
36 ibid. Letter No.236, 19 December 1812.
37 ibid. Letter Nos.199 and 200, 15 and 24 June 1812.
38 Vinter, p.162–163.
39 Cook, Chris and Stevenson, John. *British Historical Facts 1760–1830*, (London 1980), p.162–171.
40 Walker, p.180–187 and 310–311.
41 Toase, William. *The Wesleyan Mission in France with an account of the labours of Wesleyan Ministers among the French Prisoners during the late war*, (London 1835), p.24–44.
42 Thorpe, John T. *French Prisoner's Lodges*, (Leicester 1900), p.16–17.
43 Abell, p.300.
44 ibid., p.322.
45 ibid., p.355.

CHAPTER 7

An Intrepid Class of Men

George Brothers was a Portsmouth wherryman who, on the morning of 22 September 1813, bade farewell to his family in Surrey Street Portsmouth, to ply his trade across Portsmouth Harbour. Saying goodbye to his wife, he was not to know that he would never see her again, for that day was to be his last. That day would also mean the end for three French prisoners of war.

At about noon on the same day, Francois Retif, Charles Daure and Jean Sere disguised themselves as civilians and stole out of Forton Prison, making for Gosport beach. Here they bargained with Brothers to take them across the Solent to Ryde. He agreed, but just out of the harbour the Frenchmen offered him £20 to sail to France. Brothers refused, there was a scuffle, and he was stabbed to death and thrown overboard.

Retif and his companions then sailed off as fast as the wind would allow. However, this deed had been perpetrated in broad daylight not one hundred yards from other wherrys who immediately gave chase. The crew of the jolly-boat from HMS *Centaur* joined the pursuit, which continued for over two hours until the Frenchmen were overtaken and captured. The crime was the talk of Portsmouth for many days.[1]

The story of escape attempts range from the ingenious to the desperate, from the tragic to the farcical. The tale of George Brothers was one of the more extreme escape stories. Escape attempts took many forms, but before relating these in detail it is perhaps pertinent to examine the reasons for escaping, which were not always as obvious as one might suppose.

During the 1790s most prisoners of war could expect to be exchanged within a year or two of capture, as regular exchange cartels were arranged between Britain and her enemies. Often the more senior officers could expect to be exchanged quite rapidly (i.e. within a year of capture) while the lower ranks had to wait a while longer. After 1803 the war dragged on for year after year with increasing mistrust between Britain and France over the question of exchange of prisoners, although Danes and Spaniards could expect frequent exchange cartels to set them at liberty. From 1803 to 1814, of the 122,440 prisoners who arrived in Britain, only 17,607 (14%) were exchanged, sent home sick or on parole, while 10,341 (8.5%) died in captivity, and the remainder had to wait until the war ended before seeing their homes again.[2]

It is not surprising that many attempted to escape captivity, successfully or otherwise. However, it would be wrong to assume that they all escaped for the same reason. Many undoubtedly decided to 'Run' (the official manner of registering an escape) to return home to the life they knew. Others escaped not from confinement but from their fellow prisoners. In October 1810 Jean Richard escaped from Tiverton Parole Depot where he was servant to Noel Busnel. He surrendered to the guard at Mill Prison. The Agent at Tiverton reported to the Board that 'he ran in consequence of his Master attempting to commit an unnatural crime on him'.[3]

In the years 1813 and 1814, when it was obvious that Napoleon's star was finally waning, many French officers on parole declared themselves for the Bourbons. This brought them into conflict with the staunch Bonapartists amongst their number, and some simply ran to escape this conflict, giving themselves up at a prison elsewhere in the country. Officers on parole had another reason for escaping. If they were career soldiers, spending the war in captivity meant that chances of promotion would not be available to them. Regaining their freedom would allow them to return to active service and their military career path.

A final reason for escaping was simply for something to do. A group of men confined in a hulk, with no imagination or ability to produce handicrafts or gain an education, would find planning and executing an escape an exercise to occupy their time and their minds. Planning an escape kept a man sane and hopeful, especially

if he was young, fit and resilient. Many were persistent if unsuc-
cessful escapees, and not a few suceeded, rejoined the French
forces, and were captured again. Freedom for a French soldier or
seaman was a subjective concept, as most of them had been conscripted into the French forces and thus would have experienced
far greater hardships whilst on campaign compared to the captivity experienced in Britain. Who is the better off? A French soldier
on the terrible retreat from Moscow during the winter of 1812–13
or a French soldier in a prison ship moored in the Medway?

To be successful, an escaping prisoner had first to get out of
the prison, then to travel through a sometimes hostile countryside until he arrived at the coast where he might find a boat to
cross the Channel.

In the Land Prisons, tunnelling was attempted on a number
of occasions. In August 1812 a small group of Frenchmen in
Portchester Castle excavated a tunnel from near the hospital
to the outside of the prison, a distance of about 80 yards. Three
prisoners escaped before the sentries discovered the tunnel.
There are no further records of mining at the depot after this
date, but it remained a fairly common method in other prisons,
especially Dartmoor and Perth. In 1811 four prisoners in the
former establishment tunnelled their way to freedom, reputedly
taking nearly a year to complete their task.[4]

Evidence still exists of a Spanish attempt at tunnelling from
Portchester Castle. Just inside the entrance to Assheton's Tower,
at the north-east point of the medieval castle, there is a partially
excavated hole in the outer wall that extends for about four feet.
This unfinished task took place in 1798 when this part of the
castle was used to house Spaniards.

A somewhat faster approach was to go over the prison walls,
usually at night. The records for Portchester note a number of
such attempts in 1811. In July seven Frenchmen got over the
wall, but on observing a sentinel pointing his musket at them
from the rampart they climbed back over again! September saw
six prisoners acquire a rope with which they slipped over the
wall, although four were recaptured the next day.[5]

The Land Prisons had one advantage over the hulks for
would-be escapees. If they were ingenious enough they could

simply walk out of the prison. Five Frenchmen managed to elude the guards at Norman Cross and walk out of the depot, reaching the outskirts of Portsmouth before being recaptured. One dark and stormy night in 1809 the guard at Norman Cross was changed with no one noticing the extra soldier marching with them. He was a French prisoner who had made a military greatcoat, cross belts and shako from scraps of cloth and leather, and carved himself a musket from a length of wood, complete with tin bayonet. He waited for the weather to aid his escape and simply marched out of the prison. Alas, his attention to detail was not what it should have been, for on entering the soldier's barracks it was noticed that his musket was a few inches longer than those of the guard for it would not fit into the musket rack. He was promptly marched back into the prison.[6]

This method of escape was relatively common. Two Frenchmen observed that fifty soldiers marched into Dartmoor prison with the turnkeys each evening. These enterprising prisoners made uniforms of greatcoats and fatigue caps out of odds and ends of cloth and blanket, and carved muskets from lengths of wood, with strips of tin shaped as bayonets. One dark night they calmly fell in at the rear of the guard as they left prison, leaving the troops as the latter marched into their barracks. Their defection was not noticed for a couple of days as their colleagues caused a disturbance next morning at roll-call to cover their absence. Encouraged by this success, three other prisoners tried the same trick a few nights later, successfully absconding.[7]

Some were blatant enough to decamp in this manner in broad daylight. One Sunday morning a sentry on duty at the Water Gate at Portchester Castle saw three Royal Navy officers walking towards him from the church. Thinking that they were part of the congregation he saluted and allowed them through. Later that day it was discovered that three French privateer officers had escaped dressed in uniforms obtained in the prison market.[8]

A simpler means of walking out was to bribe the guards. The first two prisoners to escape from Dartmoor in July 1809 did so by bribing four sentries. The Frenchmen were recaptured and admitted who had helped them, each soldier having received eight guineas from the prisoners. Two of the soldiers (from the

Nottinghamshire militia) were sentenced to be shot. Four privates from this regiment were involved in another escape from Dartmoor in February 1811. They were heavily bribed by two French officers. One soldier, thinking that he was unfairly treated in the division of the money, gave information to his officers and the guards were waiting for the escaping Frenchmen. The three guilty soldiers were more fortunate than their colleagues two years previously. They were sentenced to receive 900 lashes each; two were pardoned, but the one who had given the prisoners firearms received 450 lashes. Soldiers who were bribed with forged banknotes also ran the risk of being tried and convicted of uttering the same.[9]

Civilians allowed into the markets were also implicated in escapes, even though security was increased during market hours. Edward Palmer, a 'moorman', was fined £5 and imprisoned for twelve months for procuring a disguise for a French prisoner named Bellaird at Dartmoor in 1812. Labourers admitted to prisons to work were also involved in escapes. Pierre Petit, a privateer seaman, was 'supposed to have escaped in the evening with the workmen coming out of the prison' at Esk Mills in March 1811.[10]

Escapees on board the hulks had the additional problem of crossing an expanse of water after leaving the ship. Escape from the vessel was either by going over the side or through it. The General Entry Books for the prison ships contain many references to prisoners 'cutting out' of the ship, despite the security both inside and outside the hulk. Thomas Rabert was '...a very bad character and detected cutting through the ship's side' on the *Vengeance* in 1812[11], while Izidor Bercouger was 'concerned with four other prisoners in cutting in the larboard quarter of the orlop deck and effecting their escape at 11.00pm 2 August 1812' from the *Crown*. Their efforts were wasted as they were retaken at 11.30pm.[12]

No matter how quietly the prisoners attempted to saw through the ship's side the guards often discovered inmates in this act of illicit carpentry. Some Frenchmen on the *Vigilante* sawed a hole in the side of the ship. They were too noisy however, for they were joined in the contemplation of their task by the sentries!

Nothing was wasted for the wood obtained from these escape portals was often used by other prisoners for the manufacture of trinket boxes.

Invariably there were always some small boats alongside the hulks, as contractors brought provisions to the vessels; the ship's crew rowed back and forth to the shore on official duties; civilian officials and sight-seers visited the vessel; prisoners were taken ashore or brought to the ship. The water around the hulks was a very busy place. There were prisoners who tried slipping over the side of the vessel when no one was looking, making use of any boats moored against the ship. During the afternoon of 4 August 1811 two Frenchmen escaped in the gunners boat of the *Crown*, while one evening in January 1812 five French prisoners escaped in the jolly boat. Such prisoners took advantage of any opportunity to use a boat moored alongside, these escapes taking place both under cover of darkness and in broad daylight.[13] If such escapees had procured civilian clothes and could pass themselves off as Englishmen, they might be able to hire a local boatman – such as was the case with George Brothers – who could be persuaded to take them around the coast away from the hue and cry they had generated at their place of confinement. The less scrupulous of the local boatmen might even take the escaped prisoners all the way across the Channel, but for a price.

Reaching the open sea was no guarantee of success, as the Channel was constantly patrolled by Royal Navy vessels, Revenue cutters and British Privateers, who frequently recaptured escaped prisoners of war, often when they were within sight of France. This would have been a bitter blow to men such as Joseph Boutellier, who absconded from Plymouth on the night of 30 June 1811, and within a few days managed to steal a boat in which he set sail for France. He was recaptured on 7 July by a Revenue Cutter; the official records states that 'he was taken up at sea in a boat', only to be returned to the hulks at Plymouth.[14]

The more desperate escapees tried swimming, many drowning while struggling against unfamiliar tides or being shot in the process. The aptly named *Vengeance* had a large number of the more troublesome prisoners incarcerated on board, and the 'Accounts of Prisoners who died at Portsmouth' make frequent mention of captives from this vessel who drowned while making a bid for freedom, such as Pierre Talray who drowned on Christmas Eve 1812.[15] The records of such escape attempts give the impression that while many were planned, many others were performed on the spur of the moment. Some of the more troublesome characters onboard the hulks used escape attempts simply as a means of annoying their captors.

Once out of the hulk the prisoners made for land. In 1808 seven Frenchmen escaped from the *Assistance* and swam for the shore, arriving on the mud flats in an exhausted state, to be greeted by the local militia. Two other prisoners from the same ship tried this method, one being recaptured as he waded ashore while the other drowned. May 1810 saw twenty French prisoners successfully cut their way out of the *Vigilant* and make for land. Ten were retaken after a sharp fight when they attempted to seize a small boat. The others were recaptured a few days later.[16]

Parole prisoners escaped by walking out of the depot wearing civilian clothes. If they timed it well they would not be missed until the roll call the following day, as happened with Greve Lambert, a Dane on parole at Peebles in 1810. The Agent reported that Lambert 'did not appear at this days muster, and on enquiring understood he had gone a fishing yesterday and has not since been heard of'. Detailed descriptions of these escapees were published in local newspapers, including descriptions of their physique, clothing and ability (or lack of) to speak English.

Three officers absconded from Alresford and the Agent reported that Francois de la Nougarede, a major in the army of Naples 'has a green coat, brown pantaloons and top boots. He speaks a little English'. Pierre Pabau, a French infantry captain captured on Guadeloupe 'speaks very good English and is supposed to be dressed in a dark green coat, pantaloons and half boots and appears very much like an Englishman'. Angelo Santo Cauro, a captain in the Royal Corsican Infantry 'cannot speak any English and is supposed to be dressed in a black coat, pantaloons, white waistcoat and half boots'.[17]

The records for all the parole depots detail some escapes, with often a group of prisoners absconding together. Wincanton and Chesterfield stand out as places from which a large number of

Number of all French Commissioned Officers, Prisoners of War, on Parole in Great Britain

Year Ending:	5 June 1810	5 June 1811	5 June 1812	Total
Total number parole prisoners*	1,685	2,087	2,142	5,914
Number that broke parole	104	118	242	464
Been retaken	47	47	63	157
Escaped	57	71	179	307

*This figure relates only to commissioned officers on parole.

prisoners escaped. In June 1812 the Board published some statistics relating to prisoner escapes in response to questions that had been asked in Parliament about the large number of French officers effecting their escape from the depots, and the general increase in violation of parole agreements.

Besides the above figures, other prisoners of rank were entitled their parole such as officers of privateers and merchantmen. Of these, 218 broke their parole and attempted escape, 85 were retaken and 133 successfully absconded. This brings the total number of parole prisoners who successfully escaped during this period to 440. The report also notes that a considerable number of officers were ordered into confinement for various other breaches of their Parole Engagements[18]. The increase in the number of escapes and parole violations by 1812 was due to the lack of any opportunity for exchange between Britain and France by that date. Also by early 1812 it was apparent that a major campaign was to be fought against Russia. This fact was known to the French in captivity, and no doubt many of them viewed such an event as a glorious career opportunity, one that would be wasted if they remained in Britain.

The escape of a prisoner could be facilitated with the help of local civilians. While most inhabitants of the country were patriotic and would willingly assist the authorities in recapturing escapees, there were some who would assist prisoners for financial reward. The prisoners did have money, either remittances from home or what they earned whilst in captivity. General Philippon, Governor of Badajoz, is reputed to have paid £5,000 to some Englishmen to help him escape from Oswestry in July 1812. The records simply state 'He got to France'.

Francois Belliard escaped from Wincanton but was recaptured two days later along with the three Englishmen who aided his flight. Some Frenchmen, if retaken, even resorted to informing on the civilians who helped them, if it would ultimately assist them in returning home. J. Aubertin escaped from Andover in October 1812. The report of his escape reads:

> He and seven others escaped together. They were retaken at Lymington ... one of the prisoners (named Vantilbourgh) gave evidence against the Englishman who assisted them to escape and was allowed to go home to the Continent.[19]

The authorities offered rewards of up to 5 guineas for the recapture of escaped prisoners, with a reward of 20 guineas (in 1812) on the conviction of any British subject aiding an escape. In 1814, when the French prisoners of war had been sent home to leave only Americans in confinement, the Board felt sufficiently generous to increase the reward for the recapture of escapees to 20 guineas.

In 1807 Commissioner Searle visited the Devon Parole Depots, and aside from a general inspection of prisoner affairs here, he was enlisting the aid of the magistrates in preventing escapes. He reported:

> With respect to the escapes which have been made from the several depots, I have been given to understand that they have been chiefly effected by means of vagabond Musicians, Jews, and pretended Italian Hawkers of pictures, little images and toys. I have desired the Agents to apply to the magistrates constantly not to permit such persons to remain in the towns.[20]

If escaped prisoners could not find civilians willing to help them, then it was usually only a matter of time before they were recaptured. Four French officers who broke their parole and escaped were retaken at Ryde, where they were loitering until it was dark enough to seize a boat. Seven Frenchmen left Wantage and marched for eight days through the country to Sleaford, where they would have stolen a boat but for the vigilance of the New Shoreham Volunteers. A detachment of the 35th Foot came across eight absconding French officers at Selsey on the south coast who, through force of arms, were persuaded to march back into captivity.[21]

Americans who escaped could blend into the civilian population very easily because of their common language. Single French, German or Italian escapees might get away with it as there were many foreigners in Britain at that time; French Emigrés, foreign troops in British service, and merchants from countries not at war with Britain. A group of foreign-sounding gentlemen was bound to arouse suspicion, especially if the authorities had alerted the population to a recent escape.

While individual civilians and prison guards were sometimes willing to assist an escape, some made a living out of it. Smugglers bringing French brandy from across the Channel were just as willing to take Frenchmen the other way – for a price. Occasionally an escaped prisoner would be able to bribe a south coast boatman to take him across the Channel, such as the French officer who found a Gosport waterman to sail him to France for 100 guineas. The organised trade in escaped prisoners became so lucrative that some smugglers set up well-organised escape lines.

A number of such lines were set up by smugglers in Kent, due to the proximity of this area to the continent. These smugglers traveled throughout the country to acquire Frenchmen for the journey to France. In 1811 a Folkestone smuggler by the name of Stevens was driving a cart near Thame in Oxfordshire, in which was discovered two French officers.[22] There is evidence that such escapes were arranged not only by the prisoners themselves, but also by friends and relatives on the Continent who contacted the smugglers on their side of the Channel. Many of the escape lines culminated at Whistable in Kent.

The escaped prisoners either made their own way to London and then to Whitstable or, if the individual concerned had sufficient money or importance, he would be collected by chaise from the general area of his confinement. The chaise would travel by day, off-loading its occupants on the outskirts of a town at dusk and collecting them in the morning. In London the escaped prisoner would be placed on board one of the Whitstable fleet of Hoys that regularly traded in the city. In addition to the Hoys, there were many private fishing boats from the Kent coast that visited Billingsgate.

The prisoners were transported to a landing site two miles west of Whitstable Harbour, in an area much used by fishermen, wild fowlers and those with other legitimate activities. Their arrival ashore would thus appear to be part of the usual activity of the area. The vessel would then proceed to Whitstable and survive any examination by the Customs authorities.

The area at the time consisted of reed grown dykes in which a prisoner could hide until it was safe to move on. The next stage of the journey was to Pye Alley Farm, owned by one Thomas Goodwin, actively involved in the escape trade. He would collect the prisoners and lead them to the farm, they walking a safe distance behind his horse, ready to dive for cover at an alarm. At the farm they would receive food and fresh clothing. The escapees were hidden in a local wood, being supplied with food by a number of farmers in the area. They stayed here until darkness, tide and safety made it possible to board a smuggling ship and be carried across to France.

Helping prisoners of war to escape was a lucrative business. One James Moore purchased a fishing smack in 1809 for the express purpose of transporting escapees from London to Whitstable. By the following year he had earned enough to buy a second boat with which to sail his charges across the Channel. He used the name Captain Thomas Harman for security when helping prisoners, and was also known by a number of aliases. He had friends in high places, for although the authorities came to know of his activities, they could not catch him in the act of assisting prisoners to escape.

He was eventually caught assisting General Pilet and Commander Paolucci to escape from Alresford in March 1810. The house in Hastings in which they were being hidden was known to the authorities, and Moore and his charges were taken into custody. Moore was tried and sentenced to serve in the Royal Navy. He deserted very quickly and took up his old calling in Whitstable under the name of Thomas Feaste Moore. The authorities suspected that here was the same Thomas Harman they had caught some time before, but lacked any tangible proof.

He was eventually caught in December 1811 off the Goodwin Sands with a cargo of silks and spirits from Dunkirk. He was found to have a complete account of all the prison and parole depots in England, with the ranks of all the principal prisoners. He even had letters of recommendation from many of the officers whose successful escapes he had negotiated! Now under the name of James Feaste he was sent to the convict hulks at Woolwich, later being sent to the hulks at Gibraltar, his career as an escape agent over.[23]

By 1812 the involvement of civilians in the escape trade was becoming so prevalent that Parliament passed 'An Act for the more effectual punishment of persons aiding prisoners of war to escape from His Majesty's Dominions, 29 July 1812'. Anyone convicted of assisting an escape, either directly or indirectly, was liable to transportation for life, or for periods of fourteen or seven years as judged by the Courts. Often civilians sentenced in this way had their imprisonment terminated at the end of the war.[24]

Finding a boat that the prisoners could sail themselves was often relatively easy. The *Crown* lost ten prisoners one night in January 1812, for they slipped over the ship's side, seized a boat moored nearby and sailed across the Channel to freedom. In some cases the boats capsized at sea and the bodies of the prisoners washed ashore along the south coast. Others were retaken by British ships when within sight of France, while a few were never heard of again.

There were other means of escape tried by prisoners of war. The *Hampshire Telegraph* reported a desperate attempt by some prisoners being transported from Portsmouth in 1811:

The French prisoners which the *Gorgon* sailed with from hence to Leith, formed a conspiracy to take possession of the ship, which, had it not been frustrated would, from the superior numbers of the French prisoners to the crew of the *Gorgon*, have caused much bloodshed. The principle abettor of the project was Henry Polite de Cruize, Ensign de Vaisseau in the Italian Navy, who was aided by sixty other officers, chiefly Captains of Privateers - a daring intrepid class of men. The design was to have been put in execution when the fifty prisoners which were allowed to take the air at one time, should be on deck: they were to rush on such officers who might be on deck who, with the sentinels, were to be thrown overboard or murdered. One of them was to go below and cause the sentinel to open the prison door, for him to go in, when the sentinel was to be dragged in. The prisoners were then to rush upon deck from the prison entrance, burst through the hatchways, and seize such arms, handspikes and iron bars as they could lay hold of. The destruction of every officer was determined upon along with all the marines. They were to run the ship on the Flemish or Dutch coast. The *Gorgon* had 300 prisoners on board, one hundred and fifty of whom had heartily engaged in the conspiracy. About eleven o'clock at night the prisoners were heard by the sentinels at work about the bulkhead, and on the strictest search being made, it appeared they had been cutting squares around the spikenails, and had one plank ready to be moved, with the least exertion, at the fore-hatchway. Had this discovery not been made, they would have attempted their well-arranged plan. These particulars were afterwards confessed by two of the prisoners.[25]

When the Spanish rose against the French in 1808, there was at the time a large number of Spaniards held in the hulks and prisons of Portsmouth. These prisoners, now allies of Britain, were ordered to be released. The *San Damaso* and *San Antonio* yielded 1,188 in number who were to be removed in six transports to Spain. Many Frenchmen tried to smuggle themselves into the groups of Spaniards, but were exposed by the latter, who had no great love of the French. At the same time the guards at Forton had to separate the two nationalities. A large body of French prisoners fell upon some Spaniards who would not acknowledge them as their countrymen, for the purpose of boarding the transports to Spain.[26]

Forton appeared to have a turbulent history for escape attempts. In July 1793 a report recorded a series of incidences at the prison:

> ...the guard discovered a plot by which several prisoners had planned an escape over the wall by tying together their hammocks and blankets. The sentry on duty fired in at the windows and hit one of the rioters who is since dead.
> ...three French prisoners were dangerously wounded while endeavouring to escape from Forton. One of them with a drawn knife rushed upon the guard, a private of the Anglesea Militia, who fired at him. The Frenchman seized him by the coat, whereupon the guard ran the offender through the body.[27]

When a prisoner was recaptured he was immediately sent under secure guard to the nearest prison ship depot and placed in the Black Hole, or cachot, on half rations, until he had monetarily made up the cost of his recapture. The report on Aubertin and his friends continued:

> ...the expenses for recapture were £113 7s 10d ... Captain Woodriffe was directed to put them on short allowance to make good £102 17s 10d...being £10 10s less than the above expenses, being the reward paid [to] Vantilbourgh which they ought not to be required to make good.[28]

Vantilbourgh took advantage of an opportunity to inform on the Englishman who had assisted him to escape, thus securing his own freedom and a reward into the bargain! The Transport Board was generous enough not to require his erstwhile companions to repay the money given as the reward, while they languished in the hulks at Portsmouth. The expenses incurred in the recapture of escapees were not going to be paid by the Transport Board, who had to justify their expenditure to a Parliament that was quick to question any increase in moneys spent on prisoners of war, or indeed, on any aspect of the prosecution of the conflict. General Simon, captured at the Battle of Busaco in 1810, escaped from Odiham on 13 January 1812 only to be recaptured at Camdentown (London) four days later. He was sent to Dumbarton Castle (not a regular parole depot but a place of security and relative comfort for a high-ranking officer) '...under the care of Vickery and Lavender (Police Officers) who took the entire mail coach for the purpose'. The total cost of his recapture and transportation north came to £198 11s 9d, which was deducted from the allowance paid to him as an officer on parole.[29]

While escaped parole prisoners were immediately confined on board a hulk, they could later re-apply for parole. If their behaviour on board the vessel had been exemplary, then often their request was granted. Persistent parole-breakers were denied this privilege.

Prisoners could be regularly exchanged as and when an exchange cartel was agreed. The exchange system will be discussed in detail alongside the political aspects of prisoners of war, although here it should be said that during the 1790s a prisoner could expect to be exchanged within a year or two of capture. After 1803 the chance of exchange diminished rapidly between Britain and France as neither could agree on the exact terms and conditions of such a cartel. However, invalids, boys and women were sent home regardless of any exchange agreement being signed, and individuals could apply to join these batches of returning prisoners if they could offer medical assistance to the returning invalids or had good reason to be exchanged, such as a verifiable health problem. One Martin, a French medical officer on parole at Bishops Waltham, requested 'to accompany some invalids to France on parole' as he had 'been confined two years in dungeons in Portugal and has a large family'. Parole officers in England could apply to return to their own countries on parole if they were suffering ill-health; but not so ill that they were incapable of any further service to their country. Severely ill prisoners were sent home without waiting for an exchange cartel. If these requests were supported by a surgeon's recommendation then they were always acceded to without hesitation.

Even the relatives of a prisoner of war would write to the Transport Office in an attempt to secure the release of their loved ones. In 1811 a French naval gunner by the name of Nicholas Noel was imprisoned at Chatham. His mother wrote from France to request that he be released or sent home on parole, the reason put before the Board being '...his mother, an aged woman, begs he may have parole, he being ill'. Noel was indeed ill, and was ordered to be sent home on the next available cartel.[30]

This letter-writing to the Admiralty was placed on an organised footing by the officers at Ashford, Kent, in early 1796. A letter to the Board reads:

My Lord,
Having heard of your great goodness in getting the passports for my superior officers, I am thereby emboldened to petition to your Lordship to procure that favour for me as I have a wife and family of small children who must severely feel the loss of my absence, and if your Lordship with your usual goodness will procure me my liberty, I promise to give my parole not to enter into any service with any nation whatever during the war, as getting home to my family is all that is desired of your Lordships.
Most dutiful and ever obedient servant,
William Bakker
Dutch Officer Prisoner of war,
belonging to the Dutch Frigate *Alliantie.*

The letter had been written for him, probably by a fellow prisoner with skill at the English language. There was nothing unusual in that, but the Board received another letter from Ashford dated 21 March, from Joghem Gras, a Dutch officer also taken on board the *Alliantie*. This gentleman wanted to return to his wife and seven children, who had 'long been destitute of succour' through his absence. A few days later Joe Pemerle, Captain of the French Privateer *Le Lempeur* expressed a desire to return to his 'wife and innocent babes' who had also been 'destitute of succour' through his absence. Jan Lohotsel, Joseph Proye and S.Bierman also wrote to the Board about the large population suffering through the absence of their men folk. All the letters are in the same hand and have the same basic content, and one gets the impression that this was a group effort in returning home, with one parole prisoner perhaps earning a few pennies acting as scribe.[31]

Pursuing diplomatic channels was yet another escape route, more so during the Revolutionary wars when most of the German States were fighting against France. In September 1796 the Admiralty received a letter from Baron Kutzleben, Minister of the Landgrave of Hesse Cassel at the Court of St James, requesting the release of five persons taken on board a Dutch East Indiaman at the Cape of Good Hope, and confined as prisoners of war in Portchester Castle. All five swore statements before a magistrate at Fareham that they were subjects of Hesse Cassel, and were ordered to be released.

This was a common occurrence, for the following month the Bavarian Minister in London requested the release of nine Bavarian subjects captured at the Cape. A month later the Saxon and Prussian Ministers asked for the release of some of their nationals taken during the same conflict. The Consuls from Sweden and Denmark were also quick to request the release of their people taken on board French or Dutch vessels. In the interests of diplomacy these prisoners were always set free.[32]

From 1803 such requests became less common as the French Empire expanded. Some prisoners however, when captured in the service of Britain's enemies although their own country was neutral, would still try the legal approach to escape the prisons. The Agent at Portchester Castle received a reply to his correspondence about an American in the prison in July 1810, a time when Britain and the USA were not at war:

> With respect to the application of Thomas Robinson, an American in your custody ... it appears by a communication from ... the West Indies, that this man is a most inveterate enemy to the British, and wantonly went into the Batteries of Basseterre, Guadeloupe, for the purpose of firing on the boats belonging to the British Squadron ... consequently he cannot be regarded as a neutral.[33]

Escape from a British war prison was not always because of a desire to return home. To many soldiers and sailors, their profession was their home, and it was of no consequence to them whose army or navy they served in. Many prisoners of war were only too ready to enlist in the British forces if it released them from confinement.

During the 1790s there were many Emigré Corps based in Britain who found lucrative recruiting in the prisons. They were expressly forbidden to recruit French or Dutch, but Germans were allowed to enlist. In April 1796 one hundred Germans taken while in the service of Holland were recruited into the Legion of Baron de Montalembert at Portchester. That same month two negroes in Mill Prison were released to serve in the band of the North Devon Regiment of Militia.[34]

After 1803 many of the German States were either overrun or allied to France through political expediency. These nations furnished many troops for the French campaigns in Spain and Portugal, and many of these soldiers became prisoners of the British Army and its allies. Some enlisted whilst still in Spain, and this recruitment on the spot was actively encouraged by the Board to alleviate pressure on the prison establishment at home. The regulations stated that no 'Frenchmen or Italians of dubious character' were to be recruited, but 'Austro-Hungarians, together with all Germans north of the Rhine, particularly Hessians, are those upon which we can place the most dependence'. They were recruited into the King's German Legion, the Duke of Brunswick Oel's Corps of Jager, the Chasseurs Britanniques and the 5th Battalion 60th Foot.[35]

Many prisoners decided to enlist after experiencing conditions in the war prisons, and after listening to the recruiting parties who were frequently allowed into the depots. The Royal Marines gained sixty Dutch recruits in Forton in January 1810. That same month saw Josh Losar (on board the *Vengeance*) volunteer to serve on board HMS *Orion*. As he was a native of Palma in the Canary Islands and had a good character reference from the Commander of the prison ship, he was allowed to serve in the Navy [36]. In 1806 a number of Russian merchant vessels were detained at Portsmouth and their crews lodged in the hulks. These prisoners were very quick to volunteer for the British merchant service as many of them were prisoners of war for no more than a month or two.[37] Livert Jonsen was a Danish seaman in the

Royal Navy who became a captive on the outbreak of hostilities with his nation in 1807. Two months and numerous applications later he was allowed to return to HMS *Isis*.[38]

While many prisoners volunteered for British service, their more patriotic colleagues regarded this action as despicable. Those who volunteered but were found unfit for service were removed to other prisons for their own safety. Volunteering for British service prompts the question of whether this a ploy to arrive in a situation where they could desert to their own side?

In the Peninsula many Germans deserted from the French armies and eventually enlisted in the British Army, to campaign again in that theatre. For such a soldier, fighting far from home for an Emperor and a nation he did not have strong feelings for, it was better to fight for the winning side, where he was at least fed regularly and where the feared Spanish guerrillas were on his side. Some of these soldiers did desert from their new units; some to regain the French forces, and not a few to escape any form of military service. Of those prisoners of war who were recruited into the King's German Legion in England, many were not sent to the units of this Corps on campaign in the Iberian Peninsula. Instead, they were sent to the Legion Depots in England, and more trustworthy Legion troops dispatched to join Wellington's Army. However, this did not prevent many such soldiers deserting from the King's German Legion in Spain.[39]

Those prisoners who volunteered for service in the Royal Navy or Merchant Service were unlikely to be able to desert to the enemy. Volunteering for the Royal Marines got them out of the hulks but no where near their own countries. When this Corps was required to send detachments abroad, invariably the foreigners amongst them were left for duty at home; a duty that found them guarding prisoners on board the hulks. It was asserted that Marines who had once been prisoners of war themselves became somewhat brutal guards, perhaps in an overzealous attempt to impress their new employers.

Rendering a service to their captors was another means of returning home without waiting for an Exchange Cartel to be agreed. The story of Joseph Maudet rescuing a child from the jaws of a lion in Oswestry has already been related, and those prisoners who assisted the Bank of England in detecting forged banknotes, but other prisoners obtained their release by deeds of heroism or compassion that impressed their captors. In 1807 some Frenchmen on parole at Andover in Hampshire assisted the townspeople in extinguishing a serious fire in the town. This was brought to the notice of the Transport Board who instructed that the officers concerned should be sent home immediately as a reward for their efforts.[40]

A more permanent means of escape was death. While prisoners died of natural causes, some were shot in the act of escaping, and a few murdered by their fellows, there was a small number who took their own lives. Either a desperate desire to escape their confinement or even a desire to escape from bullying colleagues; their reasons died with them. Francois Russard, aged 17 years, hanged himself in Portchester Castle in December 1799. Brother Bouvain, a 23 year old negro taken in the West Indies, 'leaped from the upper storey of the Tower, and killed himself'. The Coroner recorded a verdict on him of 'insane'.[41]

Francois Retif and his companions were but one example of the desperate lengths some prisoners would go to escape their confinement. For their deed they were sentenced to hang. A collection was made for the widow and children of George Brothers and reached a total of £263. The three condemned men even contributed £7 while they languished in Winchester Gaol, and their fellow prisoners at Forton subscribed £20 as a mark of disgust at their colleagues' action.[42]

Prisoners of war were, after all, simple men with consciences, as well as a desire to see their homes again.

Notes

1 Pescott Frost Collection, p.118.
2 Abell, p.6.
3 TNA:PRO ADM103/607. General Entry Book of French Prisoners of War on Parole at Tiverton.
4 Pescott Frost Collection, p.118.
5 TNA:PRO ADM105/45. Escapes of prisoners of war 1810–14.

6 Walker, p.161.

7 Joy, p.51.

8 Abell, p.169.

9 ibid., p.235.

10 TNA:PRO ADM105/45. 7 March 1811.

11 TNA:PRO ADM103/440. General Entry Book of French Prisoners of war on board the *Vengeance* 1812–14.

12 TNA:PRO ADM103/85. General Entry Book of French Prisoners of War on board the *Crown*.

13 ibid.

14 TNA:PRO ADM103/491. Escapes from all depots 1811–14.

15 TNA:PRO ADM103/646. Accounts of Prisoners of War who died at Portsmouth.

16 Pescott Frost Collection, p.62.

17 TNA:PRO ADM105/45. 1 June and 23 June 1811.

18 TNA:PRO ADM105/44. 25 June 1812.

19 TNA:PRO ADM103/491. Escapes 4 July and 1 October 1812.

20 TNA:PRO ADM105/44. 2 October 1807.

21 Pescott Frost Collection, p.62.

22 *Kentish Gazette* 29 October 1811.

23 Harvey, Wallace. *Whitstable and the French Prisoners of War* (Emprint, Kent, 1983), p.11–40.

24 *An Act for the more effectual Punishment of Persons aiding Prisoners of War to escape from His Majesty's Dominions* (London 1812).

25 *Hampshire Telegraph*, 16 March 1811.

26 Pescott Frost Collection, p.60.

27 Abell, p.215.

28 TNA:PRO ADM103/491. 1 October 1812.

29 ibid., 17 January 1812.

30 TNA:PRO ADM105/52. Prisoners Applications.

31 NMM ADM/MT/415. Transport Board Letters, January–June 1796.

32 NMM ADM/MT/416. Transport Board Letters July–December 1796.

33 TNA:PRO ADM98/252. Admiralty Letters to Agent, Portchester Castle 1810.

34 NMM ADM/MT/415. 18 and 26 April 1796.

35 TNA:PRO WO25/672. Description and Succession Book Foreign Regiments in British Service 1810–11.

36 TNA:PRO ADM98/261. Letters relating to prisoners of war at

Portsmouth 3 and 10 January 1810.

[37] TNA:PRO ADM103/371. General Entry Book of Russian prisoners of war at Portsmouth.

[38] TNA:PRO ADM103/344. General Entry Book of Danish prisoners of war at Portsmouth 1807–14.

[39] Gray, Daniel Savage. *Prisoners, Wanderers and Deserters: Recruiting for the King's German Legion, 1803–15*, Journal of the Society for Army Historical Research Volume 53, p.153.

[40] TNA:PRO ADM103/44. 2 October 1807.

[41] TNA:PRO ADM103/645. Death Certificates Portchester Castle 1799–1814.

[42] Pescott Frost Collection, p.119.

CHAPTER 8

French Trophies of War

We were marched off to Dunkirk, each carrying the few clothes he was allowed to bring with him from the ship, slung on his back. We were tied to each other with a strong cord, much as you may see a number of horses coming to Smithfield, and escorted by a party of soldiers headed by two drummers, beating what, I suppose, we should call the Rogue's March, to give dignity to the scene. Before we reached Dunkirk we were much fatigued, partly from want of rest for some nights past, and partly from want of food, but chiefly from depression of spirits.[1]

Thus was the tale penned by Alexander Stewart, captured in the English Channel by a French Privateer within sight of Brighton Battery. Indeed, his narrative gives an interesting insight into the fortunes of war during that time. He was a Scot; working on an English merchant vessel, captured by a French Privateer crewed almost exclusively by Danes and Swedes who had once been in the English service. His vessel and its captive crew were sailed to Gravelines, and from here they were marched to Dunkirk:

We arrived in Dunkirk towards evening, on entering which our guard, to our great annoyance, again beat their drums at our head, to summon the idle, the curious, and the simple, to witness French trophies of war.[2]

The number of Britons taken by the French was never comparable with the prisoner total in Britain, and France was not the only country to take Britons prisoner.

Holland, Spain, Denmark and the United States of America all captured British soldiers and seamen at various stages of the war.

To understand the problems that faced the Transport Board when attempting to formulate exchange cartels for prisoners in their care, and to explain the attitudes displayed by the authorities when discussing prisoners of war, it is necessary to examine the fate of Britons captured by the nation's enemies.

The French had an ambivalent view of prisoners of war during the early years of the Revolutionary War. At times they were regarded as slaves of oppressive regimes and to be treated with humanity, if not pity, and introduced to the benefits of *Liberté*, *Egalité* and *Fraternité*; at other times to be treated as instruments of the privileged aristocracy still in power throughout Europe; in other words, enemies of the French people. During the Belgian campaign in 1792 against the Austrian Army, some ill-disciplined French troops actually hanged some Austrian prisoners of war held in the town of Lille, although it has to be said that they also murdered some French officers including their own commanding officer. This act horrified the Legislative Assembly in Paris, who proceeded to reaffirm the earlier eighteenth century 'laws of war' that provided for the humane treatment of prisoners of war. Their belief was that if the French Armies committed atrocities on captives, the same could happen to French soldiers taken by the opposing forces. This situation would also seriously affect the exchange of prisoners.[3] Certainly by late 1792 the French were exchanging prisoners of war with the Austrians.

In 1794 there was much posturing and rhetoric in Paris regarding the taking of English and Hanoverians as prisoners of war, but this remained nothing more than bombast, the French soldiers at the front taking a professional view of captive-taking – the role could so easily be reversed and they become the prisoners.[4] As the Government in Paris became less extreme and the numbers of captives taken by all the nations increased, the treatment of these men settled into the format that had developed throughout the wars of the eighteenth century, in that captives were the unfortunate victims of war, to be cared for until they could be exchanged. Thousands of Frenchmen held in Britain were men denied to the French Army and Navy, and so exchange was a practical necessity.

From the outset of the war in 1793 captives were acquired by both Britain and France. While the vigorous prosecution of the war by the Royal Navy resulted in many thousands of prisoners arriving in Britain, there was a flow of captives, albeit not as great, into France. The ports of Cherbourg, St. Malo and Le Havre were home to many active privateers who preyed upon the shipping in the Channel and eastern Atlantic. The records for 1793–95 list those Britons captured and later released from France, and the majority of such entries are for men taken on privateers, merchant vessels and neutral ships.[5]

During the abortive campaign in the Low Countries during 1793–94, a British force under the Duke of York fought a number of actions against the French, losing men as prisoners. The arrangements for housing prisoners of war in this theatre were primitive on both sides. While disease accounted for many deaths in the ill-equipped armies of both combatants, it also spilled over into the prison depots, resulting in many deaths. The depots during this campaign were not as secure as they should have been, with many prisoners escaping back to their own side.

The major depots in France from 1793–1800 were Arras, Douai, Dunkirk, Messieres, Saumer, Sedan and Valenciennes, while minor depots were located at Bordeaux, Brest, Cherbourg, Gravelines, Morlaix and St. Malo. The coastal prisons were convenient for the transfer of British prisoners across the Channel when exchange cartels were arranged.[6] These early prison depots were not as organised as they later became, with their records often being incomplete. This did not matter so much in the early years of the war as prisoners of both sides were often exchanged after only a brief spell in captivity. As the war continued and men remained prisoner for much longer, more detailed records were kept.

British prisoners taken by Spain were held at Alicante, Barcelona, Cartegena, Corunna, Ferrol, Majorca and Malaga, most being released via Gibraltar. These sites were in use as prisons from 1798 until 1807. As in France, small numbers of British were held at other sites, although only for brief periods.[7]

During the wars with Revolutionary France, a number of British civilians found themselves on the Continent during this period. As will be seen later, the number of such people taken captive by the French did not compare with the larger number of such Britons taken in 1803. Throughout the 18th century France had been seen as part of the cultural tour for an English gentleman. Many such gentlemen left France as the Revolution took hold, and few ventured forth into a country that was in the grip of an often-violent ideology. Those that did so were either trying to pursue their business interests, or to open negotiations with the French Government over the exchange of prisoners of war or the potential for peace. British civilians whose reason for being in France was not acceptable to the authorities were promptly sent home, if they managed to enter France in the first place. Two bankers, Boyd and Ker, made their way to Paris in 1797 in the hope of recovering confiscated property, only to be unceremoniously packed off home with no sympathy being given to their claims. Aristocratic Britons were tolerated in France as they were always potential envoys for peace negotiations. Lord Malmesbury deserted his wife in January 1793 to follow his mistress, Aimée de Coigny, to Paris where he was promptly arrested. He applied to her previous lover Lauzun to procure his release, which was granted without any formality. Malmesbury was to be found in Paris again in 1796, and in Lille in 1797. On both occasions he received an offer from Barras to assist in peace negotiations.[8]

While prisoners of war during the 1790s were treated humanely and usually exchanged after only a matter of months in captivity, the French authorities did on one occasion treat one such captive more harshly than most.

Sir Sidney Smith was a colourful character whose exploits were known on both sides of the Channel. In 1793 he took the *Swallow* into the port of Toulon after it had been evacuated by the Anglo-Spanish force, for the purpose of burning the French shipping moored in the docks. He not only burnt some of the vessels, but also evacuated many of the terrified inhabitants who knew the justice they would receive when the city was occupied by the besieging French army. In command of the frigate *Diamond*, he cruised off the coasts of Normandy and Brittany intercepting French coastal shipping, placing agents ashore, picking up Royalist fugitives and landing supplies for the Royalist partisans fighting in La Vendée.

On one occasion, hoisting the tricolour on board the *Diamond*, he calmly sailed into Brest harbour to see what ships were about. In the spring of 1796 he burnt nine ships in the harbour of Herqui while his landing parties captured and destroyed the shore batteries. Within the area of his command, he pursued an aggressive policy towards French privateers. To the British public he was a hero. To the French he was little more than a pirate.

His undoing arose because of his audacity. In April 1796 he discovered that the privateer *Le Vengeur* was moored off Le Havre. The water was not sufficiently deep for the *Diamond* to sail close to her, so he mounted a cutting out expedition. The night attack was successful, but during the conflict a Frenchman cut *Le Vengeur*'s cable and the tide swept the vessel up the River Seine. Sir Sidney and his crew secured their captives in the hold and attempted to sail the ship out of danger, but the wind had fallen away. The captors then attempted to tow the vessel using the boats from the *Diamond*. This activity became evident to the French coastal batteries as dawn broke. These guns were manned, and a corvette and some armed luggers put off to rescue the privateer, followed by longboats full of troops.

Seeing that battle was imminent, Sir Sidney released his captives ashore on parole. The first attack was beaten off, but more and more vessels arrived from Le Havre and His Majesty's newly and temporarily acquired ship *Le Vengeur* returned to her rightful owners, with Sir Sidney Smith and his crew now receiving a taste of captivity.

When it was known ashore that the redoubtable 'Commodore' Smith had been captured, a large crowd assembled to witness the spectacle of Sir Sidney being landed. The crowd was not hostile and there were many cheerful cries of '*Vive la Republique*' to which Sir Sidney replied with an equally cheerful wave and smile. The crew was sent to Rouen as prisoners of war, while Sir Sidney, his servant John Bromley[9] and his secretary, Midshipman John Wesley Wright, were conveyed to Paris where they were lodged in the Abbaye Prison. The authorities in Le Havre were ecstatic at capturing the great British 'pirate' Sir Sidney Smith. They wrote to the Government in Paris, who in turn published the letter in *Le Moniteur*:

> At last we hold Sidney Smith, that British incendiary who burned our ships at Toulon, the same who attempted, some time ago, to set fire to the buildings and stores of Havre; he who, in a word, has promised Pitt to make of all our harbours and shipping only a heap of cinders... We warn you that, not having at Havre a place strong enough to hold him, we are sending him off to Rouen under good and strong escort to await until national justice gives its verdict on all the attempts of this monster.

To this piece of good news the *Moniteur* added that '...the Directory has just given orders for him to be taken to Paris as an incendiary'.

Smith, Bromley and Wright were transferred to the Temple Prison, which was then regarded as only a stepping-stone to the guillotine. This was in contravention of the accepted practice of allowing such officers their parole, a matter that caused the British Government considerable concern. The impact of this event upon the prisoner population in Britain, and the diplomacy surrounding captives, will be discussed in the next chapter. Sir Sidney and his colleagues were separated and confined in solitary cells. John Bromley's real identity was never discovered, and after fifteen months he was released and allowed to return to England. After two years of captivity, Sir Sidney Smith and John Wright escaped with the help of some Royalists.[10]

Following eight years of conflict, peace came with the Anglo-French treaty signed at Amiens on 25 March 1802 after the formal Preliminaries had been signed the previous October. While this interval of peace lasted only fourteen months, that was time enough for many Britons to sample the delights of France. The Dover to Calais mail-packets resumed sailing on 18 November 1801, and one of the first brought to the shores of France no less than sixty-three English ladies, all desirous of a glimpse of Paris fashions, entertainment and perhaps even a sight of the First Consul, Napoleon Bonaparte. The influx of civilians into France was to have a serious effect on prisoner of war diplomacy after the resumption of hostilities in 1803. It is estimated that among the British visitors during this short period of peace there were five dukes, three marquises, thirty-seven earls and countesses, eight viscounts, seventeen barons and forty-one elder sons and other heirs; all but one-third of the then House of Lords.[11] On 16 May 1803 Britain, having grown distrustful of Napoleon's intentions, declared war on France. All French and Dutch ships in British ports and waters were 'detained by the Admiralty'; *letters of marque* were issued; and French ships in the Channel were attacked and seized. On the Continent these actions were reciprocated and resulted in an immediate population of captives that would influence the outcome of prisoner negotiations for the next eleven years.

On 23 May a decree was passed by Napoleon that:

All the English enrolled in the Militia, from the age of 18 to 60, holding a commission from His Britannic Majesty, who are at present in France, shall be made Prisoners of War, to answer for the Citizens of the Republic who have been arrested by the vessels of subjects of His Britannic Majesty before the declaration of war.[12]

These civilian captives or *détenus* amounted to seven hundred, of whom four hundred were tradesmen, with many of these détenus taken as they attempted to leave France.[13] Napoleon hoped that a large haul of eminent Britons would prove useful bargaining counters at future peace negotiations. They were however, to prove a stumbling block in future negotiations over the exchange of prisoners.

These détenus signed parole documents as did the officers who were taken in armed conflict, and were allowed to reside on parole, mainly at Verdun, but some of the higher-ranking Britons were allowed to choose their own place of residence. Thus Lord and Lady Boyle resided at Verdun for a while, but later obtained permission to live in Paris, where the social life was more to their liking while the Duke and Dowager Duchess of Newcastle resided at Tours until they were released in 1807. The list of détenus included the great and the not so great, from dukes to gentlemen to circus proprietors such as Philip Astley, who joined many of his fellows at Verdun.[14]

The détenus differed from the military officers taken captive in that they observed their parole obligations more strictly than the latter. Army and naval officers taken captive after 1803 were prisoners for far longer than they would have been during the Revolutionary War. The higher-ranking détenus regarded their parole as part of their character as gentlemen and their captivity did not affect their careers as much as it did the military parole prisoners. Wealthy détenus could live in relative luxury in the parole depots, obtaining drafts of money from England, while British tradesmen taken captive had the opportunity of setting up in business catering for their wealthy compatriots and the local French population.

During the 1790s the short period of confinement experienced by most prisoners of war resulted in few accounts of their incarceration and general treatment. The accounts we do have of French prison depots come from the period after 1803, when a long captivity of up to eleven years was a significant part of a man's life. After Waterloo the long conflict from 1793 to 1815 became known as The Great War, and many of the participants put their experiences down on paper. It was a major part of their lives and they related their story as soldiers, sailors or civilians caught up in the war, including periods of captivity. From such accounts we have a detailed story of the prison depots in France, though not of those in Spain, Holland, Denmark or the United States of America.

While British victories generated large numbers of captives for the depots in England, the nation did not have it all her own way when it came to the conflict. British ships were taken at sea, either in small naval actions or by enemy privateers. Peter Bussell, thirty-two year old part owner of the *Dove* sloop, set sail from Weymouth on the morning of 22 February 1806. When off the Needles they saw a lugger coming towards them under English colours. This vessel tacked and stood towards the *Dove*, which made Bussell suspect that all was not quite as it should be. His suspicions were confirmed when the lugger hauled down the English colours, hoisted the French flag, and fired musket shots at him. The lugger was the French privateer *Les Deux Frères* from Boulogne and the *Dove* and Peter Bussell had become victims of the privateering war.[15] The privateer and her prize only just managed to reach Cherbourg as they were chased for much of the way by two Royal Navy cutters.

Captain Frederick Hoffman commanded the sloop *Apelles*, seeing much service in the Channel from 1810 until May 1812, when his ship ran aground between Boulogne and Etaples while patrolling close inshore in the company of HMS *Skylark*. When dawn broke both vessels found themselves under the guns of a large shore battery, which opened fire with considerable effect. Both ships were stuck on a sandbank and they threw equipment and stores overboard in a desperate effort to lighten the vessels and escape. Both ships remained stuck fast, and the crew of the Skylark set fire to their vessel and abandoned her, making off in their boats. However, some of the *Apelles's* boats had been destroyed by the shore guns, and so only part of Hoffman's crew could effect their escape. Captain Hoffman decided to remain with those whose fate was obviously to be taken captive.[16] The gallant captain and his remaining crew were taken prisoner by a force of 150 French soldiers who waited for the tide to recede until they could '...board us without wetting their delicate feet'![17]

Aside from accidents at sea such as running aground, the elements had their say in the fortunes of the Royal Navy in that many ships succumbed to storm and were wrecked, occasionally on an enemy coastline.

HMS *Hussar* was one such ship lost at sea in early 1804, when a fierce storm drove her onto the rocks of the Saints Islands off the coast of France. One of the seamen onboard, John Wetherell, later recalled how the crew and marines made their way to shore, formed up, and marched as if on parade to the local village, which they captured. Taking possession of the local fishing boats, Wetherell and his comrades attempted to sail for home, only to be thwarted by yet another storm that drove them into Brest. Here they were captured by a Guard Boat from the harbour.[18]

Britons were taken prisoner in the many land campaigns fought not only in Europe but also during attacks on enemy colonies overseas. It was not until the Peninsular War began in 1808 that appreciable numbers of British soldiers were taken by the French. Many were taken as stragglers when British forces were forced to retreat, such as during the Corunna campaign of 1808–09, while others were taken when they became wounded. Generally they were treated well, as Captain Charles Boothby discovered on being injured at the Battle of Talavera. This was a victory for the army under General Wellesley, but on learning of the approach of fresh troops under Marshal Soult, he prudently withdrew leaving the wounded from the battle quartered in the town under the guard of some Spanish soldiers, who promptly deserted their charges on the approach of the enemy. The town was open to the advancing French, who took possession of the houses not only for shelter but also for a strong desire for plunder. Boothby feared for his few clothes and personal effects.

The servants of two French officers entered the house in which Boothby was recuperating from losing a leg, and he seized his chance and invited them to lodge their masters in the same building as he, for there were a number of rooms so far unoccupied by either British wounded or their attendants. Boothby's reasoning was that if he shared a house with some French officers, he was not likely to be molested or plundered by any of the common soldiers roaming the streets.

One of the Frenchmen who decided to reside in the same house was one Captain de la Platière, who took pity upon Boothby and readily offered him protection. During the Peninsular conflict many French officers who fell into the hands of Wellington's army experienced kindness and courtesy from their British counterparts. The French would reciprocate whenever possible, as Boothby found to his relief. The second French officer introduced to the wounded Briton was a Captain Simon who had experienced captivity after being taken on the capitulation of the French colony of St. Domingo. He had nothing but praise for the kindness he had received from his captors on Jamaica and 'thus he had received a most favourable impression of English character and English society'. The two Frenchmen kept Boothby company whenever they could, saw that he obtained food and even procured some books for him.[19]

British prisoners were initially held in local gaols until they could be escorted to the main prison depots. This temporary confinement was usually basic in the extreme, with little or no sanitation and only straw to sleep on. Peter Bussell was fortunate in that his first prison was a little better than most:

> The prison is a small one in the dockyard, and appears only for prisoners of war, or for detaining those who are going to be sent on board any of the ships of war...as several sea-faring men was brought in while we were here. Our gaoler was an elderly man, very friendly to us but loved the bottle ... Our daily allowance each was three quarters of a pound beef, one pound bread, and a pint of cider. I got a bed for ten sols a night in a cockloft amongst the poultry, the entrance to which led through a trap-door in the floor by means of a step ladder, which was taken away after I had ascended.[20]

From these temporary prisons the captives were marched to the depots at which they would spend many years of confinement. If they were fortunate they might travel part of the way by cart or carriage, especially if they had money with which to purchase such a luxury or they were suffering from wounds received in action. Boothby was conveyed in a wagon from Talavera to Madrid, where many British prisoners of war were being collected prior to their journey to France.[21]

Soldiers taken captive were used to marching and so travelling on foot was no hardship to them, whereas seamen found such travel tiring. Midshipman Maurice Hewson found his journey 'uncommonly fatiguing', made even more so by travelling in the company of some common criminals. Prisoners of war and civil prisoners were marched throughout France under the escort of mounted gendarmes and often mixed parties of such captives were conveyed together for convenience. Hewson and his four British companions 'were joined by eleven poor culprits from the city prison' before they left Brest for Verdun.[22]

While Britain had purpose-built prisons and prison ship depots, the border fortresses of eastern France were the destination of most British prisoners of war. Such fortresses were ready-made and very secure prisons, and could cope with the number of inmates they were to receive. Each left a different impression upon the minds of those who lived there. Officers were given the same parole conditions as their counterparts in Britain although the main parole depot in France was Verdun. When attempting to compare the treatment of French in Britain and Britons in France it should be remembered that during the Napoleonic Wars no more than 20,000 British soldiers and seamen became prisoners of war and languished in French prison depots, with a maximum at any one time of about 15,000 in 1813. Compare this with the 72,000 held in British depots the same year, and it becomes obvious that if any captives were to be exchanged at all then the French authorities could not afford to treat their British captives harshly. British nationals usually fared as well as their counterparts across the Channel, but not so those taken prisoner during France's campaigns against Austria, Prussia, Russia and Spain. These men were used to replace the depleted male population on the land and used as a cheap source of labour, often becoming little more than slaves.

Many of these men who were housed in French prison depots later put their experiences down on paper, partly perhaps to come to terms with the past, and partly to explain to their family and friends what exactly became of them during their long disappearance from home. These accounts are a valuable source of information on the French depots, and while some prisons are described very generally others are related in detail by a number of Britons who stayed there. These personal accounts are used here to describe the depots used by France to hold prisoners of war and the détenus, and to relate the treatment experienced by British captives in French hands, as a comparison with the description of the hulks, land prisons and parole depots in Britain.

Arras

This name is more associated with The Great War of 1914–18, but one hundred years prior to this the town was home to British soldiers and seamen. The only detailed, but somewhat dull, description of this depot comes from the pen of Peter Bussell who arrived there in 1806. The early prison depot was situated in buildings set against the town walls but later moved out to the Citadel, half a mile from the town. Bussell described the earlier buildings thus;

> ...situated near the ramparts, the yard is very small, and the walls very high, so that there is but little room for us and scarcely any air. Each room is to contain eighteen prisoners. The furniture of the room is a stove, kettle, table, two long stools, one earthen dish and a pitcher. A straw bed with an old blanket is allowed for every two prisoners. Straw is served out every four months.[23]

Arras was certainly used as a depot for British prisoners during the 1790s as there are records detailing those released from this depot in 1799 and 1800, but no description of the depot from this period exists.[24] According to Bussell many Masters were allowed to reside on parole in the town while other prisoners were given permission to go into town between the hours of seven in the morning and four in the afternoon. Most of the prisoners held here were merchant and naval seamen. In June 1806 for example, Arras was home to 249 seamen, marines and boys taken on HMS *Calcutta*, while 76 crew members of HMS *Ranger* also resided there.[25]

While Bussell painted a very drab picture of the depot, he was writing about a period in the depot's history when the accommodation was very cramped. In 1809 this overcrowding became so serious that a new depot was opened at Cambrai. Arras was then used mainly to hold merchant seamen and evidently improved, as Alexander Stewart has left us with a more positive view of the depot. He had been marched from Briancon northwards in 1813 as the Allied Armies closed in on France. He joined a prison population of about 2,000 in a well-kept depot;

> The Barracks formed a great square, whose inclosure was allowed the prisoners for walking and recreation: the avenues were guarded by soldiers ... This was the best depot I had seen in France. There being plenty of room, the prisoners could keep themselves more separate from each other than in any of the other depots I had seen.[26]

Auxone

Of this depot there is no surviving eye-witness account. Bussell makes only a few passing references to it in his account, and then only to refer to prisoners he met who had marched from that depot to other prisons. The depot would appear to have been an unpopular prison to reside in, if the number of escapes is an indication of conditions there. Of the 355 British prisoners who escaped from France up to 12 September 1812, no less than 92 are reported as having run from Auxonne – this is more than from any other depot. The only good thing to be said about Auxonne is that in 1809 some of the British prisoners there did great service by helping to put out a fire in the town, which was threatening to consume many of the buildings. Their assistance was acknowledged in many letters of thanks from prominent townspeople.[27]

Besançon

The border fortresses were also military depots, and often the accommodation there was handed over to troops marching for Napoleon's campaigns in central and eastern Europe. Prisoners of war were relocated elsewhere after often marching many hundreds of miles to their new lodgings. Bussell was surprised to hear that all the prisoners resident in Arras were to be marched to Auxonne and Besançon – a distance of some three hundred miles – for these two depots were situated near the border with Switzerland. His first impression of Besançon was that:

> The Citadel seems to be a very strong place, situated on a high rocky hill. There are three or four rows of very large buildings, very strongly built; the backs of some of the buildings is hewn out of the solid rock. The pavement of the yards is of the same. High walls is on the east and west sides, on which is two or three watch or look-out towers. Here is two large magazines, and a small arsenal for Arms etc. here is a small church. The water which we make use of is rain water, from two or three large cisterns. There is two

or three rows of buildings in the counterscarp below the Citadel, but we are not permitted to go without the Citadel gate (except when we go for provisions etc.).

Bussell describes the people who guarded such prisoners of war. All able-bodied men from between the ages of 18 and 40 were liable to conscription in the French forces, thus leaving the wounded, infirm and elderly to serve in the prison depots. At Besançon:

> ...the inhabitants of the Citadel is the Commandant of the Citadel and his family, an old invalid gunner and his wife, an old invalid barrack master and store keeper, the people that keeps the Military Canteen, and a few wounded soldiers that does duty as sentries, beside a porter at the gate.

As the prison population expanded, so more troops arrived at the depot. Bussel's account continues;

> ...there arrived in the Citadel two companies belonging to the first battalion Des Tirailleurs du Po. They are come into the Citadel to do duty. They appeared to be all young men, and are all Piedmontese.[28]

Bitche

Of all the depots in France after 1803, Bitche had the most ominous reputation for the conditions of close confinement experienced by many British captives. While the Transport Board sent troublesome prisoners to the hulks as the ultimate punishment, the French sent persistent troublemakers and failed escapees to the citadel of Bitche, an isolated fortress in Lorraine some eighty miles east of Verdun. This site was the principal punishment depot for British prisoners who transgressed the regulations, be they naval or military officers and men, or civilian détenus. Maurice Hewson had been ordered to Bitche in consequence of a number of failed escapes while at Verdun. He recalled that the citadel was perched high above the town '..its lofty ramparts and heavy gates foreboding little possibility of escape'. He was immediately confined in the *souterrain*, a large chamber about 20 metres underground:

> We descended by stone steps to this terrific vault large enough to contain 500 men. The sides were roughly hewn from the rock with drains of salt water oozing continually, and such a moisture of atmosphere pervaded the whole that in going to bed every night, our sheets were quite humid.[29]

Midshipman O'Brien was twice confined at Bitche and relates how the *souterrains* were the main living quarters of the prisoners. Aside from short periods when they were allowed to walk about the small central courtyard of the fortress under close guard, they lived, ate and slept underground. They were allowed a wood fire in winter and rush lights at night, with a blanket for bedding and straw on the floor in which lived all manner of vermin. Rats were their constant companions. All were locked up for the night at seven in the evening during the summer and at four o'clock in winter, with a nominal roll-call each day at eleven when the gendarme in charge of each dungeon would simply count heads. Once a month there was a more detailed inspection of the prisoners and their quarters.[30]

Briançon

This fortress, situated on the Italian border, was used from 1812 until early 1814 to house many British prisoners arriving from the Iberian conflict. While it was not a punishment depot, many of the prisoners who stayed here thought that a stay in Bitche was more preferable! Briançon was an overcrowded fortress of immense strength, set in the snow-clad mountains of the Alps. The walls were designed to be bomb proof and were not less than two metres in thickness, which did not make for warm accommodation.

The barracks bordered a large airing ground on which the prisoners were only occasionally allowed to walk. Each barrack had a long corridor which was accessible to the prisoners during the day, and was frequently used for accommodation, especially during 1814 when the prison population was at its height. The corridors led to rooms in each of which fourteen prisoners were confined, often throughout the day as well as at night. There was no glass on the small windows, and Stewart recorded that their windows had panes made of paper steeped in oil.[31]

Many confirmed the living conditions described by Stewart. Thomas Williams was fed on a bread and meat allowance from which they made a soup:

> Our food was chiefly polenta or Indian meal, and part of our bread was made of that meal, which was a very loose kind of bread, and did little service. In each room there was a stove for cooking our victuals, in which we burnt a kind of coal which we were told was taken from the mountains. It was small and slimy and full of brimstone ... it would burn very well in the dark, but very badly during the day, and sent out a great deal of sulphur, which made us black as tinkers and, being without soap, you would hardly know us from real Negroes. It also caused a deal of sickness, especially fever and ague. I was some time in the hospital with that complaint.[32]

Cambrai

Of this depot, established in 1809, there is little direct evidence. The town and depot is in the same region as Arras and Valenciennes and became one of the larger prison centers. Surprisingly for a major depot, no British prisoner has left an account of the place. In December 1813, with many Allied Armies marching towards the French border, the Government in Paris decided to march all British prisoners from the border fortresses to the interior of the country to prevent them falling into the hands of the enemy. Many were marched from one depot to another including John Tregerthen Short who related how he and his comrades from Givet arrived at Cambrai in late January 1814, to join a total of

2,600 captives awaiting further marching instructions.[33] Aside from this indication that the citadel of Cambrai had extensive accommodation for prisoners of war, there is no other description of the depot.

Givet

Givet lies on both sides of the river Meuse on the border of France and Belgium. The larger portion of the town situated on the right bank was known as Great Givet, while the smaller part, or Little Givet, was on the left. The two halves were connected by a pontoon bridge whose central boats could be moved aside to allow the passage of river traffic. Above Little Givet was the fortress of Charlemont into which the first prisoners were confined. However, their numbers soon outgrew the accommodation available and they were moved out of the citadel into the horse-barracks on the outskirts of Great Givet.

The depot at Givet had a reputation of being one of the worst of the prisons, not so much because of the environment there but more to do with successive commandants being corrupt and cruel. This cruelty was alleviated somewhat by senior British naval officers being allowed to visit the depot from Verdun. John Wetherell provides a vivid account of life in the depot:

> At daylight we were roused by the Gendarmes to empty our tubs, sweep the stairs, and then all hands to muster in the yard, which was done three times a day, morn, noon, and night, by a Brigadier and one Gendarme to each passage which contained eight rooms, and each room 16 men, so that each brigadier had 128 men in his department. The sick were reported at muster in the morning so that they could be sent to the hospital directly after muster. Bread and rice or beans was served out every 4th day, 3 lb. of bread for 4 days. We also had salt at the same time. Every five days we had wood and one and half sols per day each man but we were generally under stoppages for windows, chimney sweeping, or some repairs to the prison; we also had to pay for our bedsteads and blankets, cooking pots, all out of

our sol and half per day, that is about three quarters of a cent per day, but we never received the whole, having always half a sol and sometimes more stopped daily, so that of our 5 days pay which amounted to the enormous sum of three pence halfpenny we never received more than two pence halfpenny. We had beef every two days; our rations were half a pound per day, but heads shins livers and lights were beef.[34]

While corruption in British prison depots was confined to the lower echelons of the administration, in France many of the officials involved in the care of British prisoners took their perceived share of funds sent to these men. The prisoners received their pay from their service in the British Army or Royal Navy, and a Charitable Fund was set up by the Patriotic Society to help those prisoners (i.e. civilians) who had no other source of income whilst in captivity, and to aid those prisoners who were on the march from the coast to the depots. Until such men reached the prisons they received no arrears of pay, and so any charitable relief was welcomed. All funds were sent to the prisoners via the depot of Verdun where the money was administered and distributed under the auspices of a senior officer. From 1806-07 this individual was Captain Daniel Woodriff RN, until he was exchanged. This administration of captives was put to good use upon his return to England for he was appointed Agent for Prisoners of War at Portsmouth, where he was held in high regard by both prisoners and colleagues. At Verdun Woodriff was succeeded until 1814 by Sir Thomas Lavie, a frigate captain.[35]

These officers were allowed to visit other depots in the vicinity of Verdun and to distribute funds accordingly and to listen to any complaints the British captives had. Wetherell often records how he and his compatriots had cause for complaining about the rations issued to them, and the stoppages of funds for various supplies and repairs. It was evident that the Commandant and officers of the depots were taking their share of the money allotted for feeding the prisoners. Officially the prisoners received the same rations as their opposite number in Britain, with a minimum of 1 lb bread, ½ lb meat and some salt, rice and/or pulse each day. In theory Woodriff could monitor this ration and submit reports to the British Government but in practice his reports made no difference to the food received by British prisoners. Wetherell wrote:

In the Spring we had what we called staggering bob, which might be sucked thro' a quill; this was served us for beef, and they called it veal. And in the fall they gave us Mutton, but it had the misfortune to die without the knife of the contractor or butcher and was taken off with the rot. Then it fell luckily to our lot to have a whole quarter of Mutton sometimes to each mess and sometimes the sheep were like the bullocks, for we have positively known a bullock to be killed for the prisoners that has had four heads and sixteen legs or shins and half a dozen livers and sometimes more lights and this was all served as beef.

Wetherell recorded how any complaint to the Commandant would be met with derision and even a thrashing with a cane for their temerity, it being obvious that the senior officials were making money from the contracts to supply the depot.

At both Givet and Verdun were clergymen who performed divine service for the prisoners. The former depot was fortunate in having a worthy gentleman in the shape of the Reverend Robert Wolfe, a détenu living at Verdun where he had already been instrumental in helping to organise charities and schools. The conditions at Givet had affected the men there so much that many were succumbing to illness and the remainder were demoralised. Wolfe obtained permission to go there to take charge of the prisoner's spiritual and practical well-being. In this he was a qualified success, being of sufficient character and authority to face the officials there whenever conditions needed improving. Wetherell could not speak too highly of him. Wolfe organised schools for up to 500 of the inmates at Givet; performed religious services on a regular basis; and through tact and subtle handling of men established a good working relationship with the new commandant of the depot, who was an improvement over the previous incumbent.

Longwy

Of this depot there is no account left by any prisoner who was held there. Stewart recalled passing through the place in 1811 but apart from that he left no description. Longwy became a prison depot during the latter years of the Napoleonic War. It was certainly in use in 1812 for holding Masters and Chief Mates of Merchant Vessels of greater than 80 tons, and passengers taken on such ships, and according to correspondence sent to the Admiralty from Verdun in January 1812 held no more than 1,600 men. The depot was on the border with Luxembourg, to the north of Verdun.

Mont Dauphin

Mont Dauphin, or Mont Lyon as it was also known, was the most southerly depot fifteen miles south of Briançon. It was not a large prison establishment and according to the Verdun correspondent held 900 prisoners in early 1812, mainly foreigners in British service.[36]

Sarrelibre

On the river Sarre to the north-west of Bitche stood the fortress town of Sarrelouis, whose name was changed during the Revolution to Sarrelibre. Alexander Stewart arrived there in 1805 at which time the depot was relatively small, but by 1812 it was home to over two thousand prisoners making it one of the larger French prisons. Stewart did not think much of the place:

> The building formed a square, and had some out-ground attached and enclosed with fencing, that we might have some place to walk in, as the ground within the square was too small for that purpose. Most of the rooms were very large, holding from fifty to a hundred. One of the largest was filled with Italians, another with Irish, while the rest of the prisoners mingled together

without national distinction. Most, but not all, had bedsteads with straw mattresses, and one blanket for the bedstead. Others, through deficiency of bedsteads, had their mattresses and blankets on the ground.[37]

According to Stewart the food ration was as bad as it was at any other depot, and there was no real control over the prisoner population by any of their number. Gambling and homosexuality were rife, though these were curbed to some extent by the formation of a small school.

Sedan

Sedan, midway between Givet and Verdun, was a small depot formed either late in 1811 or early 1812 for those prisoners who had attempted escape. Certainly in early 1812 there were no more than 20 such prisoners there, and none have left us with an account of the depot.

Valenciennes

The fortress of Valenciennes had one of the better reputations among the prisons as it was not as overcrowded as many of the others. In January 1812 there were 1,400 seamen and marines held there, increasing to 2,000 by 1814. This included many captured following shipwrecks along the European coastline. They were housed in a specially constructed barracks within the lower fortress, and one third of their number was allowed to go into the town to find work each day.[38]

Verdun

The town and citadel of Verdun was the major depot for British prisoners of war in France during the Napoleonic War. It became a vibrant English community, transformed by the détenus in

1803. In that year it had a population of 10,000 inhabitants, and the influx of wealthy Englishmen and women was a windfall for the townspeople. Indeed, so well did the town benefit from the prisoners, that other French towns such as Metz, petitioned the Emperor to have Englishmen on parole. However, Verdun retained the monopoly. In 1812 there were 840 captives on parole, of which about 400 were détenus.[39]

The parole prisoners signed an undertaking not to escape or cause trouble if they were allowed the liberty of the town. They were allowed to journey up to 2 leagues into the country, and had to be back in the town before the shutting of the gates at sunset. A league is about 3 miles, compare with 1 mile out of the town limits for parole prisoners in Britain.

Verdun became an English town. There were amateur theatricals, cockfights, horse racing and hunting excursions, and one witness described the English at Verdun as 'playing, dancing, singing, and drinking all day long'. Before the arrival of the English, there were 3 or 4 good shops. With the influx of wealthy Englishmen and women, the town soon prospered, with shops selling all the latest fashions in clothing and jewelry. George Call, passing through Verdun in 1810, wrote in his diary, 'Young Englishmen are much the same whether prisoners or at home, playing, driving, and shooting each other ... One might fancy oneself in London.'[40]

The prisoners formed several clubs at Verdun. Café Caron Club was the principal one, and had 120 members run in the style of a club in England. Creanges Club consisted of about 40 members, 'chiefly of the noisy, dashing young fellows of the place, – this was an extravagant institution, where high play was practiced'. There were other Clubs, such as Bishop's Palace, where women were allowed to attend with their husbands. A Mrs Concannon was the life and soul of this establishment and actively promoted the Verdun Theatricals. Many Clubs gained a reputation for excessive gambling, loose morals and resulting duels between young men who had nothing else to do. One witness wrote: .

Persons who had before never touched a card in their lives, were, from want of occupation, induced to risk half a crown, till the passion grew upon them, and then, to regain their losings, plunged deeper and deeper into difficulties. Every night some drunken guests were decoyed by girls of pleasure, placed for that purpose'.[41]

Some of the more notorious Clubs were closed by order of the Governor, General Wirion, after complaints that many French youths were taking part in all the activities on offer, and getting into serious debt.

Wirion was an unpopular Governor of Verdun who took a cut of all the gambling profits. He even imposed fines on prisoners who were late for roll call, and expected to receive fees for allowing balls and horse races to take place as well as charging commission on any funds sent to Verdun for the prisoners. So many complaints about him were sent to Paris by the English prisoners, that eventually he was ordered before a Court of Inquiry in Paris in April 1810. Before the Court could pronounce its obvious findings, Wirion put a pistol to his head and blew his brains out.

While Wirion took a cut of most financial activities, the local police were doing very well out of issuing licenses to the town's prostitutes, who looked after the younger members of the English community. Indeed, some of the more respectable English prisoners complained about being unable to walk the streets of Verdun without being accosted by some 'seductive nymph crying out – 'let us go and play some dirty tricks together'.[42] To counter these loose morals, English clergymen, resident at Verdun and at Givet, performed divine service and helped to establish schools for the younger prisoners. While the French treated sick soldiers and seamen in the prison hospitals, officers on parole employed professional doctors to care for them. Certainly at Verdun, some of the wealthier prisoners gave monthly subscriptions to care for their poorer colleagues, and to fund the schools.[43]

Britons held by other nations

The lack of frequent exchange cartels between Britain and France after 1803 meant that many Britons spent a long period in confinement. After the war many of them recorded their experiences. Prisoners taken by Holland, Spain, Denmark and the United States of America could look forward to frequent exchange cartels, resulting in very short periods of captivity. These men did not experience a period of captivity that they felt necessary to record in detail later, and so detailed accounts of prisons in these countries are non-existent.

Denmark found it relatively easy to exchange prisoners with the British garrison on the island of Anholt in the Kattegat sea, so most prisoners were held in Copenhagen. Officers were held on parole at Wibourg while seamen were confined at Holstebro and Ringkiobing on the Jutland Peninsula. Conditions were generally poor, with all prisoners short of clothes and fuel, and the food ration consisting of seven pounds of black rye bread issued every fifth day, sour milk, boiled pease and once a week a few ounces of meat or bacon. The officers at Wibourg complained to the Transport Board of the 'ill usage and insults which they daily experience from the inhabitants'.[44]

America took 15,508 British prisoners of war during the period 1812–1815.[45] They were held at Salem, Pittsfield and Worcester, Massachusetts; Schenecteday, New York; Providence, Rhode Island; Wilmington, Delaware; Annapolis, Maryland; Savannah, Georgia and New Orleans, Louisiana.[46] British soldiers captured by the Americans did not experience a long confinement, as regular exchanges took place in Canada and the West Indies; while officers of the Canadian Militia were frequently sent home on parole until exchanged. Generally Britons held in America were well-treated, but events could on occasion result in recrimination and suffering on both sides, as will be related in the chapter on prisoner politics.

Notes

[1] Stewart, Alexander. *The Life of Alexander Stewart: Prisoner of Napoleon and Preacher of the Gospel* (London, 1948), p.21.

[2] ibid., p.21.

[3] McKibbin, Michael A. 'Citizens of Liberty, Agents of Tyranny: The

Dual Perception of Allied Prisoners of War During the French Revolution', in Consortium on Revolutionary Europe 1750–1850: Selected Papers (Florida State University, 1996), p.114–115.

4   ibid., p.119.

5   TNA:PRO ADM103/474. British released from France 1793–95.

6   TNA:PRO ADM103/478. British released from France 1799.

7   TNA:PRO ADM103/481. British released from Spain 1798–1807.

8   Alger, John Goldworth. *Napoleon's British Visitors and Captives 1801–1815* (London 1904), p.14–15.

9   John Bromley was actually a French gentleman, Monsieur de Tromelin, who had escaped from France in 1795, thereafter being employed on special missions on behalf of the British Government and French Royalists in exile. His presence on board the *Diamond* was part of this employment, but when Sir Sidney invited him to take part in the cutting out expedition against *Le Vengeur*, he felt honour-bound to accept. When this adventure failed it was certain that de Tromelin would have been executed had his identity been discovered. Sir Sidney therefore passed him off as his servant, John Bromley. Shankland, Peter. *Beware Of Heroes: Admiral Sir Sidney Smith's War against Napoleon* (London 1975), p.9–10.

10 ibid., p.11–23.

11 Alger, p.23–114.

12 Lewis, Michael. *Napoleon and His British Captives* (London 1962), p.26–27.

13 Alger, p.178.

14 Lewis, p.294-308.

15 Turner, G.A. (Editor) *The Diary of Peter Bussell 1806–1814* (London 1931), p.1–2. The *Cracker*, gun brig, retook the *Dove* in March 1806, while *Les Deux Frères* fell victim to the war on 29 December of the same year when she was taken by HM Sloop *Spitfire*. Ibid., p.214–215.

16 Hoffman, Frederick. *A Sailor of King George: The Journals of Captain Frederick Hoffman RN, 1793–1814* (London 1999), pviii.

17 ibid., p.164.

18 Forester, C.S. (Editor). *The Adventures of John Wetherell* (London 1994), p.92–94.

19 Boothby, Charles. *A Prisoner of France* (London 1898), p.55–60.

20 Turner, p.5–6.

21 Boothby, p.152.

22 Brett-James, Antony (Editor), *Escape from the French: Captain Hewson's Narrative (1803–1809)* (Webb & Bower, Exeter, Devon, 1981), p.39–40.

23 Turner, p.28.

24 TNA:PRO ADM103/478.

25 TNA:PRO ADM 30/63/15. Pay Lists for the Depot of Arras June 1806.

26 Stewart, p.79.

27 Lewis, p.156–157.

28 Turner, p.106–107.

29 Brett James, p.114–118.

30 Fraser, Edward. *Napoleon The Gaoler* (London 1914), p.91–92.

31 Stewart, p.62–63.

32 Hain, Edward. *Prisoners of War in France from 1804 to 1814; Being the Adventures of John Tregerthen Short and Thomas Williams* (London 1914), p.114–115.

33 Hain, p.47.

34 Wetherell, p.137.

35 TNA:PRO WO1/915. Exchange of French Prisoners of War 1810 and 1812.

36 TNA:PRO WO1/915. Correspondence from Verdun to Admiralty, 7 January 1812.

37 Stewart, p.26.

38 TNA:PRO ADM30/63/14. List of seamen and marines at the Depot of Valenciennes 1806 and Lewis, p.150–151.

39 TNA:PRO WO1/915.

40 Alger, p.196–197.

41 Fraser, p.40–43.

42 Lewis, p.125–134.

43 TNA:PRO WO1/915.

44 TNA:PRO ADM 1/3757. 16 November 1808.

45 TNA:PRO ADM103/466. List of British prisoners of war captured by the United States during the War of 1812.

46 TNA:PRO ADM98/292. Correspondence to British Agent in USA 1812–14.

CHAPTER 9

Their Odious Calumnies

'Jenner! Ah, we can refuse nothing to that man' exclaimed Napoleon as the Empress Josephine drew his attention to a letter from Edward Jenner, the proponent of vaccination against smallpox.

The name of Edward Jenner was well known throughout the civilised world as he had performed experiments on the value of vaccination with cowpox to protect against the more serious smallpox, which ravaged the population of Europe at that time. Through his work he was universally admired and respected, and many countries adopted his method of protection against the disease. Napoleon, who had an interest in promoting scientific progress and achievement, encouraged the adoption of vaccination in France. Jenner's name was legendary and guaranteed to arouse interest and respect. So renowned was he that Jenner could correspond with his scientific counterparts in Europe throughout the war, and write to prominent people on behalf of his friends who happened to be captives detained in France and Spain.

Edward Jenner wrote to the Central Committee of Vaccination in Paris, attempting to secure the release of two détenus, namely, Dr. Wickham and William Thomas Williams. The Committee explained that they did not have the power to influence his request, but suggested that he avail himself of his great celebrity in France and appeal directly to the Emperor. Accordingly, in February 1805 Jenner petitioned Napoleon directly:

Sire,
  Having by the blessings of Providence made a discovery of which all nations acknowledge the beneficial effects, I presume

upon that plea alone, with great deference, to request a favour from Your Imperial Majesty, who early appreciated the importance of vaccination and encouraged its propagation, and who is universally admitted to be the patron of the arts.

My humble request is that your Imperial Majesty will graciously permit two of my friends, both men of science and literature, to return to England. One, Mr William Thomas Williams, residing at Nancy; the other, Dr. Wickham, at present at Geneva. Should Your Imperial Majesty be pleased to listen to the prayer of my petition you will impress my mind with sentiments of gratitude never to be effaced.[1]

So while the Governments of Britain and her enemies dealt with the majority of business relating to prisoner of war politics and exchange, individuals could play their part as well.

The treatment of prisoners would affect exchange cartels being agreed as allegations of mistreatment could delay such negotiations for many months. The matter of who paid for prisoners of war was also a source of resentment and could further delay exchange. This often-delicate business was hampered by vitriolic outbursts on the subject by the Press on both sides of the Channel. During the early years of the war with Revolutionary France, the small numbers of prisoners taken were usually exchanged within eighteen months to two years after capture, which was relatively rapid compared with the time it took later in the conflict. Although French prisoners were confined for only a brief period, and they often declared they were better fed and accommodated in the war prisons compared with service under the Revolutionary Government, this did not stop many fabricated stories about their harsh treatment being promulgated in France. So many stories were being circulated, that the French Directory obtained permission to send one Monsieur Vochez to Britain to investigate the truth of the matter.

Vochez was given free access to the Land Prisons and prison ships during 1797, and it was proved to him that out of an average total of 4,500 prisoners of war on board the Portsmouth hulks, only six had died during the preceding quarter. He expressed himself convinced that prisoners were humanely treated, and promised to report to the French government the 'gross misrepresentations that had been made to him'.[2] This however, did not prevent the Directory from continuing to make prisoners the subject of political statements. This was exacerbated by the argument over who should pay for prisoners of war.

During the American Revolution France and Britain had attempted to regulate the treatment and exchange of prisoners. It became accepted practice that each side should reimburse the other for holding their nationals captive. Therefore, France would pay Britain funds to cover the cost of holding Frenchmen in the British Isles, and vice versa. If funds could not be transferred during hostilities, then settlement would be made on the conclusion of peace. The Revolutionary conflict resulted in France having no gold reserves with which to pay Britain for the upkeep of French captives so the cost would have to be met by the government in London. Placing prisoners of war in the care of a branch of the Admiralty meant that such captives were fed with similar rations to that of a seaman in the Royal Navy. Regular food, clothing and bedding, plus immediate medical attention if he required it, meant that a French, Dutch or Spanish prisoner of war was often better off in captivity than when he was serving his country. In Britain, he was still fed and clothed even if poor harvests and high taxes resulted in the local populace starving. However, no government is going to admit that its people are better off in the prisons of its enemies, and so throughout the 1790s the French newspapers published 'frequent ridiculous tirades' on the subject. *The Times* took every opportunity to counter these outbursts, reporting on 8 January 1798:

...and yet the Directory dares to state officially in the face of Europe that the Cabinet of St. James has resolved to withdraw all means of subsistence from 22,000 Republican prisoners in England, and has shut them up in dungeons, as if such a measure, supposing it even to be true, could have any other object than to force the French Government to provide for the sustenance of the French prisoners in this country in the same manner as our Government does with respect to the English prisoners in France.[3]

The problem as far as the French Government was concerned was that more gold would be paid to Britain for the upkeep of the many thousands of Frenchmen in England, than the British Government would pay for the far lower number of Britons held in France. Lack of resolution of this matter would in its turn delay exchange of prisoners between the two countries. It was thus in the interests of the Directory to resolve the matter, which they did in February 1798. They announced that they would undertake the total subsistence of French prisoners of war in England, and by this they meant provisions, clothing, medical attendance and to make good all depredations by the captives. Britain would, so the Government hoped, escape any further diatribes on the subject from the French and thus be able to exchange captives on a more regular basis. *The Times* wrote a triumphant and gloating report in which it stated that:

> The firm conduct of our Government in refusing any longer to make advances for the maintenance of French prisoners, has had the good effect of obliging the French Directory to come forward with the necessary supplies, and as the French agents have now the full management of this concern, we will no longer be subject to their odious calumnies against the humanity of this country.[4]

The Directory was having trouble raising funds through loans and taxation to continue the war, and so once they took over the task of provisioning their countrymen in England, they immediately reduced the daily rations by one quarter. Apart from the prisoners expressing their irritation and annoyance with their own Government, this increased the invective published by continental newspapers on the subject, portraying the reduction as symptomatic of the British Government's treatment of Frenchmen who had had the misfortune to be made captive!

Matters changed with the replacement of the Directory with the Consulate in November 1799, comprising three consuls, the dominant of whom was Napoleon Bonaparte. At this stage of the prisoner of war story, Napoleon Bonaparte came to play a leading role, one that was to often hinder the fortunes of captives on both sides. Once he became ruler of France, either as First

Consul or later as Emperor, he busied himself with every detail of government, attempting to control the fortunes of France (and of Europe) without recourse to compromise. This was very evident in his dealings with Britain over prisoners of war.

On 7 December 1799, the British Agent in Paris, Captain Cotes, was informed that from 1 January 1800 'the French Government would take charge of the English prisoners in France ... and that the English were to provide for the French prisoners in England'. There was no negotiation over this and 'that such were the orders of the Consuls'. Cotes was given no time to consult with his superiors, and was instructed to liaise with a M. Bonjour over the details.[5]

This caused problems for the Transport Board, as contracts for supplying the prisoners had recently been handed to the French government, and there would be unnecessary delays and possible suffering while new contracts were put in place. This was conveyed to the French, who replied that the Consuls had investigated the arrangement of the French supplying their nationals in England and the English looking after their own people in France, and had declared it irregular! They had made their decision and this was to be implemented.[6] There is no doubt that this decision did cause suffering amongst French prisoners in England. The Board sent numerous letters to Baron Otto regarding problems encountered in supplying French prisoners with clothing and bedding. With the termination of contracts with English merchants, and transfer of the responsibility for these items to the French government, there was a delay in getting supplies to the depots.

Throughout May 1800 there was much correspondence with Otto relating to deficiencies of clothing at the depots of Liverpool, Portchester Castle and Norman Cross. The Board also complained of the serious problem of French prisoners at Norman Cross acting as unofficial merchants within the depot and purchasing food and clothing from their fellow captives, and then selling it back to them at an inflated rate. These 'merchants' also purchased hammocks and rented them back to the unfortunate prisoners at ½d per night. The prisoners themselves were exacerbating the shortage of clothing and bedding.[7] The situation became so bad that the Board received a letter from some prisoners at Portchester on the subject:

Sir,

You have often, and so generously, given us proofs of your feelings for our unfortunate situation, that we believe we may implore through you, a relief the more urgent as it becomes indispensable. It cannot be necessary to lay before you a minute picture of the state of nakedness to which we are reduced, a state the more deplorable, as our debilitated bodies are the more susceptible of the severity of the season, and the want or repose.

The many sufferings we endure from the total want of clothing, and other necessaries of this kind, are already so well known to you, that there can be no difficulty in your interceding in our favour. We cannot doubt of your complying with our expectation in this respect, or, at least, that you will contribute every means in your power to alleviate the misfortunes of prisoners sinking under the weight of such a calamity.[8]

This letter was signed by a considerable number of prisoners, and was conveyed to Otto. He replied by lamenting the 'deplorable situation to which these unfortunate men are reduced', but emphasised that he had received no authority or instruction from his own government to undertake any expenditure on the matter. His letter also contained a new reason for not supplying French prisoners in England:

I must nevertheless observe to you, that the French Government, having undertaken to clothe all the prisoners whom the chance of war had thrown into its hands, had reason to expect a reciprocal attention on the part of Great Britain; and although the prisoners now detained in France are not exactly English, nevertheless they belong to powers in alliance with His Majesty.[9]

With Britain acquiring more prisoners of war than France, and even if they were all exchanged man for man, rank for rank, there would still be many thousands held in the war prisons of the country. The Consuls of the Republic knew this and declared that Britain's allies should be included in any exchange proposals for Frenchmen in England. Inclusion of Britain's allies would be a recurring theme in all exchange negotiations until 1814.

The basis for this in 1799–1800, as far as the French were concerned, was that British gold paid for Austria, Russia and many of the German states to remain in the war against France, and thus Britain should pay for the exchange of continental prisoners for Frenchmen. This was not a concept that the British Government would initially consider. However, in 1799 an Anglo-Russian force landed in Holland and captured the Batavian fleet, but was forced to withdraw due to lack of resources and poor inter-allied co-operation. The British agreed to include the Russians taken captive by the French in exchange for French and Dutch taken by the allies, arranging for vessels to sail under a flag of truce to Flushing for the reception of the British and Russian captives.[10]

The acrimonious exchanges on the subject continued throughout 1800 with Otto citing the desperate plight of Frenchmen in places such as Liverpool and Portchester Castle, while at the same time emphasising that 'in France, on the contrary, the English, the Russians, and the Austrians, who have fallen into our hands, not only receive a wholesome and plentiful subsistence, but are clothed at the expense of the Republic, and enjoy a degree of liberty which the French prisoners are not allowed in this country'. He went on to state that many prisoners in France had received permission to leave their prison depot to carry on different trades, and 'to earn by the fruits of their labour even more than would have provided them with a comfortable support'.[11] What he did not explain was that the male population of France had been conscripted to fight the war, thus depleting the countryside of a male workforce. Foreign captives working in the countryside were inadvertently helping the French war effort, albeit improving their own situation at the same time.

Reports from the depots were drawing public attention to the distressed state of many of the prisoners in Britain, and so the Transport Board made the decision to clothe and feed the French prisoners of war at British expense. However, this did not immediately stop prominent people in England from complaining to the Admiralty about the conditions experienced by the prisoners, such complaints coming to the notice of the French government. On 30 December 1800 a meeting was held at the Council House in Bristol, at which twenty-three people were present, including

Ambrose Searle and Dr James Johnston from the Transport Office, the Mayor of Bristol and various Aldermen, Lt.General Rook and a number of officers from the Militia, plus the butchers supplying Stapleton Prison. This gathering was in response to a letter sent to the Mayor by Thomas Batchelor and Thomas Andrews, who had visited the depot and had been shocked at the nakedness of the prisoners and the appalling condition of the rations. Their complaint was examined in detail, with a number of witnesses being called. The allegations were disproved, and the reasons for any naked prisoners explained, these being that the French had refused to supply provisions for prisoners in England and that many of the prisoners lost their food and clothing through gambling, with which even Baron Otto had been forced to concur.[12]

While the plight of French prisoners was a constant topic of discussion between the Board and the French Agent, other events resulted in complaints being sent to the French Government. In 1799 the Admiralty discovered that the French had been coercing Irish prisoners of war to join the French Navy at Orleans for an expedition to Ireland; a practice unacceptable to the British.[13] Five Masters of captured British merchantmen were exchanged in 1800, and on their return to England they swore before a magistrate that they had been badly treated whilst in captivity in France. They stated that they and their crews had been placed in the cachot and given no food for the first 24 hours; the rooms they were in were damp and dirty with no beds; and that an ill prisoner had not received any medical attention.[14]

The incarceration of Sir Sydney Smith was cause for concern, with even King George III putting pressure on the Transport Board to speed up the exchange process and use the cartel negotiations to improve Sir Sydney's treatment.[15] To put pressure on the French, the Board ordered that all French officers on parole in Britain be placed into strict confinement until 'it appears that Sir Sydney Smith experiences the indulgences usually granted to officers who have been captured'.[16] Sir Sydney resolved the issue himself by escaping.

Continual complaints of the treatment of prisoners on both sides of the Channel delayed but did not stop exchange cartels taking place. While the Dutch had also refused to pay for their nationals in British prisons in 1799, they had a better working relationship with the British regarding exchange. As early as 1796 they had released Captain Stap, commander of His Majesty's sloop *Scourge*, on parole to return to England with a proposal from the Dutch government respecting a reciprocal exchange of prisoners between the two countries, according to the standard exchange system. This proposal was readily agreed to by the Admiralty. All prisoners were exchanged according to an agreement between Britain and France in 1780, which was used as the basis for exchange from 1793 onwards between all belligerent nations. This table of exchange was published again in 1798 to explain how the system worked.

Rates of exchange of prisoners of war

Naval Rank	Army Rank	Common Men
Admiral	Field Marshal	60
Vice-Admiral	General	40
Rear-Admiral	Lieutenant-General	30
Commodore	Major-General	20
Post Captain	Brigadier-General	15
Master & Commander	Colonel	8
Lieutenant	Captain	6
Lieutenant/ Midshipman*	Lieutenant	4
Midshipman		
Master of a Merchant Vessel		
Captain of a Privateer	Ensign	3
Mates	Non-commissioned	
Petty Officers	Officers down to rank of Corporal	2
Seamen	Soldier	1

* Lieutenants, when all the French shall be exchanged, and in default of English Lieutenants, Midshipmen.[17]

The table gave the equivalent army and navy ranks, with their respective worth in common men. Prisoners could be exchanged man for man, rank for rank, or if insufficient of a particular rank was available; the numbers could be made up of lesser ranks using the common men equivalent. Thus Captain James Alms RN was exchanged for Jean Jacques Lee, a French Brigadier General, in May 1800, while privateer Captain Poupeville was exchanged for Thomas Lloyd, Mate of a merchant vessel and John Spooner, a Private soldier.[18]

Despite the continual arguments over the treatment of British and French prisoners, exchanges did take place until the Peace of Amiens, when all prisoners were released. After 1803 the exchange system between Britain and France broke down, so that only 17,607 prisoners from a total of 122,440 were exchanged or sent home as invalids from Britain between 1803 and 1814. This total included Spanish, Danes and Americans so only a relatively few Frenchmen were released from captivity. The reasons for this are evident from the start of the conflict.

The British attacked French colonies overseas as soon as the war began. In June 1803 the French garrisons of St. Lucia and Tobago were taken, but sent home to France on parole, the intention being that they should not serve until having been exchanged for British prisoners. The French government would not acknowledge this. October saw 177 men of the French garrison at Pondicherry returned to France on parole, while on 30 November 1803 the French garrison on St. Domingo was taken into captivity, but on this occasion these prisoners were transported to the prisons in Britain. This was in retaliation for the detention of nearly 700 British civilians who had been in France on the outbreak of war, despite the British allowing 526 French nationals to return home, expecting a reciprocal arrangement. Realising that the predominance of the Royal Navy would result in many more Frenchmen being taken than Britons, the Minister of Marine in Paris demanded that all prisoners taken in French colonies should be released on parole. The détenus in France were the sticking point as far as the government in London was concerned. These men and women had been detained in 'flagrant violation of those laws and customs by which civilised nations have so long been guided' and were to be a factor influencing future exchange negotiations.

Other events caused problems. The *Matilda*, a British cartel vessel taking French prisoners under a flag of truce for Morlaix, was fired upon. At the same time, Lieutenant Dillon of HMS *Africaine* was sent into the Dutch port of Helvoet under a flag of truce to negotiate a local prisoner exchange. He was allowed to depart by the Batavian Navy, but on his way out of port was taken by a French armed boat stationed there. Captain Wright of HM Sloop *Vincess* was taken off the coast of Brittany, but instead of being regarded as a prisoner of war was sent to the Temple Prison in Paris and repeatedly interrogated before a Court of Justice. During the early months of the war the British government had suggested two exchange cartels with France, but the stumbling block had been the Hanoverian prisoners of war in the hands of the French Army. When Hanover was overrun, the French government wanted to offset the Hanoverian soldiers taken captive against Frenchmen in England, their reasoning being that as King George III was Elector of Hanover these soldiers were British subjects. That was not the case as the government in London emphasised, refusing to include these men in exchange negotiations despite the fact that many of them had escaped to Britain where they were being formed into the King's German Legion.[19]

The war dragged on with many Frenchmen and Britons languishing in prisons with only the hope of exchange to comfort them. The war in the Iberian Peninsula in 1809 gave impetus to a fresh exchange cartel proposal from the French, who realised that many French soldiers and sailors were in British hands with no hope of release. The Transport Board was receptive to the idea, as by this time the country was also at war with Denmark, and captives were arriving in the country in their thousands. The exchange proposal of 22 November 1809 was given serious consideration by the British government, who relented on the idea of including the Hanoverian troops captured in 1803 in the proposals. They also agreed to release the French taken on St. Domingo, and had no objection to the détenus being exchanged for soldiers and seamen. The Admiralty were well aware of the cost of housing many thousands of prisoners for whom there

Proposed rate of exchange for Détenus (1810)

Détenus	Military/Naval Rank
Peer's sons and Privy Counsellors	Colonel or Post Captain
Baronets and Knights	Field Officers and Commanders
Gentlemen holding no distinction of rank	Captains in the Army Lieutenants of Ships of War
Tradesmen	Subalterns
Servants and all others detained	Private soldiers and sailors

was no hope of release, as by early 1810 there were 40,843 French in Britain, with the Peninsula campaign promising to be a major source of further captives.

Accordingly, in April 1810 Mr Colin Alexander MacKenzie was sent to Morlaix to arrange an exchange cartel with the French government, using these concessions and with a proposal for the détenus.

He was also instructed to offer to liberate without exchange 411 fishermen taken under the particular circumstance of having a soldier in each boat, but it was suggested that he reserve this as an extra card to play during the negotiations.

As soon as discussions began the negotiations looked doomed to failure. MacKenzie was not allowed to move from Morlaix, corresponding with the Minister of Marine in Paris who sent all correspondence to Napoleon for ratification, regardless of whether the Emperor was in France or touring his empire. After arguments about the Hanoverians, the détenus and the garrison of St. Domingo, the French demanded that all Spanish taken prisoner serving alongside the British in the Peninsula should be included in exchange for French in England. Initially the Admiralty would not consider such a proposal, maintaining that these men were a matter for the Spanish government.[20] The French then complained about the treatment of prisoners of war in Britain and their confinement on board ships. The response was that prison ships were a necessity as there were no large citadels available in Britain as there were in France, and further land depots were being built to alleviate the pressure. In 1810 there was accommodation on land for 30,000 men, but if regular exchanges took place then the pressure on the system would be reduced. The French were told that there was no difference in treatment of prisoners on land or in ships.[21]

To speed up the process, the Admiralty relented on the matter of Spanish prisoners, and proposed that prisoners be exchanged in batches of 1,000 at a time. Once all the British prisoners were home, the remaining French would be exchanged for Spaniards who would be sent directly to Spain, not to England. The valid point was also made that Britain would have to consult with Spain regarding Spanish prisoners in France. France would not make distinctions as to rank including the détenus and insisted that the Spanish be sent to England. A tentative 'Convention for the Exchange of Prisoners' was proposed for 15 June 1810, but the sticking point was where the Spanish would be sent. MacKenzie then received a demand from Paris that all French prisoners in Britain should be released before their British counterparts across the Channel! [22]

MacKenzie was still at Morlaix in September, waiting for fresh demands from Paris. The French government was very slow in responding to any proposals, and when they did reply it was evident that the Emperor was the driving force behind any new demands. The Admiralty began consultations with the Spanish authorities over the proposed cartel, and on 8 October MacKenzie reported that the French demanded that the Royal Navy be responsible for the conveyance of Spaniards from France. The Admiralty could not accept this proposal as they had no ships that could be diverted to the transport of Spanish prisoners. With no agreement being reached, the proposals fell down and many thousands of British and French prisoners languished in the depots until the war ended in 1814.[23] From 1810 news of the failure of exchange negotiations caused an increase in parole violations by French held in England.

Many on both sides of the Channel made political propaganda of these failed negotiations. By October 1810 the prison population in Britain had increased dramatically and the Board compiled lists of the captives in their care to refute any allegations made in Parliament that nothing was being done to alleviate the pressure on the war prison system, and to show that much was done to maintain the health of these men.

Return of prisoners of war 24 October 1810 [24]

	Total	Sick	Convalescent	Wounds
French				
In confinement	48,333}	450	283	180
On parole	3,021}			
Danish				
In confinement	2,056}	16	4	0
On parole	39}			
Russian				
In confinement	342}	0	0	0
On parole	15}			
Dutch				
In confinement	82}	2	0	0
On parole	20}			
	53,908	468	287	180

The Admiralty was at pains to point out that from the outbreak of war in 1803 until 30 July 1811, a total of 10,467 French invalids had been released from England. During the same period only 13 invalid Britons had been released from France, and the French did not automatically send such men home as was the case in Britain.[25] The only captives automatically sent home from France were women and children.

Many prominent men took an interest in prisoners of war. Sir Samuel Whitbread (the prominent brewer and Member of Parliament) received many requests from both British and French prisoners to use his influence on their behalf. He received much correspondence after 1810 when British prisoners in France heard of the exchange negotiations, and wrote many letters to the Admiralty to endeavour to assist where he could. He was a particular friend to the Transport Board when he defended that office in the Commons in the summer of 1811. Admiral Lord Thomas Cochrane, maverick naval officer, hero to the British public, and a constant thorn in the side of not only the French naval authorities but the Admiralty as well, attacked the Government over the treatment of prisoners of war. He had visited Dartmoor Prison and the hulks at Plymouth without any communication with the Transport Board, and had used his rank to intimidate the naval staff into allowing him access to the depots. Cochrane painted a deplorable picture of the prison at Dartmoor, alleging that the prisoners there were subject to inhumane treatment at the hands of the Board. Sir Rupert George sent Whitbread much information with which the latter successfully defended the Board's administration of prisoners of war. Sir Rupert informed Whitbread that he was 'grateful for your polite and liberal conduct in Parliament'. [26]

Cochrane's attack was minor however, compared with that published in the *Statesman* in March 1812. Correspondence was published from 'Honestus', in which the plight of Britons in France was described, their long incarceration being the fault of the Transport Office. Attacking the administration of the prison system in a newspaper was one thing, but the writer took it too far, saying that the Transport Office handled more than three million pounds per annum for the care of prisoners but that 'a large part is not converted to the intended purpose, but is of clear benefit to the Commissioners and their employers'. The writer went on to accuse the Commissioners of withholding remittances for the prisoners and 'employing it in stock-jobbing'; of gaining from the property of dead prisoners; and from profiting from the food and clothing contracts at each depot. 'Honestus' declared that 'the real reason for bringing so many prisoners into the country is not military, but to enrich themselves [i.e. the Government]'.

The Transport Office sought legal advice from the Attorney-General who pronounced it to be 'a most scandalous libel and ought to be prosecuted'. Proceeding were brought against the editor of the *Statesman*, Mr Lovel, who was found guilty of libel, fined £500, imprisoned in Newgate for eighteen months and had to find security for future good behaviour, himself in £1000 and two sureties of £500 each. Lovel in his defence claimed the letter was published without his knowledge and he had no idea who the author was! There was some suggestion later that 'Honestus' was in fact an ex-employee of the Transport Office who had been dismissed for irregular conduct over prisoner affairs.[27, 28]

While French prisoners realised that their prospect of exchange was minimal, this was not the case with other nationalities. The British and Dutch exchanged prisoners on a regular basis in the 1790s, with statements of exchange being sent to each government so that the process would proceed without interruption. This ensured that Dutch prisoners were returned home after no more than a year in confinement. Between 1 January 1796 and 14 March 1798 a total of 732 British prisoners had been exchanged with the Batavian Republic, with many of them being delivered to the British Consuls in Denmark and Norway.[29] Mr Van Dedam was the Dutch official allowed to reside in England and visit the depots, and in January 1800 he assisted in the exchange of 132 Dutch officers who were on parole in Holland for 623 common men held in that country. The officers were thus released from their parole obligations.[30] This working approach continued until Holland became a Napoleonic kingdom in 1806.

The Spanish Agent, Manuel De La Torre, had a cordial relationship with the Admiralty from his appointment in November 1796 through to his country becoming an ally of Britain in 1808. Spanish prisoners benefited from this relationship as he was able to get many of them simply released, rather than waiting for one of the many exchange cartels he negotiated with the government. In January 1797 he arranged for the release of Juan Munn, Pedro Munn and Jayme Casabel who were Spaniards serving in the Royal Navy. On the outbreak of war he used his influence at the Admiralty to obtain their release, as they were serving before hostilities began, and they were sent home complete with wages and prize money owing to them.[31] De La Torre was instrumental in arranging a number of exchange cartels, and assisting in the exchange of Spanish and British prisoners in the Americas. He was again Agent in London in 1805, and the following year he was informed that some British prisoners of war had escaped in the Spanish vessel *Barbarossa* at Santander. The Agent requested that this vessel be restored to its rightful owners, which was readily agreed to.[32] The Board had provided him with a glowing testimonial in May 1799:

...and we are happy in having such an opportunity of testifying our sense of the uniform propriety of your conduct in all the business that has passed under our notice relative to your situation as Agent for the Spanish prisoners in this country.[33]

Spanish prisoners held in Britain were fortunate to have such a man looking after their affairs.

Danish prisoners were rapidly exchanged. The strong British naval presence in the Baltic allowed for frequent exchange, and the Board was willing to send Danes in Britain home in exchange for British prisoners released directly to the Royal Navy in the Baltic. As long as accurate records were kept and submitted to the Transport Office, this was seen as a rapid method of exchanging prisoners.[34]

Certainly after 1811 the Board realised that once a French prisoner arrived in Britain or a Briton arrived in France, the chances of him being exchanged were non-existent. The Peninsula campaign afforded them a means of exchanging prisoners very shortly after capture, albeit on a small scale. The British and French in Spain often arranged local prisoner exchanges, but these invariably involved only officers, the rank and file being sent to the prison depots. Wellington was encouraged to exchange captives in this way, again as long as accurate records were submitted to the Board in London. Lord Wellington arranged for the exchange of Major Emain Le Gentil, who was on parole in England, for Major O'Hara of the 1st Portuguese Regiment who was being held by the French in Spain. This was readily agreed to by the Transport Office.[35] Most such exchanges took place via the outposts of the two armies.

When the United States of America declared war on Britain in 1812, the Transport Office had sixteen years experience of handling prisoners of war in a fair and humane manner, and was able to arrive at a rapid agreement with the American government over the exchange of captives. This worked very well in the Americas, where many local exchanges took place either around the Great Lakes or in the West Indies, with most American prisoners being held at Halifax, Nova Scotia; Bridgetown, Barbados; and Kingston, Jamaica. However, one aspect of the war that the

Americans found distasteful and inhumane was the transport of American captives across the Atlantic to reside in the depots of Britain. If they were held in the Americas their chance of exchange was greater than if they were transported thousands of miles across the ocean.

The British and American governments were happy to agree to all non-combatants being released on the first available cartel, these being surgeons, surgeon's mates, pursers, secretaries, chaplains, schoolmasters, surgeons of privateers, surgeons and surgeon's mates of merchant vessels, passengers, plus all other men not engaged in naval and military service of the enemy and not being sea-faring persons. All women and girls plus all boys under 12 years of age were also released immediately '...conformable to the usage and practice of the most civilised nations during war'. They also agreed that:

> ...all prisoners on both sides not being officers who have wounds, age or infirmities, are rendered incapable of further service ... shall be forthwith returned to their respective countries without regard to their numbers or equality of exchange.

This was the general agreement made with European belligerents throughout the wars. Ensuring that some men plus women and children were sent home relieved pressure on an already overcrowded prison system in Britain.

The conduct of cartel vessels used to transport prisoners home was strictly regulated. Such vessels were merchant ships hired for the task and given passports and flags of truce. Their armament consisted of one signal gun and a guard of no more than one non-commissioned officer and six men. A white flag was to be flown at the fore-top masthead, and on British vessels the British ensign was to be flown on the gaff while the American ensign would be at the main topmast head. On American ships the position of the flags was reversed. As long as regular lists were sent by each government of prisoners sent and received in exchange, this system worked well.[36]

Britain allowed an Agent from each of her enemies to reside in England and liaise with the Transport office over matters pertaining to captives. They were allowed full access to their nationals, and were able raise any requests or problems with the Board, if they felt the Agent at the depot was not dealing with the matter. These Agents, Baron Louis Guillaume Otto for France and Manuel De La Torre for Spain, did much to help their fellow nationals, and when possible arranged exchange cartels. The United States government sent Reuben Beasley to London to represent American prisoner of war interests. The American prisoners he was supposed to assist did not have a very high opinion of him. They 'accused him of an unfeeling neglect, and disregard to their pressing wants' and it was said that 'he never visited them but once [at Dartmoor], and when he did, he kept his distance from the main body of prisoners'.[37]

Events involving American prisoners did have repercussions for captives on both sides, culminating in the infamous Dartmoor Massacre in 1815. The first grievance the Americans expressed was the transport of many of their number across the Atlantic in transport ships where conditions were poor, especially for men who had never been to sea before. If local exchanges could not be arranged for everyone, and if the prisons in Canada and the West Indies were full, then the Transport Board considered the only option was to hold these men in Britain. An American held at Halifax, Nova Scotia, could expect to be exchanged after three months captivity. Once in England however, such men would likely be held for the duration of the conflict.[38]

In the North American theatre both sides made use of Indians as scouts and to harass the enemy. In January 1813 a force of Americans had surrendered to the British and their Indian allies near Frenchtown on the Raisin River. After the surrender about 80 American wounded were quartered in the town, guarded by a few British troops and some Indians. Having found a hoard of whiskey, the natives rampaged through the town scalping and killing the Americans, of whom at least 30 died and many more were seriously wounded again. This incident sent a wave of horror and indignation through the United States, with the British being accused of being unable to protect wounded prisoners of war. Thereafter the cry 'Remember the Raisin' became a rallying cry for Americans, and instilled in Americans an element of mistrust regarding the treatment of prisoners of war by the British.[39]

One of the causes of the War of 1812 had been the impressment by the Royal Navy of men they considered British citizens. At the Battle of Queenston in 1812 the British captured a number of American soldiers, including twenty-three Irishmen who had been born in the British Isles and had lived in the United States for many years. These men were sent to England to be placed on trial for treason despite American protestations. In retaliation the President ordered twenty-three British soldiers placed into close confinement as hostages for the safety of the twenty-three Americans. The governor-general of Canada, Sir George Prevost, then ordered forty-six American officers confined and threatened to execute two Americans for every British soldier executed. The Americans responded by confining all British officers in their hands, with the British responding by doing the same to all American officers they held, so that by early 1814 all officers held by either side in the Americas were in close confinement, under threat of retaliatory execution. Both sides accused the other of a 'wanton and barbarous act of cruelty'. At the same time there were accusations that the Americans were attempting to coerce British prisoners into enlisting in the United States Navy.[40]

In reality, as the Americans later found out, the original twenty-three prisoners were being held no differently from other prisoners of war, with the British realising that accusing Americans prisoners of being British citizens and contemplating prosecution for treason would not help the exchange process. Certainly by the summer of 1814, good sense had prevailed on both sides and exchange cartels had resumed.[41]

However, one further incident involving prisoners of war would sour relations between the two countries.

Notes

[1] Baron, John. *The Life of Edward Jenner* (London) 1838, Volume 2 p.36–38.

² Abell p.12.

³ *The Times*, 8 January 1798.

⁴ *The Times*, 27 February 1798.

⁵ (BL) B.P.8/9. Correspondence with the French Government relative to Prisoners of War 1801. Letter No.3 James Cotes to Commissioners for the Transport Service 7 December 1799.

⁶ (BL) B.P. 8/9. Letter No.5 Niou to Dundas 15 December 1799.

⁷ (BL) B.P. 8/9. From Transport Office to Otto Letter No.10, 22 April 1800; Letter Nos. 12–14, 24–28 May 1800.

⁸ (BL) B.P. 8/9. Letter No.20 from the French Prisoners of War to Mr Holmwood, Commissary at Portchester Castle, 10 September 1800.

⁹ (BL) B.P. 8/9. Letter No.28 Commissary of the French Republic in England to Transport Office, 29 October 1800.

¹⁰ TNA:PRO WO1/908. Exchange of British and Russians for French prisoners of war 20 and 27 November 1799.

¹¹ (BL) B.P. 8/9. Letter No.28.

¹² TNA:PRO ADM105/44. Commissioners Report 30 December 1800.

¹³ TNA:PRO WO1/908. 11 April 1799.

¹⁴ (BL) B.P. 8/9. Letter No.53, 22 December 1800.

¹⁵ NMM ADM/MT/415. Transport Board Letters June 1796.

¹⁶ NMM ADM/MT/416. Transport Board Letters 24 September 1796.

¹⁷ The *Morning Chronicle* 27 September 1798. Report of State paper for the exchange of prisoners of war between Great Britain and France.

¹⁸ TNA:PRO ADM103/506. French exchanges effected 1798–1801.

¹⁹ TNA:PRO WO1/910. Exchange and care of French prisoners of war 1803–05.

²⁰ TNA:PRO WO1/915. Exchange of French prisoners of war 1810 and 1812, 2 April 1810.

²¹ ibid., 6 April 1810.

²² ibid., 15 June 1810.

²³ ibid., 8 October 1810.

²⁴ W1/2598, 24 October 1810. Whitbread Collection, Bedfordshire County Archives.

²⁵ TNA:PRO ADM105/46.

²⁶ W1/2624, 18 June 1811. Whitbread Collection.

²⁷ Abell, p.21–23.

²⁸ TNA:PRO ADM97/130.

²⁹ TNA:PRO ADM98/293. 28 March 1798.

30 ibid., 16 January 1800.

31 TNA:PRO ADM98/303. Correspondence to Spanish Agent 20 January 1797.

32 ibid., 27 March 1806.

33 ibid., 14 May 1799.

34 TNA:PRO ADM97/130. Prisoner of war escapes and exchanges, 30 June 1813.

35 TNA:PRO ADM103/614. Parole prisoners November 1813.

36 TNA:PRO ADM98/292. Correspondence to British Agent in the USA, 6 November 1813.

37 Waterhouse, p.72.

38 TNA:PRO ADM103/571. American prisoners at Halifax.

39 Latimer, Jon. *1812: War with America* (Cambridge, Massachusetts, USA) 2007, p.119–120.

40 TNA:PRO ADM98 292, 30 March 1814.

41 Hickey, Donald R. *The War of 1812: A Forgotten Conflict* (University of Illinois Press, USA) 1990, p.175–180.

CHAPTER 10

An Honourable Grave

The confinement of prisoners of war cost the British Government money. As soon as the Napoleonic Wars ended prisoners of war were shipped home as fast as transport vessels could be found for the task. Napoleon Bonaparte surrendered to the Allies on 11 April 1814, and over the next six weeks the British released French prisoners as quickly as they could, so that by 9 June a total of 47,628 Frenchmen had been embarked for France. By July there were only 1,485 French prisoners remaining in captivity at Malta, Barbados, Halifax, Bermuda and the Bahamas. Distance delayed their release.[1]

The effects and money of deceased prisoners were also returned and bills submitted to the French Government for all costs relating to the upkeep of prisoners during the wars. The French liquidated their debts for prisoners of war by the Treaty of Paris of 30 May 1814, and again by the Treaty of Paris of 20 November 1815 for those Frenchmen taken during the Waterloo campaign. However, peace was an opportunity for British merchants to submit claims to the government in Paris for the subsistence of French prisoners in 1799, when the French had agreed to pay for the upkeep of their nationals in England, entering into contracts with English merchants. Forty three of these merchants were still pursuing their claims in February 1834, expecting to be reimbursed a total of £41,996 0s. 2d for unpaid bills, including $33\frac{1}{3}$ years of interest. The Commissioners of Arbitration and Award in London were sympathetic to the debt, but were not confident that the French Government could be made to pay such a debt since the two Treaties of Paris had settled the account for prisoners of war.[2]

While French prisoners returned home in 1814, American prisoners remained confined until the following year, by which time more French were arriving to fill the prisons once more. In 1814 the war prison system was speedily run down to operate at minimal capacity for American prisoners of war, and in this capacity was able to cope with prisoners taken on the resumption of hostilities in Europe. The last prisoners taken during the Waterloo campaign finally left British shores in February 1816, thus bringing to a close the story of Napoleonic prisoners of war as far as the Admiralty was concerned. However, the legacy of these captives is with us today, with much to remind us of their sojourn in a foreign land.

The return of prisoners of war did not always go smoothly. May 1814 saw a fleet of cartel vessels sailing the Channel, a fact that the Port authorities in France were not slow to realise. The Admiralty received many complaints that the British vessels were being forced to pay exorbitant port dues on arrival in France. After complaining to the new Government in Paris this practice was stopped and the flow of ex-prisoners into France was not impeded.[3]

The most serious event occurred at Dartmoor Prison in 1815. Here American prisoners had seen their French colleagues return home the previous year. Hostilities between Great Britain and the United States officially ceased with the signing of the Treaty of Ghent on 24 December 1814. When the news reached Dartmoor in January the Americans naturally expected to be repatriated at once. Yet there was a serious shortage of shipping due to British forces being transferred home from various theatres, and Reuben Beasley could only find three vessels to repatriate American prisoners.[4]

By April 1815 there was almost a state of mutiny in the prison, worsened by shortages of food, especially bread, as the local contractors were making less frequent deliveries to the depot as many of its inmates had returned to France. The prison authorities issued biscuit in place of the bread, which the prisoners refused to accept. To alleviate the tension amongst the Americans, the Transport Board allowed any who had money to make their own way to Plymouth and purchase their own passage across the

Atlantic if they could find a merchant ship willing to take them. The majority of Americans however, remained at the depot.[5]

On 4 April a large body of prisoners rushed into the market square of the prison demanding bread instead of the issued biscuit. Fortunately a delivery of bread had recently been made and so these men were placated, returning to their barracks.

Two days later, at about 6.00pm, the guards discovered a large breach in one of the prison walls, big enough for a man to pass through, and it became evident that other attempts had been made to demolish parts of the wall. At the same time, a number of Americans had climbed over the fence erected to prevent them having contact with the sentries on the walls, and were tearing up pieces of turf, and 'wantonly pelting each other in a noisy and disorderly manner'. This incident would have been treated as the skylarking it was, had not large groups of prisoners been assembling at the various breaches in the wall. One of these openings, if developed further, would have allowed prisoners access to the guard barracks, where there was a supply of muskets. This combination of events induced the Agent Captain Shortland, to give the order to sound the alarm bell. This action was to have tragic consequences.

Many of the prisoners were in their respective barracks as the alarm sounded, and curiosity brought them out. At the same time, Shortland was informed that the chain locking the gate to the market place had been broken, and a large mass of prisoners was surging into the square. The official enquiry found no evidence that the sequence of events was premeditated, but rather that the prisoners were reacting to a number of spontaneous occurrences, either directly or simply out of curiosity.

Captain Shortland and the officers of the garrison concluded that a mass escape was being attempted. Shortland and fifty soldiers entered the market square and faced the prisoners. Both he and the surgeon, Dr. Magrath,

...endeavoured by quiet means and persuasion, to induce the prisoners to retire to their own yards, explaining to them the fatal consequences which must ensue if they refused, as the military would in that case be necessarily compelled to use force.

This had no effect upon the prisoners, and so the guard was ordered to advance and push the Americans back into their own barrack yards. This persuaded some of the prisoners to retire, but they were unable to do so due to the mass of inmates in the yard. It also had the effect of provoking jeers and insults from some of the more aggressive of the prisoners, and some soldiers later asserted that stones were thrown at them at this time.

It was at this point the firing commenced, although who actually gave the order was never established. Captain Shortland denied having done so, and this was corroborated by his officers who stated that the order was not given by them. It would appear that the soldiers opened fire spontaneously and initially over the heads of the prisoners, but on being taunted further and hit by stones, began firing into the crowd. Shortland and Lieutenant Fortye of the Militia succeeded in halting the firing by the troops in the market place. However, soldiers on the prison walls continued to fire, and some even followed the by now retreating prisoners into the barrack yards, and fired upon those Americans trying to return to their barracks. This lack of control of the militia was further emphasised by parties of soldiers who took it upon themselves to run up onto the platforms along the perimeter wall and fire down on the prisoners, even shooting at those who were going through the doors of their barracks.

Captain Shortland and the turnkeys were engaged in helping the wounded in the market place, and the only militia officers present, two lieutenants and an ensign, remained in the square with their part of the guard. It would appear that no other officers, including the senior officers of the regiment, were available in the prison that day, and it was this lack of discipline and control that resulted in what became known as *The Dartmoor Massacre*.[6]

The whole affair lasted for no more than five minutes, but resulted in seven prisoners killed, and six others so badly wounded that limbs had to be amputated. Three of these later died. Fifty other prisoners received hospital treatment, many for musket wounds to their backs. Thomas Jackson, 'shot in prison yard, 6 April 1815' was 14 years of age.[7]

The affair resulted in an enraged American Government, and an intensely embarrassed British counterpart, along with an official enquiry involving a jury of British and American officials. Captain Shortland was exonerated of any personal responsibility for the massacre, the enquiry maintaining that he was right in thinking that a mass escape was imminent, but the subsequent firing was inexcusable. The official report alluded to the lack of control of the militia by their officers, and the surprising lack of senior ranks at the prison on the day, but these criticisms were couched in very vague and mild terms! Captain Shortland continued a successful career in the Royal Navy.

The only positive result of this tragic event came at the instigation of the Foreign Secretary, Lord Castlereagh, who proposed the speedy transportation of American and British prisoners of war from both sides of the Atlantic. However, there were still Americans in Dartmoor at the end of June 1815.[8] The British Government provided pensions for the relatives of those inmates killed, and for those wounded in the affray.

From May 1809 to January 1816, 1,478 prisoners died at Dartmoor Prison, and this total included 229 Americans. When a prisoner died there was no formal funeral, nor even a basic coffin or burial shroud. The bodies were laid to rest in shallow graves on the moor outside the depot. Their story did not end there.

In 1850 the depot, having lain lying empty and derelict since 1816, was reopened as a convict prison. In 1866 the Governor, Captain W.P. Stopford, discovered that many of these bones had been uncovered by animals and the elements, and were lying exposed for all to see. He had them all exhumed and divided into two piles. There was no way of knowing the nationality of the remains, but nevertheless the two piles were re-interred in separate cemeteries outside the prison walls, each fenced in and marked with a granite pillar in memory of the French or American prisoners who ended their days there. In 1928 the National Society of the United States Daughters of 1812 subscribed to the erection of a memorial gateway to the American cemetery, inscribed 'To the glory of God and in loving memory of 218 American sailors and soldiers of the war of 1812 who died here'.[9] The exact number of deaths at the depot between 1813 and 1815 has been subject of debate, but Ron Joy, Prison Officer and historian at Dartmoor Prison, has compiled a list of 271 Americans who remain buried on the moorland outside the prison. Dartmoor Heritage Centre is situated near the prison and cares for this legacy of the depot's history.[10]

During the Napoleonic Wars these prisoners were very much a part of the British community, be they in land prisons, hulks, or on parole. It is pleasing to note that those captives who died are still very much a part of the history of a locality, and their graves are often well-maintained and regarded with some pride by local people. The story of Francois Guidon in Ashburton has already been told, but the bodies of these prisoners have been instrumental in promoting harmonious relations with erstwhile enemies elsewhere, or perhaps in placating a later generation whose conscience is mindful of the deeds of their forefathers.

Prisoners who died on the hulks at Chatham were buried, without ceremony, either on St. Mary's Island or along Gillingham Reach on what was known as 'Prisoner's Banks', a marshy area owned by the Gillingham Gas Company in the mid-nineteenth century. In the 1860s there were plans to extend Chatham Dockyard, encroaching upon the Prisoner's Banks, and so preparations were made to remove the bodies and re-inter them in the existing 'French Cemetery' on St. Mary's Island, which already contained some bodies. 711 skeletons were re-interred on the island in the spring of 1869 and a short while later a memorial was placed on the grave site.

1903 saw plans for the construction of a new Dockyard Basin that would take in the French Cemetery, so it was decided to remove the memorial and the bodies to a new site, south of the Naval Chapel in the Royal Naval Barracks. The Admiralty directed that every care was to be taken and the work performed respectfully and without publicity by Dockyard workmen employed in the evening after normal working hours. The transfer of the remains took place during late August and early September, and it was reported that 521 skulls and remains had been reburied in varnished deal boxes, with the memorial being re-erected in December.[11]

It is a mystery why all the bodies in the French Cemetery were not removed in 1904. In late 1990 the island was part of a development by English Estates, who discovered that there were still some skeletons remaining. A local pathologist was called in to monitor the remains, and the site was carefully excavated. These remains were re-interred at the dockyard site behind St Georges's Church, and a short service of remembrance was held in front of a new memorial tablet placed on the site, which reads:

> This memorial was laid here on July 22, 1991, to commemorate the re-interment of the remains of a further 362 prisoners of war from the original cemetery on St. Mary's Island.

The service was conducted by the French Parish of London priest Father Jacques Coupet, and attended by the Mayor of Gillingham and officials from the French Consulate. At last all the dead prisoners of His Majesty's Prison Ship Depot, Chatham, now rest in peace in a well-kept graveyard, remembered and honoured by Briton and Frenchman alike. In November each year there is a small ceremony involving local dignitaries and representatives from Le Souvenir Français and the French Consulate, at which wreaths are laid and the unfortunate victims of war are remembered.[12] The inscription on the original memorial is just as valid now as it was one hundred years ago:

> Here are gathered together the remains of many brave soldiers and sailors, who, having once been the foes, afterwards the captives of England, now find rest in her soil, remembering no more the animosities of war or the sorrows of imprisonment. They were deprived of the consolation of closing their eyes amongst the countrymen they loved, but they have been laid in an honourable grave by a nation which knows how to respect valour and to sympathise with misfortune.

Not all memorials to these prisoners actually mark their last resting place. At Norman Cross 1,770 prisoners died and were buried somewhere in the vicinity of the depot. Legend stated that the cemetery was situated to the west of the depot, across what was then the Great North Road (now the A1M), and it was overlooking this site that the Entente Cordiale Society erected a memorial in 1914. This society existed in Britain to foster good relations with the French, and it was thought that:

> ... the erection of a memorial to the memory of these brave men would be a graceful act, which would be very pleasing to the French Army and Navy, and to our good friends the French people generally.

A fund was raised for the construction of an impressive monument consisting of a stone pillar atop which was a bronze Eagle with wings outstretched. At the base of the pillar was a bronze plate detailing the reason for the memorial. This was erected to the west of the depot site, and it would seem that the legend of the depot's cemetery also being here grew out of association with the memorial. The Entente Cordial Society certainly did not presuppose that the field next to the memorial was the actual burial place. They were simply erecting a memorial to the dead of a past conflict, to promote harmonious Anglo-French relations in 1914.[13]

The Norman Cross Memorial became a familiar landmark to generations of travellers north. In October 1990 the memorial was vandalised and the eagle stolen, either for its scrap metal value or as an antique work of art to enhance the collection of an unsuspecting collector.

Shortly after the memorial was destroyed, a number of independent groups expressed an interest in restoring the monument. Spearheaded by Peterborough Museum, the Norman Cross Eagle Appeal was launched to raise the funds necessary to reproduce the bronze Eagle and restore the memorial. Due to extensive road developments in the area, it was not possible to place the monument on its original site. The stone column was unveiled on the A15 road to Yaxley and Peterborough, near the north-west corner of the depot site, in 1998 by Sir Brian Mawhinney MP, former Secretary of State for Transport. A grant of lottery money from the Local Heritage Initiative enabled the Appeal Committee to commission the sculptor John Doubleday to recreate the eagle in bronze. A sunny day in April 2005 saw His Grace the Duke of Wellington (patron of the Appeal) inaugurate the restored memorial before an audience of over 1,000 people. The eagle had landed! However, the story did not end there. The enthusiasm for this project by many people worldwide has enabled the Appeal to fund more than just a restored monument. The project has included an information panel about the depot alongside the memorial; a Heritage Trail leaflet to guide visitors around the story of the Napoleonic period in the area; a Teacher's pack with which to educate and entertain local schoolchildren; and the production of a Community Textile Panel that tells the story of the prison through tapestry.[14]

The 1,770 prisoners of war of many nationalities who died at Norman Cross prison depot have not just their memorial, but an awareness of their story both locally and worldwide. While the Agent's house and a small part of the original boundary wall remain to remind us of Norman Cross Prison Depot, the site is a scheduled ancient monument, but the story of this prison will remain alive for generations to come.

The idea that the original monument was sited by the prison cemetery is a myth. To investigate this legend, in 1990 an archaeological investigation of the site was undertaken by the Archaeological Officer of Peterborough City Council. A series of trenches was dug in the field next to the monument, but no trace of any human bones was discovered.[15] A grave containing 1,770 bodies would occupy a large area, so if the field in question had been the burial ground then some evidence of human remains should have been discovered. So where were the bodies actually buried? Nothing has been found to indicate where the depot had its cemetery. However, the records for Dartmoor, Portchester Castle and Forton prisons indicate that land was acquired just outside the prison walls for burials. Extensive agricultural activity in the vicinity of the depot site has yielded no human remains. It is possible that they lie to the south of the site in marshy and wooded land, but their exact location remains a secret. Unless the ground is disturbed and yields up these men, then let them rest in peace. They have their memorial, and their story is evident to all who visit the area.

Since the end of the Napoleonic Wars, many communities in the British Isles have remembered their 'foreign gentlemen' by erecting memorials. Such edifices may be found at Penicuick, Leek, Princetown and Forton, to name but a few, while the gravestones of parole prisoners are often well cared for.

While these prisoners are remembered after their death, it should not be forgotten that many prisoners returned home at the end of the war, and lived on into the nineteenth century. Even returning home could be hazardous for some of these men. Some French ex-prisoners (possibly Germans fighting in the French Army) who had enlisted into the British service were discharged at the end of the war in 1814 and sent home, to be murdered on their arrival at Morlaix.[16]

Many prisoners who returned home and lived out their lives free from conflict felt the need to put their experiences down on paper, as a legacy for their family, or perhaps to remember the glory and hardship of life under the Emperor. The mid nineteenth century saw numerous memoirs published on both sides of the Channel. Frenchmen such as Louis Garneray wrote accounts of their life in the English prison hulks. Garneray's book *The French Prisoner* (translated into English in the 1950s) is a semi-factual story of how Louis Garneray took on the British war prison system single-handed. In his book he vividly describes life on the hulks, in Portchester Castle, and on parole at Bishop's Waltham. He maintains that he resided first on the *Prothée*, then the *Crown*, and after innumerable escape attempts, on the *Vengeance* (the repository for troublesome prisoners in the hulk depot at Portsmouth). After a spell in Portchester Castle, he was eventually granted his parole at Bishops Waltham. He actually only spent time on the *Prothée* before being allowed his parole.

Garneray became a successful marine artist after the war and extended his talents to writing. His stories were a mix of his experience, plagiarism of other published accounts, and pure fabrication, designed to entertain his public and earn a living. While many authors have used these stories as an accurate account of life on board the hulks, they should be viewed for what they are – fiction based upon fact.[17]

The Napoleonic prisoner of war story is very much alive today, fuelled by interest in local and family history. These men and women have their memorials, including the many bone models in museums and private collections, which sell for large sums when they come onto the market. While the Emperor Napoleon is remembered for his contribution to world history, the ordinary men who were the bedrock of his achievements are remembered as well, especially in this, the bicentenary of the Napoleonic period.

Notes

[1] TNA:PRO ADM98/304. Letters to French regarding prisoners of war.

[2] BL 08227.cc.22(1) French claims.

[3] TNA:PRO ADM98/304.

[4] TNA:PRO ADM99/260. Transport Board Minutes 27 March 1815.

[5] ibid., 31 March 1815.

[6] Report of events regarding America in The *Pilot* 18 August 1815.

[7] Trafford, Dr. P.A. *Dartmoor Prison and its American Prisoners 1813–15.* Journal of the Prison Medical Association, Spring issue 1985, p.9–11.

[8] TNA:PRO ADM98/291. Transport Office letters to US Agent in Britain, 29 April 1815.

[9] Joy, p.97–100.

[10] ibid. p.125–131.

[11] Inscription on Napoleonic prisoner of war memorial, St Georges Centre, Chatham Maritime, Gillingham, Medway.

[12] *Chatham Evening Post*, 23 July 1991.

[13] Proposed Norman Cross Memorial, Entente Cordiale Society 1913. Peterborough Museum and Art Gallery.

[14] The Norman Cross Eagle Appeal Souvenir Programme 2 April 2005. Peterborough Museum and Art Gallery.

[15] *Sample Trenching at Norman Cross, Cambridgeshire 1990–1991: An Archaeological Evaluation.* Peterborough Museum and Art Gallery.

[16] TNA:PRO ADM98/135. 31 May 1814.

[17] Garneray's original work has recently been translated from the French by Richard Rose, complete with an analysis of the account and an historical background to the stories.

Bibliography

Abell, Francis. *Prisoners of War in Britain 1756–1815*. London, 1914.

Alger, John Goldworth. *Napoleon's British Visitors and Captives 1801–1815*. London, 1904.

Barker, Rosalin. *Prisoners of the Tsar: East Coast Sailors held in Russia 1800–1801*. Highgate Publications, Beverley, 1992.

Baron, John. *The Life of Edward Jenner*. London,1838.

Bennett, Joan; Parrack, Colin; Poole, Ray; Walton, Cathryn. *French Connections: Napoleonic Prisoners of War on Parole in Leek 1803–1814*. Leek, 1995.

Bernard, Léonce. *Les prisonniers de guerre du Premier Empire*. Paris, 2000.

Boothby, Charles. *A Prisoner of France*. London, 1898.

Branch-Johnson, W. *The English Prison Hulks*. London, 1957.

Brett-James, Antony (Editor), *Escape from the French: Captain Hewson's Narrative (1803–1809)*. Exeter, Devon, 1981.

Brown, J. Howard & Guest, W. *A History of Thame*. Thame, 1935.

Burgoyne, Lt. Col. Sir John M. *Regimental Records of the Bedfordshire Militia from 1759 to 1884*. London, 1884

Byatt, Derrick, *Promises To Pay: The first three hundred years of Bank of England notes*. London, 1994.

Campbell, Charles, *The Intolerable Hulks: British Shipboard Confinement 1776–1857*. Maryland, USA, 1994.

Casse, George Richard. *A Prisoner of France*. London, 1976.

Childs, W.M. *The Town of Reading during the Early Part of the Nineteenth Century*. London, 1910.

Clayton, Time and Graig, Phil. *Trafalgar: The men, the battle, the storm*. London, 2004.

Costello, Edward. *The Adventures of a Soldier or Memoirs of Edward Costello*. London, 1841.

Cook, Chris and Stevenson, John. *British Historical Facts 1760–1830*. London 1980.

Crowhurst, Patrick. *The French War on Trade: Privateering 1793–1815*. Gower Publishing, Aldershot, 1989.

Cunliffe, Barry and Garratt, Beverley. *Excavations at Portchester Castle Vol. V: Post Medieval 1609–1819*. London, 1994.

de Curzon, Alfred. *Dr James Currie and the French Prisoners of War in Liverpool 1800–1801*. Liverpool, 1926.

Ditchfield, P.H. *Reading Seventy Years Ago: A Record of Events from 1813–1819*. Reading, 1887.

Donald, A.J. and Ladd, J.D. *Royal Marines Records 1793–1836*. City of Portsmouth, 1982.

Dupin, Charles. *Voyages dans La Grande Bretagne, Entrepis relativement aux Services Publics de la Guerre, de la Marine. et des Ponts et Chaussées, en 1816–17–18–19, et 1820. Deuxieme Partie, Force Navale.* l'Institut de France, Paris 1821.

Endle, Rufus. *Dartmoor Prison*, Bodmin, 1979.

Forester, C.S. (Editor). *The Adventures of John Wetherell*. London, 1994.

Fraser, Edward. *Napoleon The Gaoler*. London 1914.

Freeston, Ewart C. *Prisoner of War Ship Models 1775–1825*. London 1987.

Fregosi, Paul. *Dreams of Empire: Napoleon and the First World War, 1792–1815*. London, 1989.

Garneray, Louis. *The French Prisoner*. London, 1957.

Garneray, Louis (Translated by Richard Rose). *The Floating Prison*. London, 2003.

Garneray, Louis (Translated by Roland Wilson). Seaman Garneray: Voyages, Aventures et Combats. Argyll Publishing, Scotland, 2003.

Gates, D. *The Spanish Ulcer: A History of the Peninsular War*. London, 1986.

de Goutel, E.Hennet. *Mémoires du Général Marquis Alphonse D'Hautpol*. Paris 1906.

Gleig, G.R. *The Light Dragoon*. London, 1850.

Grover, G.W.M. (Ed.). *History of the Royal Marine Divisions*. Portsmouth, 1931

Gurwood, Lt.Col. J. *Selections from the Dispatches and General Orders of Field Marshal the Duke of Wellington*. London, 1851.

Hain, Edward. *Prisoners of War in France from 1804 to 1814; Being the Adventures of John Tregerthen Short and Thomas Williams.* London, 1914.

Harvey, Wallace. *Whitstable and the French Prisoners of War.* Emprint, Kent, 1983.

Haythornthwaite, Philip J. *The Napoleonic Source Book.* New York, 1990.

Haythornthwaite, Philip J. *The Armies of Wellington.* London, 1994.

Hickey, Donald R. *The War of 1812: A Forgotten Conflict.* University of Illinois Press USA, 1990,

Hoffman, Frederick. *A Sailor of King George: The Journals of Captain Frederick Hoffman RN, 1793–1814.* London, 1999.

James, Trevor. *Prisoners of War in Dartmoor Towns.* Orchard Publications, Devon, 2000.

Jenkins, E.H., A *History of the French Navy.* London, 1973.

Johnson, W.Branch, *The English Prison Hulks.* Phillimore, Chichester, 1970.

Joy, Ron. *Dartmoor Prison Volume One: The War Prison 1809–1816.* Halsgrove Publishing, Devon, 2002.

Kennedy, Ludovic. *Nelson and His Captains.* London 1975.

Kincaid, John. *Random Shots from a Rifleman.* Spellmount, Kent, 1998.

Latimer, Jon. *1812: War with America.* Cambridge, Massachusetts, USA, 2007.

Latimer, John. *The Annals of Bristol in the Eighteenth Century.* Bristol, 1893.

Lavery, Brian. *Nelson's Navy: the Ships, Men and Organisation 1793–1815.* London, 1989.

Lejeune, Baron Louis François. *Memoirs of Baron Lejeune.* London, 1897.

Lewis, Michael. *Napoleon and His British Captives.* London 1962.

Liddell Hart, Captain B.H. (Ed.), *The Letters of Private Wheeler 1809–1828.* The Windrush Press, 1993.

Lowe, J.A.(Editor) *Records of the Portsmouth Division of Marines 1764–1800.* City of Portsmouth, 1990.

MacDougall, Ian. *The Prisoners at Penicuick.* Midlothian District Council. 1989.

McGrigor, James. *The Autobiography and Services of Sir James McGrigor; Late Director General of the Army Medical Department.* London, 1861.

Munch-Petersen, Thomas. *Defying Napoleon: How Britain bombarded Copenhagen and seized the Danish Fleet in 1807.* Sutton Publishing, Stroud, 2007.

O'Brien, Donat Henchy. *My Adventures during the Late War*. London, 1902.

Palmer, Benjamin Franklin. *The Diary of Benjamin F. Palmer, Privateersman. While a prisoner on board English warships at sea, in the prison at Melville Island and at Dartmoor*. The Acorn Club, Connecticut 1914.

Parkinson, C. Northcote, *Britannia Rules: The Classic Age of Naval History 1793–1815*. Alan Sutton, Stroud, 1994.

Penny, G. *Traditions of Perth*. Perth, 1836.

Pescott Frost Collection of the History of Portsmouth, Central Library, Portsmouth, Hampshire.

Pilkington, Francis. *Ashburton: The Dartmoor Town*. Devon, 1981.

Reilly, Robin. *The British at the Gates*. London, 1976.

Rendle, Joan. *Gateway to Cornwall*. Bodmin, 1981.

Robertson, Ian. *A Commanding Presence: Wellington in the Peninsula 1808–1814*. Spellmount, Stroud, 2008.

Sanderson, Robert. *The Prison on the Moor: The Astonishing Story of Dartmoor Prison*. Westway Publications, Plymouth, Devon, 1974.

Seaman, L.C.B. *A New History of England 410–1975*. Harvester Press, Brighton, 1981.

Shankland, Peter. *Beware Of Heroes: Admiral Sir Sidney Smith's War against Napoleon*. London 1975.

Stanbrook, Elizabeth. *Dartmoor's War Prison and Church 1805–1817*. Quay Publications, Brixham, Devon, 2002.

Stewart, Alexander. *The Life of Alexander Stewart: Prisoner of Napoleon and Preacher of the Gospel*. London, 1948.

Teissedre, F. *Pontons et Prisons sous le Premier Empire*. Paris, 1998.

Thorpe, John T. *French Prisoner's Lodges*. Leicester 1900.

Toase, William. *The Wesleyan Mission in France with an account of the labours of Wesleyan Ministers among the French Prisoners during the late war*, London 1835.

Toller, Jane. *Prisoners of War Work 1756–1815*. Cambridge, 1965.

Turner, G.A. (Editor). *The Diary of Peter Bussell 1806–1814*. London 1931.

Walker, Thomas James. *The Depot for Prisoners of War at Norman Cross Huntingdonshire, 1796–1816*. London 1913.

Waterhouse, Benjamin M.D. *Journal of a Young Man of Massachusetts*. Boston, 1816.

Index